FINDING SOUL
From Silicon Valley
to Africa

"Finding Soul: Silicon Valley to Africa is a travel memoir that invites reflection.

The reader not only enjoys the varied adventures of a refugee of success from Silicon Valley to re-discovering soul in Africa and the delights of sights, sounds, and smells while being an armchair traveler, but the invitation to reflect on where your own life is and where it is going."

—Catherine Ann Jones, *Buddha & the Dancing Girl*

FINDING
SOUL
From Silicon Valley
to Africa

A PERSONAL JOURNEY THROUGH
TWENTY COUNTRIES IN AFRICA

KURT DAVIS

NEW YORK

LONDON • NASHVILLE • MELBOURNE • VANCOUVER

FINDING SOUL, From Silicon Valley to Africa
A PERSONAL JOURNEY THROUGH TWENTY COUNTRIES IN AFRICA

Published in New York, New York, by Morgan James Publishing. Morgan James is a trademark of Morgan James, LLC. www.MorganJamesPublishing.com

All pictures are owned by KDAlive LLC except where noted that Niklas Faralisch of Farali Production in Germany gave rights to use his photos. Please contact him at faralisch.niklas at googlemail dot com.

ISBN 978-1-63195-272-2   paperback
ISBN 978-1-63195-273-9   eBook
Library of Congress Control Number: 2020916860

Cover Design by:
Rachel Lopez
www.r2cdesign.com

Morgan James is a proud partner of Habitat for Humanity Peninsula and Greater Williamsburg. Partners in building since 2006.

Get involved today! Visit
www.MorganJamesBuilds.com

TABLE OF CONTENTS

ACKNOWLEDGMENTS

To David Hancock and Morgan James Publishing, thank you so much for believing in this project and my platform, KDAlive.

To David Wolf and Mark Shipman at Audivita, thank you for working with me on the audiobook project, with over 40 different voices, and running with it.

To Pip Strickland, my first editor who helped me get it all on paper to start, thank you for your initial help consolidating all of my travel logs.

To my editors Catherine Ann Jones and Brunella Costagliola of Kevin Anderson & Associates, thank you for your editorial assistance.

To my parents (Henry and Cynthia Davis), who read through this countless times, thank you for your patience. I know I'm crazy.

To Clarence Chang and Brian Isleib, who gave me crucial feedback as my target audience, thank you for your time and precision.

To Traci Kanzawa, who gave me the confidence to follow my creativity and passion for finishing this and rendezvousing with me in Kauai at the Kauai Writer's Conference, a soft, sweet thank you very much.

To all of the people in the book whom I met and who contributed to this book, thank you for the experience of many lives.

As they say in Africa, "It takes a village to raise a child," and in this case, "It takes a lot of amazingly dedicated friends to write a good book."

INTRODUCTION

This book is about what I learned in Africa and how it inspired change. I've posted pictures and videos of the journey on my website, KDAlive.com, to add some visual action to this book. The audiobook includes over two dozen unique voices, so it provides an exceptional listening experience. Through my brand, KDAlive (Kurt Davis Alive), I share my travel, well-being experiences, and entrepreneurship tips—in essence, living a better life, and how you, too, can live up to your best potential.

Before Africa, I didn't know much. In 2002, with my long-time friend Gerry, I visited South Africa and Zambia. I knew this immense continent was more than TV images of impoverished kids with bloated stomachs, big-game wildlife—sadly far fewer now—and Tarzan, which are the limits of most Americans' knowledge of Africa. At least that's what Rick, my Ivy League-educated friend, joked when I met him traveling on our overland trip.

The African continent, with 1.2 billion people and growing, offers tremendous opportunities in the coming decades. Not just that, I also wanted to realize my dream of visiting a new continent on my quest to see half the world, and Africa was the final frontier. Little did I know the profound impact it would have on me.

Upon returning to the United States and overcoming my not so minor stomachache, I was searching for what to do next while working on my blog. There was no plan to write this book, yet so many people asked me to tell them more. To my surprise, they didn't ask about safaris, but more profound questions like: What was the most meaningful experience and why? How did it change you? I would reply, "Let me get back to you or look at my blog," but I couldn't articulate the deeper meaning that lived unvoiced.

I skimmed my blog posts, journal entries, email updates, and WhatsApp conversations before concluding that I should, indeed, write this book. While it doesn't highlight just one experience or story, it does offer takeaways from each country and what was learned there. To that end, many books about Africa focus on an outer development story in one country, like building a school; this book focuses on my inner personal development through interactions and experiences.

Each chapter reads like a vignette while developing the critical themes in the book: experiencing deep empathy for others, releasing ego and identity, and discovering a deeper meaning for life. Then other "Aha!" moments appeared, such as understanding the roots of racism, experiencing the power of entrepreneurship, and learning how to enjoy a journey without a plan. And what would a travel novel/memoir be if it didn't have a bit of romance, right? So there is a storyline about how my interactions with women evolved throughout the trip.

I know it's cliché: Successful, white businessman goes to Africa and grows a new heart. That's not me; I've always enjoyed helping others, though, I hadn't committed my life to it. I'm an explorer, and I went to Africa to learn about the rich, the poor, cities, nature, business, culture, and more. Meeting people on the way, I looked for technology business opportunities and volunteer experiences at humanitarian non-profits; and, of course, I played tourist games. Traveling anywhere teaches one about one's self, and this trip did so in spades. These experiences gave me a new lens to look at my career.

To my African readers, this assuredly isn't a white savior story. I've versed myself in Wainaina's satirical essay "How to Write About Africa" so as not to write offensively or stereotypically To my African friends, I thank you for your hospitality and all the knowledge you shared with me. In turn, this is my attempt to pass on that wisdom to a broader Western audience.

When memory is the primary source of information, the facts will only be as accurate as the ones I can recall. In many cases, I worked with other people to rehash the dialogue. Thank you to all of you who helped and contributed to the audiobook. What happened in the book is 99 percent true. If you can guess one of the two parts that I exaggerated in one shot, I'll donate your entire book purchase to a charity mentioned in this book. You can email me at kd@kdalive.com. Furthermore, I am donating 50 percent of my profits to non-profits, herein, and you can track the donations on my website.

Whether you're a traveler searching for a few tips, a student learning more about the continent, an entrepreneur or businessman/woman interested in Africa's potential, or just a curious reader of exciting stories, this book is for you. And deep down, I hope this helps a handful of people to change the way they see others, develop empathy, and empower others to create a better world.

The Journey

The Map of the Journey I went on.

PROLOGUE

"May each soul find your Africa."
—KD

Head between my hands, I stared at the cracked white tile floor—a stream of tears flowing between my feet. The tears told of a six-month journey to townships in South Africa, Nigerian slums, slave castles in Ghana, Uganda's Karamoja and Batwa Regions, Rwanda's genocide, slums in Nairobi, and more. Depressed. Defeated. Delirious. I couldn't take it anymore. I had to get out, but where?

The five-room hotel outside Kakuma Refugee Camp, Kenya, didn't have much except a lopsided bed, mosquito net, and a dimly lit orange-yellow light. But here was luxury, and my host, Innocent, wanted the best for me; he didn't want me to sleep on the dirt floor of his small mud house. A Congolese refugee who dressed like a businessman and wore glasses like an academic, he'd lived in the camp for ten years and set up Wi-Fi networks at country-sponsored non-profits earning $70 a month, the standard United Nations wage for refugees. He escorted me back just before sunset, and now night had come.

Left alone with just my emotions, which in the past had proven to be somewhat dangerous, I lifted my head. That orange-yellow color coming from a fading lightbulb in the bathroom burned my face as I peered into it. Through the glaze over my eyes, I saw a mural of people I met throughout Africa. Depression had compounding effects, and the emotions built up were now being released all at once. "It's never good to bottle these experiences up," said Dawn at the Team4Tech evening reflection sessions in Johannesburg. After those heartfelt discussions, I had ceased to share anything with anyone for the last six months. I bottled them up, and now they were erupting like the volcano in Congo; unwanted thoughts stirred like lava. My heart pounded, and the air supply to my lungs diminished, causing me to breathe faster and deeper.

Forget this life. It means nothing or at least mine means nothing. My right hand turned into a fist, my eyes closed, I stood up and punched the air with a 1–2. I had been caught off guard by how Africans view life as a short journey of existence. To them, death is just death, part of life, and nature.

I head-butted the wall like an American football player. No more should I fear death. I swayed and spun in a circle, getting dizzy. Focusing my sight on a specific dirt spot, I stabilized. Focus, concentrate on that little dot in the cylinder brick as in concentration meditation. Life was racing through my veins. I could feel something impermanent and that one day would not be there. I pounded my chest with my fist. I took a deep breath.

I dreamed big dreams yet now realized those were temporary and disconnected from a why, only tethered to identity or money, and with a firm, breeze collapsed like a house of cards. Bold ideas and lofty goals, driven by ego alone, couldn't be the foundation for dreams. No, they must have substance, real meaning, and deliver value in a concrete, lasting way.

The essential meaning of my life should be to find meaning and purpose in what I do, anywhere, anyhow. Many Africans prioritized family and community first. Even the refugees found meaning in helping those around them. Look no further. Right here. Right now. Right in this refugee camp.

A revelation. I discovered what Buddha meant by releasing the ego and giving up all existence and substance entirely, as stated by Shun Ryu Suzuki in *Zen Mind, Beginner's Mind*—the one paperback book I carried on the journey. Now I get it. With no ego, there is no identity and no label, color, or creed. Racism would vanish, and respect would reign. There is only the soul.

That's why women get the brunt and were last in line for food, clothes, and necessities—not just in impoverished countries but all over the world. Not only western, but all women must be treated equally, or the world will never get better. Why are so many men so aggressive, competitive, and manipulative? It's called the male ego. Sometimes I too have been that way, and that's not how I should be. No, it must be equality for every individual. I stood back up to pace the floor.

Innocent was unique. Unlike many of the refugees at the camp who had lost their joie de vivre to hardship, he had boundless energy, enthusiasm, and drive. Like many educated refugees, Innocent had a proper engineering degree but nothing to do with it. Sitting in the desert, baking in the burning hot sun, drinking dirty water, and eating whatever they could find was their daily existence. Some painted, and others created small businesses with the pennies they had. Still, others toiled and just waited for the next United Nations plane to deliver rations. It's understandable. How can anyone keep going until they get sustenance? Not everyone does.

Innocent was so positive about life. "You just go, keep the brain active. Learn new things, learn. Learn and go." Then he would say, "Just go to the next. There is no other way; just be positive." He wouldn't let his emotions overcome his brain—he had full mental control and used mental stimulation to block out his feelings. Positivity is a choice. Moving on is a choice. I kind of get it, I sort of understand what these refugees are going through. Through mental stimulation, he created his work. He epitomized entrepreneurship.

Empowerment through entrepreneurship. That is how to help! Entrepreneurship gives others meaning, hope, and control of their destiny—all while supporting the community.

My tears dried up, my thoughts became lucid. I opened the door and walked outside, chest-high like a gladiator facing battle. The moon and stars lit the night enough to navigate the stony, bumpy terrain inside the hotel courtyard. Just across from the little five-room hotel was the United Nations landing strip. Pushing open a crack in the barb-wired laced fence, I leaped inside an opening portal, spinning hypnotically into some new galaxy. I visualized the morning runs, the rising sun over tin-roofed huts, and the local kids who chased me up and down the landing strip. "Run! Run!" They yelled until they got too tired and walked backed home to their tin shacks. It's the little memories of the voyage—

not necessarily the outcome that made it worth it because the result is often what wasn't planned.

I knew I'd miss this endless African sky. Every constellation so clear: Orion, Capricorn, Sagittarius, Scorpius, and Cassiopeia—what a sight to see! It reminded me of childhood and my obsession with stars and outer space, an interest that fell by the wayside as I moved down the road—so many options in the West, none in a refugee camp.

To be grateful for the endless paths and opportunities we can take is right. To be true to my deepest self, strive for excellence, and find ways to empower others is correct. Just like a refugee, I'm whoever I want to be. There is power in having no identity. And I would start right here, with a cleansed soul.

I gazed at the stars, and they twinkled as if in response to the insight.

My mind was now truly a beginner's mind, open to any possibility. Welcoming new paths, without judgment, I have only one rule: to follow the guidance of my true self, my soul.

Thank you, Kakuma.

Thank you, Africa.

May each soul find your Africa.

Chapter 1
F* IT, I'M GOING TO AFRICA

"Never submit to any arbitrary action."
—Gandhi

This is how I went mad.

October 2016. Knoxville, Tennessee. Fox News blared in the living room, echoing behind me in the kitchen and all around the house. My dad sat on the recliner angrily, crunching on pork rinds and sipping satisfactorily on red wine I had brought from Napa. He felt vindicated by the Fox News commentary and the rise of Trump, who divided all parts of society right down to the core family. His support of Trump—like many others—was buoyed by family circumstances.

My sister battled mental health issues and drug addictions, leaving my parents to raise her four kids, which came with an endless cycle of custody battles with her ex, prison visits where she stayed for various crimes, and courtroom meetings. In my dad's mind, a more ruthless and relentless president would solve America's problems, and he didn't give a hoot about progressive values or libertarian ethics—by the way, if you thought this was another *Hillbilly Elegy*, it ain't.

Looking down at him in the recliner, I asked, "Do we have to listen to this all of the time? Why not another source?"

"Cuz' they are lying." He replied with eyes fixated on the TV.

"Look, I get it, we need to invest in other parts of America—like Cleveland." We had just returned from Cleveland—my dad's hometown and my birthplace—where we watched a World Series Game and a Cavaliers ring ceremony parade. Everywhere I looked, I saw Cleveland Indians hats interspersed with red hats inscribed with "Make America Great Again." The irony.

"We could balance out the perspective a bit." I paused, contemplating my next provoking question. "How about CNN?"

"The Communist News Network? All liars."

"So is Fox News. They give one-side of the coin only." I looked out the window and sighed.

"Look, I listened to CNN for a decade then switched to Fox because they give both sides, Democrats and Republicans."

"They do? Whatever. Trump is still a liar, a jerk, and most of all, an unsuccessful businessman—he didn't even beat the market in his lifetime. He would not have survived a month in Silicon Valley."

"You think Clinton is any better? She pocketed millions from foreign governments, not to mention Bill outsourced our jobs to China—you know that, you saw it when you lived over there!"

"She's been doing this for forty years. I trust she would have good insight and at least knows what not to do—even with China."

"Insight? I don't think so. Having someone who isn't part of the system, who worked in the global environment, will bring a new perspective. He'll drain the swamp." He didn't back down. My anxiety caused my shoulder to twitch.

"Perspective, I have my perspective, and yours sucks." I pointed at him, tossing some peanuts on him.

Jumping out of his recliner, spitting pork rinds, he yelled, "Let me show you. Put 'em up!"

"Dad, forget it," I replied but then with two fingers, gently pushed him back in his chair. He was an ex-Marine and still acted tough.

"Grandma! Grandpa and Kurt are fighting!" yelled my niece, Izabella, to Mom, then she scampered out of the house. Izabella was my sister's youngest daughter. She called her Bella. I called her Izzy.

Why was I here, anyway? To visit family, vote in the election, and go crazy. I grew up in South Carolina and went to Davidson College in North Carolina. I would visit my parents in Knoxville, Tennessee, once or twice per year. After I graduated from college, they moved there, and I took the first flight to Japan in 1999 to teach English to middle schoolers with the Japan Exchange Teaching Program.

I could always go back to San Francisco. The ultra-liberal, capitalistic utopia, now part of Silicon Valley. I didn't want just to go back and do what I did before—fall in line with the rest of the technology soldiers: work hard, run the rat race, and hope that I'd catch a break. By the time I turned thirty-five, the startup I worked at had turned into a decent job that made me good money—though like all startups at the time, the first few years were a slog. But it did allow me to travel the world, relishing the best fine dining—at least, that's what my CEO always said. So, what was my problem? What in the world was I complaining about?

I had saved up some money, was a Vice President, and done decently. In my mind, this little success was an abject failure, especially when compared to others around me in Silicon Valley. I admit, one of my problems is that I like to make up a story, set a goal, work like mad, and then complain about it to myself when it doesn't happen. It's how I drove myself crazy.

Nevertheless, for eight years, I steadfastly stayed at the company from the first day until a feasible outcome was clear. I knew it wasn't an attractive company to those looking in from the outside. While Silicon Valley exploded, I remained patient, worked diligently, dismissed other opportunities, and waited for our chance to succeed. Then we did. I told myself—and was told by others—that completing the mission and being loyal would pay off in the long run. How naive. In the end, relationships soured – as things do, when things go unexpectedly well, not when they fail. After it was all said and done, those who promised introductions to their hot companies never came through. Loyalty isn't a contract; it's a hard lesson to learn.

Dude, settle down. You could have left the company or started your own. It's your fault. So what if you made billions or even a million during the most significant economic and technological revolution the world has ever seen? So, what. What would you do with it? Buy a Porsche or baseball team? I listened to my own diatribe.

Even if I made F*You Money as they say in Silicon Valley, I'd still have to work; I'd still be searching for meaning. Even billionaires are working harder than ever. Bill Gates still works like he is at a startup—while trying to save the world. And the company I worked for pocketed him big bucks since he was an investor through a fund. I made up some stupid story that if I worked in technology long enough and made it big, then I could do something meaningful. *There's gotta be more,* I thought. It wasn't money I was searching for.

"I'm just an idiot," I mumbled to myself. My blood pressure rose; my heartbeat thumped in my neck. I needed out, where could I go?

Returning to Japan crossed my mind. I had lived there from 2013–2016, helping to build that startup, which later made billions in transactions there, propelling the company to success. Peering out the window at the beautiful Tennessee orange-yellowish leaves, a crisp, calm and soothing feeling penetrated and settled my chaotic thoughts. That's how I felt whenever I landed in Narita, a Tokyo airport. Delicious delicacies, outdoor excursions, and exquisite experiences filled those years. I met a woman, a lovely lady who had skin as smooth as the petals on a sakura (cherry blossom) tree. She walked away from me because she had the emotional IQ of that tree. Easy to blame her when I was the one who couldn't open up. Or perhaps wouldn't.

After I returned from one trip, she let her feelings out ever so slightly (which was a lot in Japanese culture): "I missed you so much. Didn't you miss me?" I paused and couldn't reply. I could have just lied and said yes. What's the truth—who tells the truth today, anyway? Idiot. Instead, she stared right through my eyes, burning a hole in the back of my head, grabbed her stuff, and walked right out the door. *Don't let the door smack you're beep on the way out,* I thought. Nope, not heading back to Japan!

So then, what else could I do? More times than I could stand, people—especially and ironically, those in California—referred to me as the privileged white guy who had too many options to make the correct decision. What was the right choice, anyway? Should I go back to sell software? That's what I am. I am a sales and business development expert. And I dread and despise that person. They just wanted me to do what was best for them. Stick a needle in my eye!

I thought about life goals. Was there anything I, personally, really wanted to do? I had always wanted to explore all of the continents. Perhaps, now was a good time to get out of Dodge. Yeah, just get out of Dodge. I can buy a ticket and get on a plane better than anyone I know.

I could go on an adventure and do something that didn't matter—to anyone, not to me, not to them, not to no one. Stuck in this western world of climbing the ladder, running the hamster wheel, and playing the game of monopoly when you can't pass go because the American system swamps you with endless taxes and bills. To support that system, you do something that just really didn't matter to society, all while keeping the same rich people on top—that's the systematic preservation of power.

And the system sucks. There's gotta be something else. I want to explore the unexplored, touch the untouched, stretch my comfort zone. No more nice hotels. No more black Ubers. No more foodie restaurants. It's time to backpack—not flashpack—but to go as rogue as possible.

"I hate when you talk to yourself. It worries me, honey," said my mom.

"He can talk to himself as long as he doesn't answer himself. Ha-ha!" yelled my dad across the room.

"Africa?" I whispered to myself.

"Africa?" repeated Izzy.

"Yeah, Africa! You don't even know where that is, do you?" I stood upon the chair and placed my other foot on the table.

"Yes, I do. And don't lecture me!" Her eyes wide opened, taking a bite of her chicken

nuggets.

"You can figure out life yourself then. Don't you eat anything besides chicken nuggets?" I curled my lip.

"OMG, Grandma. Here he goes again! I'm eating fries!" She was ready for a fight.

"OMG, right . . ." I said under my breath. "I'm going to Africa."

"Grandma, he is so extra." (Extra was what the kids called dramatic.)

"Extra awesome," I added.

"Cray-cray, you really need help. Get your dirty shoes off the table!" She slapped my shoe and then walked away.

It was my friend Gerry who seeded the idea to return. A tall, northern New Yorker, level-headed straight shooter, he and I had been friends since we met in Hong Kong from 2000 to 2003—visiting Africa together in 2002 for about a week. Recently, when I visited him in Singapore after departing Japan in 2016, I used his home as a hub to jaunt around Southeast Asia. He would remind me and often urged me to "Go back; you've always wanted to backpack Africa. You keep talking about it. Now is the time." Then he would always bring up my stomach issues. "If you go, don't get a parasite again like you did the last time!" He bellowed out. He reignited the fire then poured gasoline on it.

"Africa," I softly said again. The chaos around me disappeared, and I suddenly felt like I wanted to sleep in a jungle next to lions, dive in the ocean with sharks, visit the tribes in sub-Saharan Africa to see how they lived—if they eat me, well, enjoy it!

My thoughts started racing. Africa was more than animals, deserts, and tribes. There was cool music, new technology startups in the TechCrunch news, and Ethiopian food, which I love. Bill Gates is there tackling illnesses. There are successful South Africans all over Silicon Valley and that funny guy on TV. "Trevor Noah!" A billion people are doing all kinds of stuff, and I'm missing out—I felt the FOMO (fear of missing out). Africa's on the up and up and the next place to be. Wonder if my frequent flyer miles go there?

I paused at the idea and thought about other Africans I might know besides Trevor Noah. Then it dawned on me. "Tessa," I whispered. She was my life coach, who happened to be from South Africa and had just returned from a trip. *I should get her sage advice. Not just follow my crazy ideas,* I thought.

I pulled out my phone and typed in WhatsApp: "Tessa, thinking about getting out of here and going to Africa. I want to look around and maybe volunteer. WDYT?"

Ten minutes later—which felt like an eternity to me, as I stared at the phone, waiting for the double tick marks to turn blue. Check, check.

"OMG! That's a lovely idea. Why do you want to go?" Her questions always stirred up more thought.

"Africa is in the news a lot, it's the last unexplored continent and the next decades of economic growth will be there. Why not go check it out?" My reasons were clear to me, at least.

"Africa is amazing, and it will help your soul. It has mystical healing power."

"Glad you agree. Let me research and get back to you." I felt the rush.

"Great. Keep me posted. I have friends I can introduce you to as well," she kept on, and I felt the corners of my lips turn upward. A good sign.

"You think this is an OK idea?"

"Yes, it's a fabulous idea. But come back with a plan please so you are not all over.

Africa is a big place!" She knew me too well.

"Stay tuned," I replied.

"Get your vaccines, please."

"Check." I wasn't about to forget those.

I felt a rush of adrenaline run through my veins, highlighting the sensation at my fingertips and down to my toes. Was I going to Africa? Or was it just another grand master plan? The adrenaline rush was so intense that I had to restrain myself from screaming out loud. I had been diagnosed with ADHD (attention deficit hyperactivity disorder) a few years back while I was in Japan. It had been around for years, even decades, but I had never done anything about it. *After all, I was doing OK in life*—or so I thought.

ADHD was a blessing when creating new ideas and a curse when it is not satisfied. Sometimes—well, I admit often—I just enjoyed lying in bed, staring at the white ceiling and dreaming of new ideas, then suddenly I'd be hyper-warped to one after another before finishing the preceding one. Chaos and hallucination—no drugs included. I'd hear my ex-fiancée's voice echo, "You should get some medication." Forget her! Meditation helped, so I relied on it as often as I could, even though it could only help so much.

That's what I need. Headspace, on. Suddenly I was no longer in the kitchen. I was in my head.

I should have stayed in Bali. I should have surfed and chased ladies. Should have. Should have. I'm going die should'ing myself! I've got to stop saying that.

Back to the nose. Focus on the tip of the nose.

Africa, safaris, shark diving . . . I didn't get to dive with the sharks in South Africa when I went there last time, so I got to go back. Hit the stop button. I can't do this. I need to plan Africa.

Meditation wasn't going to help me this time. I was too excited. For once in my life, I wanted to plan, not impulsively shoot from the hip—even though I was darn good at it and rarely missed. I had to research, talk to people, and come up with some projects. Just wandering around aimlessly in Africa didn't sound like a good idea. I filled the next two weeks by researching and speaking to friends about the faraway continent. Tennessee wasn't providing me any inspiration or connections, so I took a trip to San Francisco—*how do I always end up back there*—and reconnected with old friends, including Neal. He had just spent two years as the Managing Director of an incubator in Ghana called Meltwater. He suggested that I visit them in Ghana and Nigeria. Right on.

Then, a friend sent me up on a date, who suggested I speak to Team4tech, an organization that taught technology at schools in marginalized communities around the world. They were planning a trip to South Africa right after Thanksgiving. Although she was very helpful to me that night, she never replied to me again. Her friend told me, "She said you talked too much, no filter." Whatever. She was too Silicon Valley Politically Correct (PC) for me anyway. It's always the girl's fault, right?

A buddy of mine had told me about the Israeli's building water wells in the desert. So, I reached out to Stephen, who made an introduction to Innovation Africa. The leader, Sivan, replied immediately, "Yes, come visit us in the spring!" "That's it?" I replied. "Sure, just let us know when you are in Africa, and we'll let you know where to meet us." It was as if she questioned whether I would make it or not. That was all the boost I needed. Israel and Uganda, what connection could they have? I pulled out my phone again.

"Tessa, I got a plan. I have three projects in South Africa, Ghana, and Uganda."

Double tick marks? Blue!

"Brilliant. You can see three parts of Africa: South, West, and East. What are the projects?" she asked.

"Teaching junior high schoolers technology, visiting entrepreneurs, and building solar power wells." Three projects fell into my lap.

"That sounds wonderful. Helping others will teach you so much about yourself. Did you get your vaccines?" She knew I had a go-with-the-flow attitude.

"On my to-do list."

"Perfect. You will have a transformative experience. I'm so jealous."

"I'll send pictures so you can feel like you are there."

"Please do. When would you go?"

"Right after Thanksgiving. Let me noodle on it. I'll get back to you."

"OK. Do whatever you feel is right."

"It ain't tech."

"That's right!" *She is always right,* I thought.

Emboldened by Tessa's confidence, I followed up with a few more friends in town. First, there was Fred. I had met Fred in China fifteen years ago, and he was my go-to person for advice. At that time, he helped me navigate my way through China. When I started my company there in 2002, he told me I was crazy—he was right, I should have listened to him.

He said, "Maybe Africa will be good for you. It opens your eyes to a new perspective. You can always come home if it's not working out or if you get malaria or typhoid. No, you'll be fine. Just come home for my wedding, get a job, find a wife, and make babies. It's not too late. Oh yeah, and get your shots—did I tell you that?"

Then the day of the election, I went for a jog with Matt, who always seemed to pursue purposeful paths working in technologies that slow climate change. The fall had arrived in San Francisco, and there was a gentle breeze with a bit of color on the trees in Russian Hill. It soothed the anticipation as I walked into his house to live election results. The places I had grown up in were dropping one by one to Trump: Ohio, South Carolina, North Carolina, and the swing states—*a democracy is determined by six swing states out of fifty.* Furling up my eyebrows, I said, "This ain't no democracy. It's a country of swing states. California doesn't even matter." Then I looked at him and said, "That's it. I'm going to Africa." He had spent some time after college working on solar projects and then again during his honeymoon, so he offered some tips.

The last glance, I could see a twinkle in his eye and sense a more intense emotion that Africa confided in him. It was powerful and persuasive, and whatever that potion was, I wanted some of it. With a tentative plan in hand and my decision still lingering, I reluctantly returned to Tennessee in time to watch my Dad gloat.

"So, Trump won. I'm sure you are happy," I said, thinking I had to face the mouth of the dragon at some point.

"Yup. You watch, he will get this country back on track!"

"I think it's pretty alright, could use a few tweaks."

"It needs more than a few tweaks," my dad said, getting louder and louder with every rebuttal.

My mom interjected, "Shut it. No political talk."

I walked away, knowing this would not end well. "I don't care anyway. I can't do anything about it." Then, I took a few steps, glanced back to them, and said, "F* it, I'm going to Africa." Ahh, that felt so good.

"Crazy man, crazy man . . . stop cursing," mumbled Bella.

"What? Why?" my mom turned around, a wave of shock ruffled her face. "Just go back to San Francisco. Work hard and make some money. You like it there."

"No, I don't. I've had enough of it," I pushed back.

"Be rational. Don't men in midlife crisis buy a Porsche? You had that picture above your desk growing up of that Porsche car, you know," my mom said.

"Oh yeah, the 911: Justification for Higher Education picture."

"That's right. Just get a 911. You'll be fine."

"I am totally fine. And no, Mom, not for me, only douchebags drive them."

Mom looked at me, confused, her eyes revealing helplessness caused by the realization that nothing in this country would make me happy.

"Don't people die in Africa?"

"There are a billion people in Africa. They don't all die," I said abruptly, pacing back and forth.

"But it's not good for us. We don't grow up in their environment."

"I'll get my shots. I'll be fine." My fingers started drumming on the dining table. "This is no different than when I decided to go to China. It was twenty years ago and on the brink of an economic explosion—which it did. Even Coach Waddle, my High School baseball coach, said there were a billion people in China, and we should check it out. So that's why I did. Now I'm doing it again."

"He did not say check it out; he told you that so you wouldn't worry so much during playoff games. What does this have to do with Africa, anyway?" She said, perplexed, not following my logic.

"I went to China and didn't die."

"That's not what I remember. You almost did when you overworked yourself."

"True, but I'm not doing any business," I said with emphasis.

"Fine, take a break. Maybe it will be good for you," my mom warned me with a pointed index finger. "OK, when are you leaving?"

"The day after Thanksgiving."

"Oh, that's only a few days, better get ready."

"I'm ready, don't need much. Can get stuff there anyway."

"At least, come back for Christmas. We love you."

"Sure. I'll try, Ma."

I rolled my eyes at the thought of what Christmas was all about. The time of year when Americans buy lavishly, sending their money to China, then complain about our trade deficit. I thought to myself as I walked out of my parents' house. Merry China-mas. Screw That.

I walked out the door, got in my car, turned the engine on, placed both hands on the steering wheel, and drove down the road to the immunization clinic. *Magnificent colors this time of year*, I thought. I wonder if the red to orange to yellow shades appear the same in Africa?

Then, I took a deep breath, and another, and another. My thoughts crystallized. The power of three breaths and mental clarity. I said aloud,

"F* It, I'm going to Africa!"

Chapter 2
PEACE BE ON THE PLANE

"I am not the least thankful to be released. I prefer the
solitude and peace of prison. It gave me time for meditation."
—Gandhi

The whoop of the airplane door shut out my ADHD. A vacuum from the real world of non-stop political media, phone notifications, emails, technology distractions, even family, a plane was a place of solitude. Silence. Sedation. Only a tiny light shone on Trevor Noah's book. What solace!

Tactical timing and a scent of serendipity. Team4Tech was planning a trip to South Africa right after Thanksgiving. Their trip served as the perfect launchpad into my Africa travels. The vibes of the team were great, and the two leaders, Dawn and Paul, had pushed me over the finish line during dinner. Raising the money from supportive friends turned out to be easier than I thought. My friends knew I needed a break and that I needed to get out of town for a while. Thanks to them.

The trip came together so fluidly. The universe spoke, and I trusted, letting it do its work. Always selling, trying to make a round peg fit in a square hole, pushing hard was how I had continuously operated. This was different. Africa was waiting for me to ring the doorbell and welcome me in.

My thoughts calmed. I watched the plane creep across the map on the screen in front of my seat.

It must have been Vipassana (a ten-day silent meditation retreat) that started it all. I'd been meditating for years beginning at the Zen Center in San Francisco and had several friends who had experienced Vipassana. While in Japan, I was jumping out of my skin in anxiety and anger and could find no remedy. Those friends suggested I try a ten-day silent retreat to help me through this time. The most I'd done was two days; I couldn't fathom ten.

Most convincingly, it was free. The founder, Goenka, believed Dhamma, the laws of nature and happiness, was the only universal truth and that there should be no fee, only what one can afford to donate. The price was the self-inflicting mental and physical pain of ten days of silent meditation plus any small donation. The reward was happiness. Curious, I wanted to do it in Yangon, Myanmar, the home for this type of Buddhism.

Closing my eyes, crossing my legs on the seat, I reflected to the temple, the speeding motorcycles, and golden stupas piercing the blue sky. I arrived at a small white gate surrounded by tropical foliage with a concrete pathway that led me to a tiny white house. The white panel sign out front said, "Welcome to Dhamma Joti. Be Happy."

Arriving at the front desk, the monk at the check-in warned me, "Don't leave. Whatever you do, don't leave. This meditation will change your life." He grabbed my t-shirt by the shoulder and said in a heightened voice, "This is the most powerful thing in the world. If you can make it ten days, it will change your life." He looked over to a short, bald Asian American guy with a long beard, white tank top, and flip flops—clearly a dharma bum.[1]

The monk-like receptionist pointed at him and said, "Take him to the ground if he tries to leave." Before admittance to the retreat, each attendee must fill out a survey about everything happening in your life. Because of what I'd written, he knew I'd struggle to finish. Throughout the program, the teacher watches you closely while you meditate.

We walked to the men's corner at the base of a small hill that led up to a large stupa. The wooden huts, our lodging, had two wooden boards to sleep on with a small net hanging low to keep out the mosquitos and a bathroom about the span of my arms with dripping cold water.

So, what happened during those ten days? I woke up at 4 a.m., went to a hall with several hundred people, of which about thirty were foreigners, meditated two hours before eating a breakfast of porridge, banana, fruit, and no caffeine. From 8 to 11 a.m., I sat cross-legged, back straight with little movement. That was the critical point. By not moving, you could sense anything that happened in the body. At 11, we broke for lunch of lentils, local soup with potato, sprouts, and green veggies, and some rice. Afterward, a short nap spent looking at the ceiling in deep mental reflections—which I liked to do anyway. At 1 p.m., meditation started again till 6 p.m. the pain piercing up and down my spine doubled with an inner cry of despair. I wanted to pull my mind out of my head and stomp on it.

If that wasn't enough, the coughing, sneezing, and farting of fellow meditators along with hungry mosquitos in the humid, heat drove my senses mad. All of this suffering was all part of the process: to learn not to let external stimuli interfere with inner peace. At the end of each day, the reward was a tea and only one cookie for new meditators (none for the old) that kept me awake during the recorded discourse on a clunky VCD player from 8 to 10 p.m. by Goenka, himself. Not everyone could take the physical pain and the inner madness as the hall became sparser day by day. Over fifty percent of the 100 plus people had disappeared.

"Without judgment, try, try again," Goenka's tape-recorded discourse would repeat in the evenings. Sometimes thoughts were so redundant, so disturbing that I'd ask myself, "Am I a madman? I must be." After enough practice, the mind cleared for five seconds, then ten, then thirty, then more. And I must admit, having no thoughts for a few seconds was mesmerizing, magnificent, and mollifying. Then I'd go mad again, of course.

But during those short moments of peace, there were neither emotion nor thoughts. Anxiety is about expectations and concern for the future. Depression is about focusing on past mistakes or paths not taken. Identifying and then dismissing both of these allowed me to live in the moment, leaving anxiety and depression behind while immersing myself into whatever good or bad that moment might have been. So powerful. Even when my hips, knees, lower back, upper back, and all parts of my body screamed at me to lay down and just give up, I remained in the moment, bearing the pain each subsequent hour.

On the eighth day, I saw myself die. Maybe it was the person I was—*I hope it was that stupid tech salesman*—perhaps it was my future self, or maybe it was just any middle-aged person sitting there by a tree in the back of a small house. I wandered outside in a forest behind my humble cottage, sat down on a stump, and stared at my shaking hands. I hugged myself then fell over. Right after that, meditation was lunch, where I was holding my head in my hands, crying into a bowl of lentils. I decided to leave and, if it weren't for my Asian buddy, I would have. He walked by, tapped me on the shoulder, and said, "Don't leave, bro, don't leave—you are almost there." The next few days, I started my climb out of the valley of death and have been climbing ever since—no end in sight.

On the tenth day, the ban on talking lifted, and both men and women could intermingle. I spoke my first words as if I could read them coming out of my month letter by letter. Then, I understood awareness. Aware of every word I said, every step I took, and every thought that crossed my mind. That's when I realized I could identify emotions and feelings at the time of their origin and stop them in their paths. Catching a thought or emotion as it arose was like a breeze of wind blowing out a candle right before the match could light it. I felt completely balanced and contained, but also connected to the outer world. As I walked around, I could go deeper into the moment, focusing on all of my bodily sensations.

In this vacuum of no emotions and thoughts, new ones blossomed. Those who made it through radically transformed into new sentient beings, pure and happy. Oh, did people change their lives! One woman went to the Himalayas to work on irrigation systems while getting her yogi training over three months, six hours per day. My roommate went down the road to a monastery where he built shelters for the aging who had no place to live. Still, others took up physical challenges. A Hong Kong banker spent a month training at a Thai kickboxing gym and fought in local competitions; another extremely obese guy went on three more retreats, dropped about 100 pounds without gaining it back.

On the eleventh day, I strolled out of the temple down a hectic street with motorbikes crossing my path and nowhere to go, dreaming what my adventure might be. First, I had to quit my job. For years, I didn't accept that it wasn't the right place for me. Vipassana helped me to accept reality, detach, and move on.

The roar of the airplane engine snapped me back to the present and, I opened my eyes to glare at the simulated plane creeping across the monitor. South Africa was right in front of me, and as I moved the screen around with my finger, Uganda and Ghana were nowhere close. My lack of knowledge surprised me, and, to alleviate any negative happenings, I pulled out some paper to set guidelines for an accident-free trip. I began jotting down notes:

Ladies: Take a break from relationships and avoid flings. Focus on my journey.

I remembered a conversation with another traveler over a banana smoothie in Bali. She said, "It's best if you stick to your trip if that's what you're looking for. If you get caught up with someone, it won't be the experience YOU are searching for. I spent the last five months with some guy I ended up breaking up with, and now I only have a month to myself."

Physical health: I can use a workout app and maintain my running and swimming wherever possible.

Mental health: Meditate daily, limit the caffeine and booze, and read Zen Mind, Beginners Mind to keep me centered and steady.

Travel Depression: Identify traveler's depression and fear. Impoverished places cause unfathomably deep emotions. I've become depressed because of thoughts of privilege, reflections on or comparisons to my own life, and feelings of helplessness. Sense fear and remember that there are no heroes in tourism. Don't do anything too crazy that risks my life. Play it safe.

Learn: History, language, and cultures of each country so that I can differentiate them, appreciate the nuances of Africa, and speak about them intellectually.

I downloaded a few good books with me, such as *Dark Star Safari, Long Walk to Freedom, Fortunes in Africa, The Boy Who Harnessed the Wind, China's Second Continent, Born A Crime, Americanah,* and a few others.

Budget and Give Back: Budget $50 per day, including hotels and flights, if possible. Save 10 percent for giving back through donations, tips, buying souvenirs, or helping others.

New Project: Find something so that I can return to Africa. Don't start something; find someone to help. Starting something comes with a lot of responsibility and requires a deep understanding of local markets and pain points that I lacked, so helping seemed like a better idea.

Return Date: Fred's wedding in March? That seems long enough. *Fred's perspective was all I had needed to get on this plane*, I thought, as I dozed off. Get married and have babies or go to Africa? Ha, that was an easy decision.

Pleased with my notes, I went back to reading Trevor Noah. Colonialism had strained the relationships of ethnic groups in South Africa, adding even more combustion to pre-colonial grudges, rivalries, and context—leading to the point of genocide in certain countries like Rwanda. As it was illegal for white men and black women to procreate, Trevor Noah was literally "Born a Crime." Black and white South Africans called a mixed-race person 'colored,' and treated them as a separate race.

Trevor Noah came from the 'hood around Soweto, Johannesburg to fame in the United States of America. Amazing. I once knew a hood growing up in South Carolina, attending Southside High School for a few years, which was a predominantly black high school. Shootings, fights, and drug runs were a daily part of life. It wasn't easy to be someone born into that environment. There were few ways out for those kids. I wondered if it was anything like the Townships I was about to visit.

It'll be fun to work with junior high schoolers again. It's a nice age, just before they think they know it all. I hadn't done that since my first job out of college teaching English to kids in Japan. For this trip, though, I made a grave mistake. I volunteered to teach them how to build a website—something I don't even know. Idiot. Just because I can sell software doesn't mean I can create it. I wondered if I would learn something new as I looked out the window into Johannesburg. I had no clue about the tremendous impact that awaited.

"Ladies and gentlemen, prepare for your arrival, touching down in twenty-five minutes."

Chapter 3

UBUNTU—EMPATHY IN A TOWNSHIP IN SOUTH AFRICA

"The African philosophy of UBUNTU—best summarized as, 'I am human because of you because we are.' Through empathy and compassion, we can create a shared commitment to discovering new pathways together."
—**John Gilmour**, Founder of Leap Schools, South Africa

Having spent so much time working independently, I worried about joining a new group. Empathy rated last of the 34 potential traits I tested over a Clifton Strengths Assessment. My goal was to be the student and just take it all in. Not only would I learn from the students, I'd start my journey learning about empathy and compassion.

Trudging out of the terminal, I saw Paul waving at me with Dawn beside him. Paul was a red-blonde-haired Texan-turned-Californian surfer who spent his holidays riding the waves in West Africa, and Dawn was a lean, fresh, freckled-faced Asian girl of thirty-something who could take charge of a room even with her quiet demeanor. They were the leaders of the Team4Tech project and had just returned from a safari, and their smiley, gleeful faces eased my anxieties as we waited for the others to arrive.

"Kurt, dude, over here," said Paul, trying not to let out a yell.

"Yo. Yo. Yo. So good to see you. I need a coffee. And don't call me dude." I did hate that.

"Hey, you are a dude, that's why. You said you were on the other plane that arrived forty-five minutes ago," Dawn was agitated.

"Oops. Details. Sorry," I replied.

"You are a high-level kind of guy, aren't you?" Dawn said.

"Depends if the details matter. In this case, it didn't, you said to arrive within two hours of two." I gave her a wink.

"Let's catch up over there," said Paul. "How was the flight?"

"Good, I read Trevor Noah's book, flipped through my books on Africa, worked on the entrepreneurship presentation, and meditated."

"Watch any movies?" Paul inquired.

"Nah, I don't watch a lot of movies on planes. I use that time to read."

"That's impressive, you can read and work the entire time?"

"Yup, being in a plane is like taking Adderall—my ADHD medicine—but without the stimulant. Amazing what happens when the plane doors shut. As for movies, I can't make it through thirty minutes before my ADHD acts up."

"You are a machine," Dawn said, brushing her hair aside to gaze at me. "Oh, there are the others!" She jumped out of her chair.

The three who approached her were a typical motley crew from San Francisco: a shy, whippersnapper Asian engineer whose youthful complexion coupled with light brown eyes could stare right through you (I got that glare a few times); a talented business development expert who wanted to be a punk rock guitar player but was forbidden by his Jewish parents; and a fresh, floppy-haired, gangly Asian kid who walked out in a multi-colored Tetris-like designed hoodie (which was a hooded sweatshirt designed with many colors and shapes). I would later discover similar designs were common in the Congo. He spoke with a southern twang mixed with a breakdancer's vocabulary drowned in wannabe professionalism. Clarence was straight out of the ATL, i.e., Atlanta, Georgia.

The last three were older gentlemen. Two were my Tennessee compadres: Al, a former high school teacher and principal, and Wayne, an engineer at IBM and navy shipman. They approached with huge smiles. They were way more excited than the rest of us. The last was Tom, an older Norwegian gentleman who was a retired technology executive.

Al and Wayne looked over and laughed like old frat boys who egged each other on. "We are going to drink plenty of beer." Wayne pointed at me. I knew I'd get pulled into this at some point. I'd gotten to know Wayne over a phone call as we bonded about Tennessee, and I was secretly hoping to meet someone more reasonable politically than my at-the-moment dad.

Our group assembled, then we hopped into a white minibus.

"Dawn, you sure we should get into one of these? Trevor said these are dangerous," I said. "They're chased down by gangsters."

Dawn laughed, "Don't be silly. We have a driver, and it'll be fine."

As we drove through the city of Johannesburg, this once-booming gold and mineral industrial town that had turned into a financial center revealed an incredible contrast from past wealth and opportunity. In one neighborhood were the glass and steel skyscrapers of the business district surrounded by fetid shantytowns. In another, internationally-recognized universities were juxtaposed against an abundance of desperate poverty. I wanted to know how this came to be and how drastically opportunity was divided.

Two hours later, after small chit-chat and dozing off and on, we arrived in Pretoria, the administrative capital of South Africa, filled with embassies, universities, and research centers. We were staying at a regular, red-brick house in one of Pretoria's suburban, gated communities. It resembled a small plantation house in Charleston, South Carolina, with at least ten acres of land, a few horses grazing in the backyard, and a separate, three-door garage. The surrounding streets appeared much like any rural community in the United States with rows of houses and clean sidewalks, but with barbed wire-topped fences. A few black Africans strolled on the corner of the streets, seemingly with no place to go.

I needed to get some exercise, and the weather was perfect for a run. Anxiety was building up from lack of sleep and too much caffeine. Warming myself up for a jog, I heard a voice shout at me.

"Hey, you shouldn't go out there," said the landlord, a husky South African whose belly lopped over his belt as he walked out of the house.

"No?"

"Yeah, probably not safe to be running around alone, never know what can happen with those black folks hanging around. Stick around here. Right? Oy?" As if I didn't hear.

"Yeah, OK. Thanks."

This guy was scared to go out in his neighborhood. He stays at home in his gated farm with horses strolling in the pastures. The crime statistics of Johannesburg (Joburg) and South Africa are frightening, even as they are a reflection of severe wealth and opportunity contrasts. What a sad way to live—in fear. It was easy for me to judge; I wasn't familiar with the environment.

The first day started with a bang, an inspiring introduction by John Gilmour, the Founder of Leap6 Schools. He built the LEAP 6 schools to advance education for talented students who live in townships, with a particular focus on math, science, and leadership. With no support from the government, Gilmour raised capital from big companies in South Africa, such as BMW, Credit Suisse, and Toshiba. That dumbfounded me.

Why don't schools in the United States get sustained investment and systematic commitment from Google, Facebook, and the like rather than the occasional donated personal computing devices or one-off employee donation-match to PTA fundraising? After all, students might one day work for them.

Gilmour began by sharing his history.

"My personal journey through privileged education in post-colonial Africa did not prepare me for the real world of complexity. Society taught us to be clever and strategic—not wise and empathetic. Teachers taught us to be cautious and opportunistic, entrepreneurial for economic self-gain—not necessarily with a consciousness to work for the greater good. Our parents taught us that politeness trumps honesty—keep people happy while exploiting them. While Steve Biko was willing to die for what he believed about social injustice, I was responding strategically to keep myself safe, silent, and stay out of trouble."

John Gilmour had sacrificed his ideals and a more lucrative career so that he could create change for his community and his country. Inspirational. Impassioned. Invigorating.

Then, he described the challenges these students faced.

"Sixty-two percent don't even know their father's name. Some don't even know their birthdays. Our children are resilient, and we build around the resilience that is born out of extreme poverty, living in relative squalor, navigating drunk predatorial adults, caring for siblings, managing hunger, confronting domestic violence, and avoiding an embedded rape culture."

What do these kids *not* go through? Not only do they fight to live another day, but they also lack an identity.

I then asked him, "What should we teach them? What's the best thing we can give them?"

"Technology is great, but let them get to know you. Be humble, because you can also learn from the students. I've learned so much from them. *Leap* away from rugged individualism toward shared humanity and learning—we call this Ubuntu."

I left the room inspired and with a greater understanding that our speck of time with these kids was more than just teaching them. But let's be honest, what was I going to learn from them? I scoffed. *Open up a little and see what you can learn. You never know,* I coached myself.

The small school building of orange-reddish bricks comprised ten classrooms built in a small horseshoe. When I walked out to meet the students, the talent and intelligence at LEAP6 were immediately apparent.

The students greeted us, bombarding us with questions. "Are Americans racist?" "Do you like Trump?" "Will he help Africa?" "Why does everyone in the US have Apple?" "Are there Apple cars?" I'd later discover that throughout all of Africa, Apple stickers were plastered on the back of the cars as if it were a logo. They were boundlessly curious and fearless as they challenged us; they wanted to know who we were and what we thought.

Overtop their worldly knowledge, their artistic capabilities shone even brighter. The students had drawn much of the artwork around the school. They were musically active, too, the boys rapping to their rendition of "Cut-It" or girls singing "Love on the Brain." Their favorites were Young Thug, Rihanna, Kendrick Lamar, and Drake. The success and leadership of African Americans had inspired them.

Then the three girls—who left me with an indelible impression—jumped right into a conversation with Clarence and me.

"What does your name mean?" one asked Clarence.

"Clarence? Nothing. But my Chinese name has a meaning: Reminiscent of Peace."

"That's pretty. You are from China?" interjected another girl.

"American Chinese. I'm American, but my parents are from China."

"Oh, America. So many types of people," said a short, light-skinned Muslim girl.

They directed their questions to me, "What does Kurt mean?"

"Kurt . . . Kurt has no meaning," I replied.

"Yeah, it does, dude. It means direct, frank, to the point—just like you are," Clarence pointed at me as if he got me. "How about you?"

"My name is Mbili, and it means Be Proud."

"I'm Skilanhide, and it means Thank You."

"My name is Litawedi, which means Happiness, and I'm Muslim. Do Americans like Muslims?"

"Sure, it's OK to worship any religion in America. Of course, there are some racist people there too. There are racist people everywhere."

"Why? I'm nice to people. My friends don't like me because I'm Muslim."

"I'm sorry to hear that. You seem to be a great student and a humble person. Try to show them the beauty of your culture." Shocked that racism even penetrated the poorest of places, I now realized it had neither boundaries nor absolutes.

The students were proud of their names; if they had an identity, it seemed, it was the beauty of the meaning of their names. We left that day feeling we had a connection, one of interest, acceptance, and curiosity to learn more about each other.

That night we stopped off to get fish and chicken sandwiches at Nandos, a local fast-food restaurant that's famous for its peri-peri hot sauce—a kind of ketchup and tabasco mix. Entering the house with our bags of food, we heard the news blared the latest doings of Trump.

Here we go again.

Dawn rushed to turn down the volume on the TV and sighed, "Let's focus on today's activities." We continued to discuss our reflections of the day and share our feelings.

With Trump's mug in the background, the older members' enthusiasm drained out the sighs and groans from the younger members. "Wait, you two voted for Trump?!" exclaimed Clarence.

A palpable sense of distrust formed in the air as quickly as fog could emerge over the San Francisco Bay. I knew we needed to address it, so I opened a discussion to clear the fog.

Open thoughts came tumbling out, allowing an understanding of different viewpoints. The discussion was amicable. Perhaps because we weren't in the United States, perhaps because we were a team on a joint mission, we could be friends and talk about politics. Then Paul, who also argued with his pro-Trump father, chimed in. "The Trump issue is nothing compared to what these kids go through." Everyone nodded. *Sometimes all people need is a bit of perspective*, I thought.

That night, I laid awake with a bit of jet lag and the perspective of the two older Tennessee gentlemen echoing in my head. They gave me a better understanding of my father's viewpoints—and I had to come to South Africa to get that.

The next day our classes began, and over the week, my fellow Team4Tech teachers spent time setting up new computers and installing software then assisted the students using Google Cardboard, Makey Makey. I created WordPress websites in my class, learning as I went along.

During one of the classes, the two eighth grade girls I'd spoken to earlier—who were also top in their class—wanted to learn more.

"What else can we do with WordPress?" asked Litawedi.

"I don't know. You mean after you build a website?"

"Yes."

"I guess, start a company," I said, not thinking.

"Oooh. Can we make lots of money?"

"Maybe, if you do it right." I didn't know what door I was opening.

"Then we can leave here." She looked up to the sun.

"Possibly." I understood what she was getting at.

Mbile jumped in, "Yeah! We want to know how to build companies and make lots of money," she said, pointing at the ceiling.

"Yes! Then we will be happy," the other one chimed in.

"I'm not sure about that equation. Money doesn't mean happiness necessarily." Darn right, I'd been chasing it my whole life and wasn't that happy even as I amassed a reasonable monetary safety net. How was I going to convince them of this when I couldn't convince myself?

"With money, we can get out of here." She affirmed. How could I answer that? In her case, some money may mean happiness for sure. I couldn't argue.

"That's true, but ever heard of Mo' Money Mo' Problem?" That was my best response.

"Oh, yes. But that's an American thang, not an African thang." She improvised in an American accent. To her, entrepreneurship could be a way out, a way for her to control her destiny: Hope.

"Let's ask the boss. Dawn, these young ladies want to know about building companies. What do you think?" I wanted to impress her.

"Entrepreneurship! Yes, that's a great idea, you can teach a class in the afternoon, and we can do a demo day on the last day of school. Do you have any materials?"

"I can put together something tonight. It should be easy," I said confidently, not knowing what I would do.

"You are on the hook now, Kurt. Get busy." Then a "KUH-CHHHH," She cracked the whip as she walked away to the other classroom carrying her clipboard.

Pressure built up. I researched, reflected on my experiences, and watched YouTube videos of Steve Jobs. Of course. Synthesizing the information, I came up with a simple process for them: find a real problem you have today, find something that interests you, and then solve it. I was trying to infuse practicality with passion. Do something in your reach or your immediate community. As

Steve Jobs said, "Don't try to connect the dots going forward." This advice might help them find problems they can work on today that may take them somewhere tomorrow.

The next morning, after a quick breakfast, we piled into the bus. We were running late to be at the school when, all of a sudden, our bus pulled over.

Dawn looked disconcerted and waved her hand down, indicating to keep it down. Whispers came back from person to person. "They want a ransom," said Clarence.

While she and Paul spent an hour negotiating our ransom, the rest of us bonded in the back. Clarence turned to me and asked, "Dude, can I get some advice about Silicon Valley?"

"First, stop calling me dude. I hate that. Do I look like a dude?"

"Oh, sorry. But kinda, yeah."

"Next, I don't give advice. I can tell you my experiences, and you can decide what you want to take out of it."

"How do you succeed in Silicon Valley? You made it, right?"

"Made it? What's made it mean? Making millions, billions? Making F*You money as they say? I don't know. What's your F*You money? One million dollars, $10 million, $100 million? I just worked my butt off, saved a bit, and now here I am with you. I'm thirty-nine, you are twenty-four. The same place, same time. Now you tell me."

"Oh, good point. You had an interesting career, right? You got to live in Japan and Asia, travel, and do cool things."

"Sure, I did, and I'm grateful for it. I had some cool experiences. Look, there is no path, no prescription. You have to find out what makes you tick. Don't look at ten years. Figure it out now and do what means something to you. You are here now, right?"

"Yeah, I get you. I think."

"Why are you here?" I questioned.

"I just wanted to travel, see a different part of the world, gain a new perspective, that sort of thing. I'm working for the man right now—Cisco. I can't take it."

"Look, enjoy your time here. Then when you go back, think about it. Otherwise, you're wasting energy and getting anxious for nothing. Thinking takes a lot of energy. Try not doing it sometime."

"Not to think? How do you do that?"

"Deep meditation. It's called Vipassana. I'll tell you later." Then I flashed back to what I learned the night before. The best advice for him was what I was going to tell the kids. "Passion is a good thing, but you don't have to love everything you do. Practicality is important, and experiences are building blocks." At least that is what I convinced myself was a logical path in a reasonable world. In a few days, Mandela and Gandhi would show me a different way.

"What do you mean?" he asked.

"That's what I've done for years. I built up experience in finance and sales, then used it to enjoy the finer things in life like traveling and living abroad. I don't always love my job, but it builds my resume."

"You are saying, get specific experiences even if you don't like it?"

"Sometimes. The people and company size are important. I like small, agile companies. But then again, I'm not the wealthiest person around and didn't pick companies so well."

"I think I'm in too big a company; I'll try something smaller."

"Sure, you can always change. Sometimes, just paying the bills makes sense, so you can do other things you want that isn't work."

"That makes sense."

"And you don't always get your choice. Sometimes the opportunity picks you. I was turned down by Google three times, LinkedIn, Apple, and pretty much every successful company you can name. And things don't always work out as expected. So don't have any expectations."

"It seems like it still worked out for you, though. Your experiences have been amazing, and you seem to enjoy life."

"Yeah . . . I guess you are right. I do enjoy these experiences for sure."

"That's why it's cool. These older guys in tech seem pretty unhappy. They lived and worked their lives for one tech company after the next. I don't want to be that."

"Then, don't be. Try different things. You made it to Africa at twenty-four, that's not your normal twenty-four-year-old."

"I guess so."

"Anyways, you have a girlfriend?"

"Noooo," he replied, struck dumb.

"Pin-pong, you are twenty-four. Get a girlfriend, get a bottle of wine, and get laid—you'll be fine," I told him, only to be looked at by everyone on the bus like I was crazy.

"What did you just say?"

"Get a girlfriend . . ."

"No, I get that, before that." His voice heightened.

"Pin-pong . . ." I said like he should know what I was saying.

"What the heck is that?"

"It means bingo in Japanese."

"Man, your brain is whack." He laughed. "And I just don't NEED a girlfriend."

"I don't know, bro. At your age, all dudes need a girlfriend." The entire bus laughed at that one. Even though I poked fun at him, I appreciated his boost in confidence. Here was this young man telling me that he thought my life was interesting, exciting, and fun. I'll take the vote of confidence.

Once we paid off the local city gang who often tracked down buses with foreigners, we continued to the school to start our day of teaching. While the students were excited about the entrepreneurship class, there was one lingering issue.

"How do I make lots of money? Because money solves everything!" Litawedi kept asking me. Entrepreneurship became her answer to get rich, to get out of the hood. And while that may be the case, I wanted to move their minds from the pursuit of money to something else. Growing up here, the odds of them making lots of money were slim, so I didn't want that to be the measurement of success; it had to be something else. I didn't have the answer! I had driven myself into misery chasing money and had recently come to the realization that it didn't make me happy, nor was I uniquely even good at it. What on earth was I going to tell them?

That night I went back to researching, searching for the elusive answer. About four hours in, I stumbled upon a young Bill Gates's video. That was my "Aha!" moment. He said, "Form a belief and stick by it. Work hard to prove it right or wrong. That will give you a mission." Eureka! If these students—and I—could form a belief that they wanted to carry out and stick by, that would give them a mission, too. Whether or not it succeeded, having a purpose, they would be fulfilled.

Later that day, one of my favorite entrepreneur students, Mbili, invited me into her tiny mud-built home, half-covered with a tin awning, and still amid construction. She shared a torn-up mattress on a broken bed frame with her two siblings, had a small fridge, and a cracked TV. Her father showed up minutes later with a grin on his face, welcoming us in. He told us about his carpentry, how he loved his daughters and thanked us profusely for teaching them, and any opportunity we gave them. It was hard holding back the tears when I saw them welling in his eyes. This father was antithetical to the drunken stereotypes and one who lived to give his daughters all he had. She was as proud of him as he was her. He said, and I remember it correctly, "I pray every day that she can go to University and leave here forever." His entire life was in the hope that she could get away. His mission was to earn enough to pay his daughter's fees to University.

Back in class, I offered the students another perspective. Like Mibli's father, Bill Gates, even with his gazillion dollars, still had a mission to make the world and Africa a better place. To find his purpose, Gates formed a belief or hypothesis that technology could solve a problem, then he worked relentlessly to prove it right or wrong. Examples of those beliefs were how to distribute polio vaccines or how to invest in climate change. These missions gave him purpose. The pursuit of money alone didn't. He doesn't eat that much, I joked as I explained this to the class, but he liked to drink lots of Diet Coke. That got them to laugh and agreed that the mission was the focus for success.

Cooking a team dinner was on the agenda that evening. And I must say, cooking dinner must be the best team bonding activity ever. Dawn took me shopping at the local grocery store, which reminded me of a supermarket back home only with less variety. *Who needs 50 kinds of cereal to pick from, anyway?*

Searching my way through the aisles, I came across what was called Tomato Sauce, with two big tomatoes on the front.

Back at the ranch, we all went to work. Paul made his specialty stew, Clarence prepared a French chicken recipe, and I drummed up my bomb spaghetti—*the best spaghetti sauce in the world*. We served dinner was served and chowed down.

I noticed Dawn playing with her spaghetti. I asked, "Hey, what's the problem? Isn't this the bomb spaghetti?"

"Yeah, bombed is the right word," she replied.

"What's the matter? Tastes fine to me." I retorted.

"Sauce is a bit thick, did you add some sugar?" Dawn's cheeks rose as if she had just swallowed a spoonful of it.

"This is ketchup, Kurt, not tomato sauce," Dawn said as the sauce dripped off her spoon.

Laughter burst out around the table. I was embarrassed. Dawn appeared with the open tomato sauce: "You don't read the fine print: Best used on fries and burgers. Maybe I should pour it right on your head."

"Now you are acting like an African wife. South African wives throw boiling water on their husbands when angry," I repeated a line from Trevor Noah.

"I'm not angry. I'm laughing at you!" She pointed at my crooked nose.

"Guess I'm not a very good cook." It was a long time since I had admitted defeat. But oddly, it felt good to be vulnerable in this safe space of newly-found friends.

That was how we ended the night, with everyone in tears over my terrible spaghetti. They did get to enjoy a great casserole cooked by Paul and Clarence, and our bonds grew stronger with our shared experiences. The process, rather than the actual culinary outcome, was rewarding.

The next day was the end of the year awards ceremony and a fantastic exhibition of the students' culture. They sang and danced, then demonstrated their entrepreneurship projects. One team sold around $55 worth of burgers, claiming there were no freshly made burgers in their local area. Another group made trash cans to separate recyclables, while another made a website to help others build websites. The winners were a group that had previously started a landscape company servicing wealthy South Africans' yards.

A comment from one of the founders of the landscape company struck a chord. "Talent is everywhere, but opportunity is nowhere. That's the problem we have."

I replied, "What did starting a company teach you?"

He thought for a second while he played with his phone and then replied, "We can create our opportunities." Absolutely! The class was a success. I left him with something positive, and he unknowingly elucidated to me how I was lucky to have so many opportunities in the USA.

That night we went out for Wayne's birthday of BBQ game meat (called braai)—I later regretted eating the oryx after seeing how beautiful the blue and brown creature was.

With a little buzz, I stayed on the couch, thinking about what I had learned. Putting myself in the students' world, I learned the power of connection. Those three young souls taught me how to relate humanly. Be kind. Be compassionate. Be empathetic.

What is empathy? I used to think, "Yeah, I get it. Your life is a lot harder than mine but let me help or give advice." That isn't empathy. That is privilege, arrogance, or a combination of the two. It's certainly not the way to relate to someone. Empathy is not just to acknowledge the difficulty of another's life but to understand and experience it.

LEAP was about mutual empathy and learning together. By teaching students how to be entrepreneurs, I learned how to be one. Developing a mission based on a set of beliefs or assumptions was the starting point. There is no doubt that I learned more than they did. Glaring at the white ceiling, I started to fade but had one final thought. It can no longer be about the pursuit of money or purely self-gain. The mission must trump both money and self-interest—it has to be that way. Those kids showed me the power of Ubuntu—shared learning and commitment to make a new path together.

The girls at Leap School 6

Team4Tech team picture before eating braai

Chapter 4

LEARNING HOW TO JOURNEY

"I had no epiphany, no singular revelation, no moment of
truth, but a steady accumulation of a thousand slights . . .
There was no particular day on which I said, henceforth, I
will devote myself to the liberation of my people; instead, I
simply found myself doing so, and could not do otherwise."
—**Nelson Mandela**, *Long Walk to Freedom*

This quote lingered in my mind as I visited the Apartheid Museum, the Nelson Mandela National Museum, and his humble house in Soweto. Without considering the personal costs, without fear of persecution, he trusted the unknown because his mission was so profound.

The Team4Tech crew spent our final day in Johannesburg touring the museums and learning about Mandela and Gandhi. There was much to comprehend, remember, and reflect. Not being able to remember it all, I spent most of my time taking pictures of my favorite scenes and quotes.

Soweto began as a socially engineered settlement for gold mining laborers and squatters separating them from the white Afrikaners[2]. Now it is home to 1.3 million people, the most famous of whom is Trevor Noah. Acclaimed South African novelist, Dr. Benedict Wallet Vilakazi's wrote, "Soweto is a symbol of the New South Africa, caught between old squatter misery and new prosperity, squalor and an upbeat lifestyle, it's a vibrant city which still openly bears the scars of the Apartheid past and yet shows what's possible in the New South Africa."[3]

Tourist vendors lined the streets, new local restaurants with sports cars parked outside, hawkers sold jewelry and beverages. A short glance down the valley were shantytowns lining the side of the hill.

Strolling beside the street vendors, I stopped at one and decided to pick up a Kaiser Chiefs jersey in support of the local soccer team while at the same time shedding myself of the American tourist silhouette. Wearing soccer jerseys had become one of my favorite travel accessories.

On checkout, the young salesman asked, "You sure you want to buy this?" as though he knew something I didn't.

"Sure, why not. I like the color, orange-yellow." My favorite color.

"Maybe you should get a rugby one?" He picked up the green national team jersey for South Africa.

"Nah, I don't like rugby. I'm not that tough."

"Right. Then go ahead with this one."

"How much?"

"$10."

"OK, sure." I could have bargained, but I didn't. A few dollars meant a lot more to him than to me.

He handed me the jersey then looked at me with sharp eyes, expressing both anger and envy. Uneasiness crept down my neck, feeling like spiders crawling on my skin. I didn't understand his coldness, nor his unwillingness to sell me the yellow jersey. This interaction would come full circle a week later.

That evening, we all said our goodbyes, and soft-spoken Tom and I headed to a decent hotel near the airport where we shared a room. He was a retired technology salesman and business development professional-turned-executive from Norway. We chatted over dinner.

"Those museums in Joburg were amazing, don't you think, Kurt? What made an impression on you?" asked Tom.

"How Mandela committed his life to better society, country, and the world. To be driven by such deep purpose and meaning."

"I am lucky to have grown up in Norway. No one is poor, and everyone has access to more or less the same opportunities to pursue their dreams."

"In the US, we take pursuing our dreams for granted, too. Like here, we also have an income-divide problem. Tell me more about Norway," I replied.

"For one, the Norwegian government funded my degree in the United Kingdom and even my MBA in the United States."

"That's nice. Did you find meaning in your work?"

"I did. I thought SAP developed a lot of great solutions that benefited others. ERP software isn't sexy, but we empowered a lot of companies, non-profits, and government organizations in developing countries to run better."

"Oh yeah, like what?"

"In India, I worked on an e-commerce project with Mahindra that made it possible for farmers to get their products to market more efficiently. Some 40 percent of their product never made it to market, and they export very little. My career at SAP opened my eyes to how IT can make the world a better place."

"I didn't feel that way with my last company."

"You have plenty of time to find something you love. You don't have to go back to the rat race. If you did, it's easy for you, right?" He knew how to say the right thing.

"Good perspective. What brought you here?" I inquired.

"Now that I'm retired, I have time to do some volunteering and traveling. My passion is to help young people in developing countries learn how to use technology. I love how Team4Tech is working with global technology companies to improve education in developing countries."

"Sounds fun to me. Maybe I can find something like that in Africa?" I followed.

"Sure, why not! There's so much to do here! My kids have finished college; they have good jobs and are off the payroll. I now have time and in a financial position to focus on what I love. Anyways, want to go to Kruger with me tomorrow?"

"Thanks for asking, but I think I'm going to take a ride somewhere and explore more of this area before taking off."

"Fully understand. When do you plan to leave?"

"I don't know, to be honest. I'm thinking around the holidays, but I'd love to see this continent."

"What's holding you back? You seem a little hesitant. Clearly not another job selling software." He smiled and chuckled a bit.

I was always a bit hesitant these days, and he honed in on that. "True dat."

"Take some time for yourself. You are single and have no commitments holding you back. There may not be another time for you to see this amazing continent. During your travels, you may even find an entrepreneurial opportunity to leverage tech and help improve people's lives."

"Yeah, you are right."

"Let's get some sleep. It's been a long day."

It's nice to have the perspective of an older friend. What's the darn rush? That was my last thought before fading off. The next day, we parted ways—he on a safari and me to Joburg to plan out my trip.

In Johannesburg, I stayed at Once in Joburg, a new hostel frequented by global backpackers in the Braamfontein district. Planning my travel route through Southern Africa, drawing on recommendations from backpackers and non-profit workers who were also staying at the hostel, I spent the next few days sketching out a plan.

Then came an inbound WhatsApp message from Tessa, "How was the experience in the Township?"

"Those kids go through so much and have tough lives, but their passion for living is
remarkable."

"It must be so inspiring to meet them," she replied.

"They inspired me. Much more than the other way around."

"What did you teach?"

"An entrepreneurship class."

"That's a perfect class for you."

"Kind of, since I'm a quasi-entrepreneur. I'd like to do more teaching after this."

"Don't kid yourself. You are an entrepreneur, not just in business but in life."

"Ah, thanks."

"Teaching is such a noble profession. Maybe you can find more places to do it?"

"Not sure, I'll look around. That's a good idea. Travel and teaching sounds like a good plan, though."

"Yes, it would! Where are you now?"

"Joburg."

"Be safe there, especially at night, and make sure to go to the museums, they are wonderful."

"We already went. They were moving. I'll keep my eye out. I am going to take a drive tomorrow—thinking about Lesotho and Swaziland."

"Oh wow, I've been to Swaziland but not to Lesotho. Send me a few outstanding pictures, not too many!"

"Will do!"

That's the art of photography these days. One can take a thousand pictures, but the real skill is picking the two or three that tell it all. Right about then, my phone died, so I needed to buy a top-up SIM card at the supermarket. The streets around the hotel had homeless people sleeping in the alleys, others walking around talking loudly. Tourists reminded each other not to go out alone due to lynching. Unsure if I should venture out, I asked the receptionist who said, "Make it quick and don't talk to anyone."

On the way to the supermarket, I noticed someone tucked beside the corner of a building. I glanced at him, and he yelled at me, "Why are you walking around here? "

"Because I need a Coke. Why are you around here?" I responded.

"Aren't you scared?" he questioned.

"Of what?" I replied.

"Me, the others."

"I'm headed to the supermarket. Want anything?" I looked right at him, not showing an ounce of fear. What I wanted to ask was, "What are you angry about?" I bit my tongue.

"Some chips, a coke. Is that OK?"

"No problem." On the way back, I dropped him off a bag full of goodies and received a "Thank you."

That interaction, the angry eyes of the t-shirt vendor, and lingering emotions from the readings of Mandela all set me into deep thought about the topic of anger and prejudice. What causes anger? Better yet, what has caused my outrage? Being poorly treated, never being given a chance or opportunity, experiencing trauma both personally and inter-generationally can all summed up by 'unfairness.' My life wasn't unfair by any stretch of the imagination. Yet when my ego didn't get what it wanted, it got angry.

How to rid myself of anger? I reflected on a quote I saw at the museum. "Forgiveness is Liberating," described by Desmond Tutu, the 1994 South African Nobel Peace Prize Winner who preached across South Africa after Apartheid. The only way to liberate oneself of anger was to forgive others and oneself. By letting it all go, understanding and empathy can grow in a vacuum. Mandela took that empathy and compassion on a profound journey.

Chapter 5

MAKING A NEW FRIEND IN LESOTHO

*"Sometimes, it takes a stranger to give you
a punch in the arm dose of perspective."*

—KD

Sitting in my Nissan X-Trail. *Should I get out of my car and ask him where to go? I am already mentally lost; now physically, I don't know where the heck I am. Can't I get some data to guide the GPS on my Google Maps?* I thought. On one side of me sprawled a massive farm where cows and horses roamed. On the other, a large white house typical of any American farmer. But I wasn't in Kansas anymore. From across the yard, the farmer approached with his two (huge) dogs of a species I'd never seen.

He clenched a long stick in his right hand and stopped about 10 meters away while trying to see who I was. I let out a, "Hello! I'm a bit lost and not from around here. I couldn't help but watch that sunset. I'm heading to Lesotho."

"Oi? Lesotho?" he paused. "You should be going southeast, not north. What are you doing there?"

"Just driving around."

"Where are you from?"

"USA."

"We don't see many of you around here. You are an adventurous one." He lifted the rifle and waved it at me. I ducked below the steering wheel.

"Hey, put that thing down!"

"Oi! Don't be alarmed, mate. It's just for protection."

"We don't see sunsets like that—or dogs. What kind are they?"

"Barbarian Boerboels," he replied. "It'll kill a lion."

"Kill a lion?" *Holy cow,* I thought.

"You better get going. It's going to be dark, and you don't want to arrive so late. It's not safe on these roads. Go back that way, take the first left and then the next right, and you'll be on the paved road," he instructed, pointing the gun toward the horizon. I had secretly hoped he would invite me in for dinner.

What and where is Lesotho? Aside from the Vatican, Lesotho is the only country in the world encircled by another—South Africa—and the locals reminded me of this almost daily. It's a small country of soaring mountains and dramatic gorges that's been dubbed the 'Kingdom in the Sky' and is building a tourism industry around adventure. It's home to around two million people with a quarter of those living in the bustling capital, Maseru, which nestles in a river valley. Its government is a constitutional monarch—which means the King doesn't have power, and the people vote for the prime minister.[4] One traveler described it to me as a sprawling village, with rural huts dotting picturesque landscapes where shepherds dressed in long colorful robes graze their sheep, cows, horses, and zorses (a zebra and horse mixed breed).

The drive to Lesotho took me through mostly barren landscapes interspersed with farms and B&Bs, as well as a few game parks. Seven hours since I left and several chicken sandwiches with peri-peri sauce later (I couldn't stop eating these), I arrived at the border between South Africa and Lesotho. A scattering of vendors on wooden and milk crates sold SIM cards, Lesotho wool blankets, and packaged snacks. Underneath dimly lit streetlights that created a haze in the humidity, people scurried here and there. There was a sense of commotion as trucks, cars, and buses negotiated their way through the small red gate; there were several hundred people walking to and from the small customs gate, which resembled a one-story house with three windows.

I lined up at the windows and struck up a conversation with a tall, light skin-colored man standing behind me who wore a baggy shirt, crooked baseball cap, and slightly tilted glasses. Rori introduced me to his wife, Matheko, and we immediately bonded.

The following day, we met up at a local shopping mall that had recently been built and occupied by South African-branded stores. At one of the alfresco restaurants, we settled into their patio chairs with a Maluti—the famous local beer that South Africans come across the border to purchase. We spoke about traveling in Lesotho and how the roads had improved compared to years ago. The Chinese had built roads, hotels, and government buildings. But there were also some on-going disputes between the Chinese and Lesotho government around payment and Chinese marrying local women, which both sides didn't seem to approve.

We hopped in the car, drove down the road, and stopped off at a little shack that looked like a used tire shop with a BBQ on the side. The sign said, "Chicken Here" pointing left and "Tires There" pointing right. The chickens were running around and killed right out back. While eating the best chicken sandwich EVER, he offered to take the trip around Lesotho with me. I paused and thought he would be a safe travel partner. Matheko agreed and said this would be an excellent opportunity for him to escape for a bit, and she would tend to the kids. Without his company, I wouldn't have adventured alone due to a lack of available information about the quality of roads and safety, though these fears proved to be unwarranted.

The following morning, we navigated the hectic, potholed streets of Maseru, not only used by cars but also people, donkeys, and livestock. We passed the aptly named Lion Rock Mountain, which was said to have spiritual powers at certain times of the year then headed toward the Kome Caves in Tetanyang, a ninety-minute drive from the capital. It was the first dose of mystical landscapes that I'd get more of in Zimbabwe.

Detouring a bit off track, we decided to go to Maliba Lodge for a scenic drive of the Valley. The road ascended to an arid plateau before descending into a lush forest that blanketed the mountainous valley. Beautifully decorated sun-dried mud huts dotted the sides of the way as shepherds herded animals in the surrounding fields. They certainly did the best they could to make their homes quaint and welcoming.

Along the way, kids played on the side of the road, and we stopped to take pictures with them. Rori jumped out of the car to hand them some snacks and money. Though he was reticent much of the time, he made an occasional insightful comment. Back in the car, he remarked, "I'm glad I wasn't born out here, it's impossible to go from here to Maseru. So little opportunity for them. What do you think you'd do if you were born here?" I had no response, but I immediately thought, sell something. I cringed at the thought of selling, but then appreciated that it was undoubtedly a dose of perspective.

After a lunch of a basic ham and cheese sandwich at the Maliba Lodge, we drove through the Tsehlanyane National Park back out the road to route A1 and continued to our final destination that day, Sani Pass. This unpaved road lies in no man's land along the border between Lesotho and South Africa. Just as we passed Afriski, the only ski resort on the continent, we weaved along the top of the hills, Rori exclaimed, "We are riding on the sky!"

Driving through the clouds around a small mountain, we noticed the fog settled into the valley. Glancing to the left, over yonder, I saw what looked like a small town built on a rugged black rock in the distance—maybe half a mile away in the middle of nowhere. The sign read, Letseng Mines—I later learned this was one of the mines from which DeBeers sources their diamonds. Looking closer through my long-distance camera lens, it looked like a mining operation on the moon. No kidding.

Ahead on the street, I caught someone dressed in a brown, wool blanket walking in and out of the dense fog—though some Basotho blankets were of reds, blues, and yellow with symbolic designs. Where was he going? We followed him until he stepped off on the other side of the road where there was a small village. The crumbling mud huts about ten feet in diameter were barely standing; there were a few animals grazing around and smoke rising from the inadequate shelters where a few people popped in and out of the rain. *He waved as we drove by. Is he the labor of the mine? Maybe this isn't blood diamonds, but it surely seems like exploitation for rings.* I thought. After seeing this, I vowed never to buy that rock for anyone.

That night, we stayed in one of the old ski cabins at the Sani Lodge and sunk a few Maluti beers in what was the highest pub in Africa. Decorated with pictures of people pushing their VW Beatles loaded with ski gear along the pass, chasing their cars down the hill, or posing with their wrecked vehicles, the walls illustrated the generations of past. Imagine driving a VW Bug up this pass in the snow!

After breakfast the following morning, we continued for six hours to an adventure area called Semonkong Lodge, which ended up being the highlight of the trip. Tucked inside a mountainous valley, Semonkong Lodge was an up and coming adventure destination for tourists. In addition to mountain biking and fishing, they offered what is said to be the world's tallest abseil 200-meter (600-foot) drop.

The next day I got a dose of the humanitarian aid world while mountain biking through the hills. While I was cycling through the lush and verdant mountain ranges interlaced with small villages, I came across a US AID truck handing out food. What could this be? I listened in as a lady explained to the villagers about the rations and when they'd come next. I questioned the sustainability of it.

Rather than rations, how about helping them establish a farm or learn about irrigation? I questioned. I didn't know enough about what was happening but wanted to learn more about what US AID was doing in Africa. In general, I wanted to learn how to best help people in these environments.

After two days adventuring at the Semonkong Lodge, Rori and I parted ways. We'd explored all corners of his country, nutted out ways to make his import car project work more effectively (though it never came to fruition), and just enjoyed each other's company. Granted that I had a bit of fear to go on a trip with a stranger, I opened myself up to him. When I realized I could just be myself and not worry, I became more comfortable around him and also with the idea of approaching others in the future.

Above all else, he taught me about friendship. I had been guilty of being envious toward friends, friends with more lucrative and successful careers, and friends with lasting romantic relationships. Rori only wanted to help me have a great experience in his country. That created trust. His calmness and kindness pacified me throughout the entire trip, and he never once got upset. Upon departing, he told me I should be thankful to be able to travel like this. It was like a punch in the arm dose of perspective from a stranger.

Chapter 6

FACING FEAR AND RACISM
IN SOUTH AFRICA'S "WILD COAST"

"I was asked as well about the fears of whites. I knew that people
expected me to harbour anger towards whites. But I had none. In
prison, my anger towards whites decreased, but my hatred for the
system grew. I wanted South Africa to see that I loved even my enemies
while I hated the system that turned us against one another."
—**Nelson Mandela**, *Long Walk to Freedom*

Durban, a city on the coast, was well known for its beaches, surf, and shark diving. I feared sharks and wanted to face this, so I headed south to the coast. Not only was I about to learn about fear, but also the timeless fear of racism.

The drive was draining, and I became sick of looking over my shoulder at rest stops. Should I be scared? Was I racist? I needed to unwind. What better place to hang out than at the beach?

Cozy in its design, a surfer's house—so I call it—was located just outside of Durban in Port Shepstone, sitting right on the coast. Aside from its smooth-talking South African host and an Aussie surf instructor, the surfer's house was currently home to a group of German travelers, a couple overlanding several countries in a 4-by-4, and a few white locals coming in and out.

There were just eight beds plus a large yard for campers, backed by shrubbery that led into a beach spot. It was the perfect spot to hang my hat for a week while scuba diving and surfing. I couldn't wait to dive into the great diversity of the Indian Ocean pelagic. Diving with hammerhead sharks had long been on my travel bucket list. Scuba diving in the past was like floating in a fish tank filled with tropical fish. I wanted to dive with real predators, ones that could eat me.

The first dive spot on my radar was Aliwal Shoals, a rocky reef renowned for its large predatory marine species and cave inhabited by raggies—a type of long-toothed shark. I joined the Agulhas House dive shop, which had a pool and diving gear targeting serious divers.

Off to the ocean, a handful of us jumped into a large navy seal-type raft. We motored out a few miles, where they would drop a large feeding ball into the water, then wait as blacktip and bull sharks congregated before signaling for everyone to jump in. They assured me the sharks had never attacked anyone.

They swarmed above and then around me like bees around a hive. Gradually, I became accustomed to their presence as they did mine. Some swam right toward me, showed their teeth then suddenly change directions. Thankfully, I wasn't the tasty bait they wanted. As Vipassana taught me, my fear could dissipate if I saw it as it was and then let it go. By staring down sharks, by looking directly into the black pits in their gaping jaws, by meeting them nose to nose—or at least close to it—I'd overcome my fear.

Not satisfied as I still felt like I was just bobbing up and down in a fish tank, I searched out another dive shop at Protea Banks—another offshore reef—with African Dive Adventures. An older African lady with greying blonde hair and a charming accent greeted me, "How much diving have you done?"

"I just dove yesterday and have done plenty."

"Plenty?" Her accent rose. "Like 100 dives?"

"Not quite . . . 50-ish."

"OK, then you should be fine. The water is quick and the current strong, so you will have to be relaxed. We aren't swimming with little fishies." She smiled, looking at the chalkboard with a list of daily sightings: 10 bull sharks, 50+ hammerheads, 5 stingrays, and the list went on. Astonished and amazed, I needed a coffee to settle me down—or not. "He will get you in an hour. Enjoy your coffee, but don't dehydrate yourself," she added.

They had photos of herds of sharks plastered on the wall. *No more bobbing around in fish tanks anymore,* I thought. She continued, "That's during the Sardine Run in the summer. It's one of the most amazing sites in the underwater world. Every underwater creature in one place, at one time, chasing the migration of the sardines. Join us if you come back around."

I replied, "Maybe. Not sure I can swing it, but let's stay in touch on Facebook." If I could end my trip back here in the summer, that would be EPIC!

Then the boss arrived. He was a 6-foot, older man in his sixties who had a youthful face but a beer belly that made up for it. He walked fast right up behind me.

"Brother, you coming with us? Let's go. I'm Roland, the Skipper. You American?"

"Yes, sir."

"Good fresh bait here, honey!" She smirked. "Why, sir? Don't hear that much from Americans."

"Huh, what? Oh yeah, well, I came from the South."

"South, like Texas?"

"The other south . . . South Carolina. We try to be polite and cordial, from the British influence," I said with a southern accent.

"That's interesting. I like you guys; you are fresh, never know what can happen with you people. You are all so different. So, how many dives?"

"50-ish"

"Ish . . . fish? Like 25? Or 45?"

"Yeah."

"Yeah, what man? Look, this is a real dive. We go fast, we move. If you don't, you just stay on the boat. To catch hammerheads, you've got to find a pack and drift right through them, not wasting any time."

"OK, OK. I'll be fine. Don't worry."

"Don't worry—famous last words for Americans. If you miss them, then you can always come back tomorrow! One dive per day here. We go deep for rec diving. Most go 18 meters. We go 30 to 40 meters plus."

"Ooh, that's deep."

"Just stay with me, mate. Get down fast, follow us, and don't try to pet the sharks. You know, they aren't little doggies. They eat fingers."

"Yeah, well, I went yesterday to Aliwal."

"That's good. You see raggies?"

"No, no raggies. Just the bait dive."

"That's kids play. This ain't bait diving. This is like running with the bulls. That's dangerous anyway. One day not long ago, a tiger shark took one of my divers out during a baited dive. When we pulled him out, we only found one of his legs stuck in his wetsuit," he said, gesturing his hand across his neck with a big smile. I never found out if that was true.

We jumped into his pickup truck and headed off, meeting on the shore a few miles out beside the highway. "This is the boat, an old Navy Seal model from the US. You all make some decent boats. We touch them up and make real boats out of them, ha-ha! Can't sink this thing. No way. We go in here and drive out twenty-five minutes" He paused and looked around. "The currents are fast today—three knots. They will take you downstream like the wind pushing you down a mountain, so when I say jump, you get in immediately and descend quickly. Don't play with your cammie until you get down."

"Cammie?"

"Yeah, your GoPro (a small handheld camera). Like, Mosquitos are mozzies, cameras are cammies. Get with it."

"OK, got it."

The six passengers, driver, and skipper launched the boat into the choppy, cold waters. We thrust the boat into the waters, pushing it out over the incoming tides that were splashing in our faces. With one last heave, we got it over the crashing tides, and I fell back, nearly swept back onto the shore over a rocky bottom. Oh Geez! That hurt! *If this is an indicator of the trip, it's going to be a rough one,* I thought. I hustled back out to the boat, and the skipper grabbed me on the back of my wetsuit and pulled me in.

He started up the 100HP engines with a rumble of thunder that sounded like an 18-wheeler truck.

"Why so big?" I yelled.

"We need the power to get through these waves!" He pointed at the waves about 100 meters away.

"Oh, god! That's where I'm going?" I muttered.

"Three- or four-meter swells today. It ain't the biggest, but it's going to be a fun ride!" He smiled. "If you get thrown off the boat, just swim back to shore. You can come back tomorrow!" he laughed.

Who in their right state of mind even dreams of launching in this surf? This adventure defined as an activity that could lead to death, and I am right in the middle of it. There are no heroes in doing crazy tourist activities, and this may just be one.

Suddenly, the driver, Spike, threw his throttles from neutral into full speed forward. The engine screamed, shooting the boat like a torpedo toward a wall of water. The water broke meters in front of us, we road up the foam, and took off like a jet in midair right out of the water. The six passengers tumbled to the back of the boat on top of each other. The bow of the superpower raft took off almost at a 90-degree angle to the water.

"Holy!" I yelled, and so did all the others.

"Wahoo!" screamed the skipper holding onto the handlebars as if he were hanging from midair. Spike sandwiched into the driver's seat in between two padded seats. The boat came crashing down, and the incredible speed shot us over the comb of the next wave. Spike then turned the wheel to 45 degrees to glide over the third wave, almost like surfing out of the danger zone.

"All good!" yelled Roland.

"Is that a question or a statement?" I replied.

"Both!" he proclaimed. "Get up and in your seat. We are off!"

These guys were fun and outright mad. I wanted a retake.

After riding out in the choppy waters, we came to a stop kit up our diving equipment and sat around looking at each other.

"Hold steady, hold steady," said Roland guiding us.

We were waiting for three, four, five minutes. The driver was looking at a dive monitor, which I presumed was tracking something, although I didn't know what.

Out of nowhere, he burst, "OK, get in!"

"So fast? Hold on!" I wasn't mentally prepared. Of course not—am I ever?

The current was like being shot out of a cannon. I was descending the slowest while the others dropped fast, and I saw our fearless leader waving me down. Exhale, exhale. I pushed the deflating valve to get the air out of my vest. I had to get below 20 meters, where the water was calmer.

I finally got down and joined the others gazing up. I couldn't control my buoyancy and was bobbing up and down, struggling to stay low enough. Something kept propelling me upward—was it the lack of weight on my belt? Did I not deflate my vest enough? I couldn't figure it out. About fifteen minutes in, the current swept me upward, upward, and I shot ahead of the other divers, skyrocketing to the surface and catching sight of a single manta ray, just my consolation prize for playing.

Back at the boat, I got an earful.

"Brother! I told you to stay calm down there—the faster the current, the better the visibility and the more sharks. You missed the best pack of hammerheads we've seen all season. We went straight through them. You will have to come tomorrow. Only one dive per day at these depths."

"OK, I couldn't stay down. I wasn't mentally ready."

"We will get you another weight," he suggested, looking at my weight belt. "Man! That was amazing. We floated right through a complete pack. Could almost have touched them."

Without due, I returned the following day to dive again and felt much more comfortable—perhaps because the current wasn't as fierce. I did catch some hammerheads and bull sharks about 10 meters away. Adventure diving at its best! I'd have to return one day between May and July to experience the annual Sardine Run off Agulhas Bay. Nothing like more adventure to excite the soul.

With newfound energy back at the surfer's house, I was ready to make some friends and talk about the crazy adventure. I had a snack and scrolled through my videos and pictures while sipping on a flat white coffee. In walked the surf instructor from the back and quipped, "Nice shirt," remarking upon the orange-yellow jersey I wore and kept walking by. *What's his friggin' problem?* I thought. Not long after, he invited several hostel members out for dinner, completely ignoring me, walked right out the door. I got dissed.

Disturbed and irritated, I went out to a shopping mall to eat supper and shop for some camera gear in Port Shephard. Then, the strangest thing happened. While eating at Ocean Basket, a local fish restaurant, a black guy got up from his family meal and slowly walked over and asked me, "Can we get a picture together?" He explained that I was wearing a Kaiser jersey, and it was very unusual to see a white person wearing it because soccer was a black man's game.

We took a selfie, hugged (no kidding, we hugged), and he went back to his family dinner. Then, another clue popped up. I remembered the words of the vendor who'd sold me the jersey, "Are you sure you want to buy this?"

The next morning, I decided to get on my way, and while checking out, it came full circle when I chatted with the hostel owner.

"I have a strange question for you."

"Go on."

"Yesterday at dinner, a black man approached me, and we chatted about this shirt. He was surprised I was wearing it."

"Oh, you don't know?" he seemed surprised that I didn't understand the context.

"No. Not at all."

"We were wondering why you were wearing that. We don't like soccer here. It's a black man's sport—Mandela's sport."

"So then . . . what's a white man's sport?" I replied.

"Rugby, even though they want to enforce the quotas for more black people on our teams. When they did, we lost. So now they are relaxing the quotas for more white people again." he said.

"Thanks for letting me know. I like this jersey. I like the orange-yellowish color. I like soccer and here's a tip for the (black) cleaning lady. I hope she gets it."

"That's nice of you. Safe travels." He spoke clearly through his clenched teeth.

How sensitive can he be to something so insignificant to my wearing a soccer jersey? I had just liked the color. What inexplicable racism he attached to it. Soccer is a black man's sport, and rugby is a white man's? Ludicrous.

The mystery lingered. I skimmed through my Mandela notes and books over a coffee. In the book *In the Words of Mandela,* he explained that "soccer is one of the sporting disciplines in which Africa is rising to demonstrate her excellence." He wanted soccer to unite South Africa, not divide it. I took off driving unsettled and felt anger kindling.

How could something as futile as a soccer jersey cause such ill-will in a person? I thought. I don't know if he didn't invite me to dinner because I was wearing this jersey, but it certainly seemed like it based on his response and tone. If that was the case, a white guy expressed racism toward another white guy for wearing a shirt that represents black people. Ridiculous.

That's when it struck. Racism's perpetrator isn't a color; it is a label or set of ideas held by people who want to protect his/her own identities and preserve power. People fear change, loss, and disempowerment—perhaps they feel they are entitled to more in life. That's racism. He feared that his rugby team would lose more games because of black players; that's it. He feared change. A Buddhist, he wasn't.

How can I or anyone wash these feelings or ideas away? That question stayed in the back of my mind driving down the Wild Coast, a scenic driving route that extends from East London up to Port Edward. Unlike the more popular Garden Route for lovers, this was about getting away from everything and experiencing South Africa's wilder side. It took me to remote, cliff-lined beaches, through coastal forests and game parks, quaint looking bed and breakfasts, and past seaside villages of luxurious houses interspersed with tiny shacks. The racial divide separated this country physically, financially, and, worst of all, socially. I was perturbed and saddened to witness such disparity and malevolence.

Then the strangest thing set me off. At a Western-style convenience store and gas station, I could fill up my water bottle from a mega bottle—about three feet tall—produced by Absolutely Water. It cost only 2 Rand or about $.10 per liter to fill up. A liter of bottled water was ten times that amount. What a simple, impactful solution to eradicating plastic bottles. Why the heck are people and companies so lazy?! Why don't all governments force all corporations to do this? Cuz' it's always about profits, not people, nature, or what's best for society.

It wasn't just about the big water bottle, it was the absurd and illogical racism I'd experienced rotting inside, and the fears that had previously defined my life. It had all come to a crux right here.

I spotted a small game park and pulled off to grab a sandwich, coffee, and chit-chat with the white owner behind the counter. She pointed me to the place I could feed the giraffes, then view the springbok, kudus, and a few elephants in the distance. What beauty, what peace. Amazing how animals can cure the human soul. They strip the ego away. They lack a sense of past and future, and exist wholly in the present moment, utterly void of self-identity. Focusing on them, I could tranquilize my body.

Mandela was unknowingly a Zen master, always courageous and polite. I wondered if he too observed animals to calm his mind. I wondered how he would eradicate the anger and feelings he had against those who did him wrong. I wondered how he conquered the fear of going on an unknown odyssey. He had the right to be angry, but he chose to forgive instead.

I walked by a caged lion, looked into its eyes, almost burning a hole in its head, and for a split second, he turned into an oncoming shark. I'll conquer every emotion—fear or anger—by staring it straight in the eyes from here on, *and I vow to Mandela I won't sit silently in the face of oppression or unfair systems*, I thought. In a Zen state, I settled back into my car and continued driving to Eswatini (Swaziland).

Chapter 7

LOSING IDENTITY IN SWAZILAND

"He who defines himself can't know who he is."
—Lao Tzu

"To change yourself, you must first lose yourself."
—KD

Learning about empathy and experiencing racism, I started doubting myself. Was I too racist deep down inside? Did I value my identity and ideals above others? *What is my identity?*

The day turned to dusk as I drove through irrigated fields framed by palm trees and farms before arriving at Swaziland's border patrol. As night fell, I drove speedily over the newly paved roads, then spotted a textile manufacturer with Chinese letters. A scattering of houses illuminated the mountainside like fireflies flickering in the night. I was relieved to see that, unlike most of Lesotho, there was electricity at night. That night I stayed at the Mvubu Falls Lodge located just a stone's throw from the Ezulweni Valley.

Even though Swaziland has one of the top 10 Gross Domestic Products (GDP) per capita on the African continent, poverty remained widespread, and it had one of the highest—if not the highest—rates of HIV infection in the world.

The current ruler, King Makhosetive, wanted to change that by using his English education and foreign ties to spur investment. Locals said that he desired to turn Swaziland into one of top African economies by 2022. Yet, as an absolute monarch, he practiced polygamy with fifteen wives and lived a lavish lifestyle. *So much for his Western education,*[5] I thought.

At the restaurant lounge, I ordered a chicken dish fitting for Africa, chicken parmigiana, one of my favorite dishes. The owner—a young looking blonde in her fifties—came over to chat. She explained that she had come to Africa from the USA after her husband passed away. After several months of traveling, she settled in Swaziland. She concluded that the easiest way to make money was through tourism, and in turn, she could promote the local economy and non-profits. The more we spoke, the more my restlessness became apparent. She left me with this, "Everyone comes here for a reason. If you listen closely enough, the soul may tell you what it's searching for. Be patient and listen. Have a nice rest." She glided out of the door like a fairy godmother. *Maybe my soul was searching for something.*

The following afternoon, I visited the highly reviewed Legends, a large hostel with a sprawling backyard where people could set up their tents and observe an occasional animal passing by. It boasted a prime location next to Swaziland Adventures, which organized hiking, biking, and rafting excursions, as well as a restaurant dishing up clay oven-roasted pizzas outside in the courtyard.

Walking toward the cluster of stores and the yellow clay oven, I saw a tall Asian girl dressed in Khaki Gap-looking shorts, a short-sleeved white t-shirt, and red ballcap—100 percent US of A. She was walking in the same direction. Perfect! Pizza and a new friend. I sat down directly across from her.

"Hey, how are you?"

"Fine, and you?" she was receptive if a bit reserved.

"What brings you here?" I asked.

"I'm traveling around before my parents come to South Africa," she explained. "I did something a bit crazy; I just hitchhiked from the airport, and it was a bit weird. I jumped into a truck and squeezed between two guys."

"Yeah, that is crazy. Why did you do that?" I responded stupefied.

"I don't know; I didn't have much money."

"Hitchhiking is probably not the best idea for an attractive, young lady, you know?" I could tell she was one of these travelers who wanted to travel as cheaply as possible, like a local – even if it risked her well-being.

"Yeah, I guess." Then a long pause.

"I have a car . . . if you need anything, let me know."

We ordered pizza and kept talking.

"So, where are you from?" I hesitated for a second because asking that question would upset Asian people in the US. I appended the question. "I mean, it seems like you are from the US, so where did you grow up?" The question, "Where are you from?" particularly offended Asian and Indian Americans, in my opinion. I—as do others—needed to do a better job framing questions so others could adequately understand me.

"The Midwest. I was working in healthcare after college but couldn't take sitting there all day, so I ditched it."

"That's cool. It's nice to see the world at a young age and not do what you're supposed to do."

"Tell my parents that, please. They always tell me that I should stay focused on a job and not to travel."

"A job. You will be able to find a job back home anytime, right? What's right? What's wrong? Asian parents can be strict, huh?" I sympathized.

"Right, tell me about it. You know Asia?"

"Yeah, lived out there twice, almost ten years."

"You've traveled. Sounds fun."

"I've been doing this for years. I think it's good for people to do different things, travel, and try new jobs when they're young. When it comes time to work, if/when they have a family, then they've already had a taste of adventure."

"You want a family?"

"Yeah, thinking about it, not now, of course."

"You already have a fulfilling life. Kids will slow you down."

"Maybe. It gets tiring running around all the time—a bit lonely." I paused. "At your age, just go as much as you can. I don't think enough Americans get out, but the millennials certainly do. I hope more do so they return and change people's perspective in the country," I said with a big grin.

Was she interested in me, or was this just a friendly conversation? At this point, I deliberated about what to do. Don't move too fast, I said to myself. Just play it cool. But I knew it could fall into the friend zone if I didn't play my cards right. *Just go with the flow,* I thought.

Then the adventure began. After our thin crust pizza, we decided to hang out and visit the Mantenga Cultural Village together to discover the ancient traditions and culture of Swaziland and watch an exciting dance performance. After, we went for a hike and stopped on the drive to buy fruit and vegetables from a roadside store.

She excitedly jumped out and said, "It is like visiting a farmer's market, but it's open every day in Africa, and the produce is bigger!" Having a lady around was lovely; she slowed me down and appreciated the little things. She walked over to two men grilling corn on the cob, bought two, and we salted them down with some spice, peri-peri style. It made for the perfect lunch.

We stocked up on goods to have a picnic in the woods. As we hiked, we chatted a lot about our lives and careers.

"You know my last boyfriend was like twenty years older."

"Really?

"It doesn't matter when you are my age. I'm not getting married anytime soon." She popped a smirk.

We approached a stream in the woods where several tourists were swimming in a freshwater stream.

"Let's hop in!" she said.

"No way. Freshwater in Africa has a lot of parasites and bacteria."(I'd later regret not heeding my advice in Malawi.)

"That's good to know, and I just heard from my friend who got an infection swimming in freshwater in the US."

"Well, I wouldn't do it here," I said. "Nor in the US, as there is a lot of stuff there too now, like brain-eating amoebas."

"Really? That's terrible!"

"But true. You know, my lodge has a pool if you want to take a dip."

"Now that could be fun," she responded but tapered her initial excitement as if she was still trying to figure me out.

"Let's grab some dinner at my lodge, they have great pasta," I offered.

"I don't eat carbs," she replied.

"They have lots of stuff, like Italian-style chicken with flavorful marinara sauce and sautéed veggies." I didn't know what Italian-style chicken was.

As we drove back, the clouds slowly turned grey and green.

As we exchanged more tales about each other, she told me she wanted to go to Burning Man and hike the Appalachian Trail. She was more adventurous than I. *Better drink faster,* I thought. I finished off our second round of beers and decided it was time to have a little fun.

"Want to go swimming now?"

"Are you crazy?" she exclaimed. "In the rain?"

"Why not, it's just rain!"

"Umm, OK."

We headed to the pool, stripped down to nothing, and jumped in. We splashed around, and I flirted a little while at the same time keeping my distance. Right when the wind calmed, and the rains subsided, lightning struck right in front of us. We both leaped out of the water.

"Bloody Hell!" I yelled in British English. "We better go inside!" Grabbing our clothes, we ran into my room and awkwardly dressed. We laid down on the bed staring at the ceiling, with the room illuminated only by a small night light in the corner, which was in the shape of a dog—no really, it was.

"Are you OK?" I asked.

"Yeah, but I should go."

"Of course, I'll drive you back."

The storm had subsided. The wind blew lightly against the windows of the car; the lightning flickered in the distance; the silence was the thunder in my mind. As we arrived, I suggested we get breakfast or lunch the next day when I'd move to the same hostel. I said I'd text her and hugged her.

The following day, it got weird. She wasn't answering her phone, so I drove over to the Backpackers to check. I found her, alone, in a room with about two dozen empty bunk beds.

"Hey, are you OK? You didn't pick up." She picked up her head from the pillow and pointed at her throat.

"No, I'm sick. I can't talk." That's what I interpreted she was trying to say. She pointed to her mouth. I offered her some medicine, which she accepted at first, then refused once she realized it was Dayquil. She shook her head. "It's bad for you." Cough, cough. I think that's what she said. Then she murmured, "I need to sleep."

"OK, sorry that you got sick. If you need anything, call me. I'm going for a bike ride but will be back by noon. I can check in with you." I felt terrible about what happened. She waved bye but didn't want to see me.

Why did she think I was a bad guy all of a sudden? No more bad karma, I don't need that. Why can't I just meet girls as friends and leave it at that?

Venting frustration, I rented a mountain bike and took off riding for miles and miles. Overthinking, I'd lost track of where I was. I stopped, sat on a rock, and looked at the encroaching clouds. Something inside of me had to change. Then thunder clapped behind the trees.

It was about to blow up a storm so I hurried back only stopping for a snack. On the side of a road, a man waved at me behind a popcorn machine. Right on the dirt road in front of traffic, he ran his popcorn-popping business. For some pocket change, I bought a paper sleeve, one that you'd get at the movies, full of popcorn. Seriously. I'm not kidding. I really did.

Back at the hostel, the storm passed, right when another was about to begin. I found my crush hanging out with some locals and tourists at the patio table in the back and walked over to ask how she was. No hello. No response. Just a sharp stare and a nod of the head.

WTF? I'm asking if she was friggin' OK. I briskly walked away.

Almost falling off the back of the porch on the way to the yard, I took a walk. *Put yourself in her shoes*, I thought. I, a stranger in Africa, made an aggressive move on her in less than a day of meeting her. Now she's sick, annoyed, and probably scared of me. OK, I can see this. I have to get rid of this womanizing mindset once and for all. What happened to my travel rules? I need to change them.

Ladies: Take a break from relationships and avoid flings. Focus on the journey—that was the rule. I broke it. But was it possible not to have a link? I amended the law.

Ladies: Play it slow and take it easy. Let her make the first move. That way, I'd have no worries, no misunderstandings, no bad feelings, no bad karma, and no #MeToo.

After my walk, I jotted down the new rule on my phone, came back up the porch and walked over to another table and started chatting with a lively threesome. They must have picked up on my interaction for one guy who broke the ice.

"She doesn't want YOU, bro." He smiled broadly with a big golden tooth reflecting my face of disappointment.

"What?" I hesitated.

"These girls come to Africa for the local flavor. They don't want what they can get at home." He knew what he was saying. He was having a go at me, and I liked it. The other two guys at the table were a bit more buttoned up. One was an economics student with plans to work in the ministry while the other, his cousin, was studying to be a teacher. They introduced themselves, and let's just say Monsinee with his golden tooth soon had us all in stitches. They were all friends, despite their different backgrounds and diverse opinions on life. There was no small talk amongst the three.

"My friend doesn't agree with my lifestyle," Monsinee explained. "But it's the only way I can earn." He hustled marijuana—called Insangu—for a living. "I grow it, sell it, and make money. And I'm good at it! And I don't agree with his white man's God. Why should we believe in him? I believe in humanity—I'm good to you, you are good to me, and that's it."

His friend just shook his head in disagreement. "There is a God, mate. He will condemn you."

"Condemn me? He already did! Look at how I live! Why do you believe in that white man's god? Do you think the Chinese believe in that God? And you?" he asked.

"Oh, the Buddha Christ."

"What?! Oh, I like this guy, you mean Buddha and Christ? See, he is hedging his bets: white man's God and the Chinese man's God. That's smart!" he looked at me, smiling and laughing with a loud gasping sound.

"One gives me inner peace and the other some hope," I explained.

"God never gave me anything. Hard work did."

His mind was an encyclopedia with a cynical assessment of the topics of religion, politics, rap, culture, and philosophy. We took a break from our in-depth discussions to go on a beer run at the shopping mall, passing the mansion-esque US embassy.

"Colonialism," Monsinee pointed at the US property. I held a long glance, swerving to the side of the road in amazement.

"The road! Man, watch the road! America is watching everything we do, too. Now Trump will colonize us." He laughed. "You like Trump?"

"No, I don't think he cares about what's going on here."

"At least he wants to do business here, just like the Chinese. I'm telling you, this is colonization. Chinese and American," he warned. "What kind of beer do you drink?"

"Whatever, lager."

"You got to try the dark stuff. It is local, and it helps you make babies."

"She left me already man, so I don't need any of that."

"Ha! Yes, it's OK. But you have to try it, the Milk Stout. They put something in it. It gives you a little extra." He winked.

"I'll try a little. Just a little." *I should really cut back,* I thought.

Then back to the Chinese. "Chinese want our resources, and Americans want to spy on us."

"Spy, why? What secrets does Swazi have?" I asked.

He glared at me like a deer in the headlights then yelped, "How to grow the best Insangu! And this beer! Bet you don't have this stuff at home."

"Let's see." I accepted the challenge. After making light of America's intentions in Africa, I said on a more serious note, "Trump doesn't care about Africa. They're going to reduce aid to Africa."

"Reducing aid?" Monsinee scoffed. "You just give it out to a bunch of villagers, and they keep asking for more. Keep your money!" He laughed loudly, and I had to agree that he was probably right after what I'd seen in Lesotho.

At the Bi-Rite shopping mall, we bought a six-pack and watched a Michael Jackson impersonator singing and dancing to "Billy Jean" outside. His name was Tito Jackson, and he'd later find the video I made on YouTube and follow me.

We headed back to the hostel to distribute the beers, then Monsineee offered, "I think you should see where I live, not just hanging out around these tourists."

"Let's do it," I replied with a bit of skepticism. When he went to the bathroom, I asked his economist friend if it was safe to go with him. He responded, "He's crazy but a good guy."

That's how I found myself at the Ezulweni Mini Market—a convenience store—sitting on crates drinking Milk Stout. Monsinee introduced me to some of his friends and showed me around. Just behind the convenience store was a place where the knife fights took place to resolve disputes. Rundown cars rolled in and out with people making purchases, greeting each other with handshakes, smiles, and small talk.

"You are chill, man. I like you because you are different. Not afraid to hang out and see where we are from." He handed me another beer.

Holding the bottle without an opener, I said, "What do you want me to do with this? Bite it off?"

"Bro, don't go black on me!" Monsinee replied. That was one of his favorite lines.

"Nah, the country boys do this at home," I replied. "It's not a black thang." He laughed in surprise.

"If you have time, you should stay with me, see how we live." He pointed up the hill.

"Thanks, I would, but I have to get going tomorrow."

"Come back and bring some of the black Americans. I never see black Americans in Africa."

"I'm sure they come. Maybe you don't see them."

"We see all of these gangster rappers and rich athletes on TV. They don't know a thing about Africa, not a thing about their roots. They should learn about their heritage and build respect for it. It would help us, too."

"I don't know."

"Just tell them to come to Africa. Where are you headed to next?"

"Not sure, probably back to Joburg." I never really knew where I was going. Does anyone?

"You are lucky to travel so freely."

"Can't you take any trips?" I asked.

"No, I don't have money. Besides, I have to support my mom and sister."

"You are a good man."

"You too, man. Do something real when you get home."

"Real?"

"Yeah, now you know Africa. Do something with it. Do something real."

"OK, thanks for the advice. I'll have to think about it. Before I go, let's get a selfie." I snapped a picture without the flash.

"This is Africa bro, turn on the flash!"

I bid him farewell, jumping into my truck, slightly buzzed.

On my final morning in Swaziland, I woke up early for a coffee and a quick pizza. As I departed, I saw my crush walking around with two European guys who glared at me as if I had done something wrong. Despite the peculiar nature of the whole situation, I waved goodbye and was happy for the lesson she taught me. She helped me to get rid of that old self, the former womanizer.

On my way to the South African border, I stopped for a photo op at Sibebe Rock, which is said to be the second biggest in the world after Australia's Uluru. I passed the Malolotja Nature Reserve and the oldest mine in the world before turning left toward Nelspruit at the old gold prospecting town of Piggs Peak, where I arrived at the border town of Bulembu. I looked around and realized the face of the city had transformed. An old mining and commercial capital metamorphosized into a place of healing, social development, and community.

What is an identity, anyway? The answer came to me in a Lao Tzu quote: "He who defines himself can't know who he is." I created an identity within a story I told myself or even, possibly, someone placed on me, perhaps erroneously. No longer just a salesman, I needed to do something bigger, something real. Just like this town could be become something new, I felt I could, too, thanks to Swaziland.

Chapter 8

BEING MINDFUL IN MOZAMBIQUE

"Readiness, Mindfulness. It is the readiness of the mind that is wisdom."
—Shunryu Suzuki

S itting at the airport waiting for my flight, I jotted down a new rule.
Be Mindful: To maximize experiences, I need to be more aware of my interactions with both travelers and Africans. No more bad karma. Give the right impression; do the right thing.

My mom wanted me to return around this time, but after a long chat, I told her I was going to continue exploring. *I am going to live it up in Tofo, Mozambique* is what I thought. When I checked on the visa situation at the Mozambique Embassy, I'd heard from the last employee who was locking up for the holidays that New Year's Eve in Tofo was a big party. Celebrating Christmas there would be more exciting than in Tennessee.

Then came a message from Tessa.

"Merry Christmas!"

"Oh, hey, you, too, Merry Christmakah!" I'd forgotten about it.

"Ha-ha. Thank you! What have you been up to?"

"I just visited Swaziland and drove to Nelspruit—now back in Joburg."

"Sounds amazing and exhausting!"

"Yes, both."

"Enjoy . . . you are on an extended vacation!" She flipped my mindset.

"True." I felt guilty.

"What did you do for Christmas?"

"I drove through Kruger and took animal pictures."

"Sounds marvelous. That's the best Christmas gift ever! Send me a picture."

Flipping through pictures on my phone, I treasured how much I'd seen already. With the map features on the iPhone, I could sort my photos by location. I sent her my picture of a giraffe in a Santa hat.

"That's superb! Lol! So, what's next?"

"I'm thinking of celebrating NY in Mozambique to do some diving in the Indian Ocean."

"The Indian Ocean is spectacular. Say hi to it for me!" She made decisions sound so easy.

With almost 2,500 kilometers of coastline dotted with untouched coral reefs and pristine islands—many still Portuguese-owned—Mozambique has been dubbed the Pearl of the Indian Ocean, and I was about to see about a quarter of it. Pulling out of the airport in my Nissan pickup, I swerved around kids splashing about, women carrying heavy loads, and motorbikes jetting in and out between traffic.

This pinky finger-like country running up the side of southeast Africa was home to 29 million people who make an average of $1200 per annum. The capital, Maputo, had pockets of wealth, however, with some upscale condominiums along a beach that extended for miles. A bit of investment in this city and it could be the next Miami crossed my mind.

The lady at the rental car agency said Xia-Xia was four to six hours and warned me not to miss the turnoff. There, I would stay before continuing to Tofo, a beach, and diving mecca the next day. I turned on the radio and cranked up the volume, Latino dance tracks interspersed with Portuguese-speaking MCs stimulated me to keep driving. *Sometimes a little chaos was the medicine to drown out my fears and create inner quietness.* That was difficult to achieve when dodging people in very crowded streets, using a stick shift with my left hand, and driving on the opposite side of the road.

I was on high alert. Leaving Maputo came as a relief; the hectic city transitioned into a more desolate countryside. Agricultural fields dabbed with palm trees took over as I turned away from the coast, driving inland. The poverty also became visible, with small villages clustered with tiny mud or concrete houses colored red, orange, red.

I looked closer, swerving off the road and getting out of the car. Vodacom, Coca-Cola, and Mcel (the Mozambique mobile phone company) branding covered every building and every mud hut like graffiti on a Detroit street. I grabbed a mandazi (fried dough like a doughnut) and a Coke (made with pure cane sugar), then kept on. Supply trucks, poultry cargos, gas tanks, and motorbikes were all competing on the narrow streets riddled with potholes. And they were coming head-on like a game of "chicken."

After a night in Xia-Xia and six more hours on the road, I arrived in Tofo. The resort town hugged a curving stretch of sand lined with beach lodges and backpacker inns. A hub for scuba diving—appropriately called scuba safaris—was my main reason for being here, followed by a close second to party for New Years. Swimming with whale sharks was the main attraction, and there were plenty of dolphins, mantas, devil rays, and whitefin sharks, as well.

I checked into a little beach lodge called the Varandas do Indico about a mile north of town—and far enough away to escape its noise; I grabbed my day pack and strolled to the square for a bite to eat. A few small shops lined the outside perimeter of the courtyard, selling everyday necessities and freshly caught barracuda and prawns, and they would cook them right there on the barbecue stalls. With the addition of tropical fruits and refreshments sold in the main square in town sold where? It was the perfect beach setup.

I sat down at one of the restaurants and ordered curried Portuguese sauce on prawns over rice. While waiting, I saw three travelers who looked a bit younger than me, smiley and energetic. They entered the restaurant and walked towards me.

"Can we have a seat?" asked the Asian girl leading the pack. *Here we go again*, I thought.

"Please," I replied with a tentative smile. "The food seems decent here," I said, swatting mosquitos off my leg.

"Where are you from?" she asked.

"California," I said as if it were its own country.

"I'm from Singapore, he's from the UK, and she's Brazilian," she said without hesitation.

We made a bit of small talk to get to know each other, explaining what we were doing here. The brown, spiky-hair Brit wore a tank top, had a great laugh, and a real, down to earth calming demeanor, and he was a freediver (i.e., diving with no oxygen tank). The Brazilian girl was stylish and cute, with longish brown hair, flowing African red pants, and an encyclopedic memory. The Asian, a Singaporean, looked like she wanted to go swimming immediately with flower shorts, a bikini top, and flip flops. They were all there to see the whale sharks and party. Part of my brain urged me to stay solo while the other part lured me to live it up on New Year's Eve, at least getting a kiss for my fortieth.

"Are you staying at Fatima's?" the Singaporean asked.

"No, I got a lodge. You?"

"Fatima's is booked, so we are looking around."

"Let me know, my place has a huge bed, couch and lots of space."

"We are trying to find a budget place."

"OK. It's $50, and I didn't want loud noise and mosquitos in my ear, so I thought it was worth it. Feel free to crash if you guys need to."

"Is that what you consider a budget? Anyway, how was the drive, and why did you drive? We took Fatima's bus." she pried.

"I had just driven around Swaziland and South Africa, so I thought I could do it here. A lot of trucks and cars were on the road. It was dangerous. In hindsight, I wouldn't do it again."

"Sounds like a bad idea and expensive. You must have lots of money. Let's head to the beach and find an ocean safari." She had just told me that said she had a good job in Europe with lots of vacation days to travel the world. I ignored the comment.

"Sounds good to me. I heard Peri-Peri divers is a good dive shop. And it's great on chicken." I threw in a joke.

"So how did you hear about the dive shop? And what is great on chicken?"

"You know, peri-peri chicken? Everyone eats it in South Africa."

"I don't know what you are talking about." She was getting annoyed.

"Forget it, back to diving. I stopped in and met the dive instructors. They were knowledgeable and run ocean safaris several times per day. It seemed good to me."

"I better read the reviews; I'm not sure I can trust you since you drove all the way here."

Over the next few hours, we roamed the beach together, then went on an ocean safari. While we didn't see any whale sharks on our first attempt, we did catch sight of a pack of running dolphins. Everyone should swim with dolphins once in their life; it was a cathartic experience that rejuvenated me with energy and love. I could feel my soul connect with the dolphins.

Later that night, we met up again over some dinner and beers. I struck up a conversation with the Brit, and we exchanged work notes. He built fences, and I told him I was a teacher, which went over well until I disclosed my prior self. Then, I vividly remembered how she labeled me.

I said, "Before teaching, I sold software. It allowed me to travel the world. I lived in Japan for the last three years and spent lots of time in Singapore and India. Have you been to Singapore or Asia?" But before the Brit could answer, she jumped in.

"Oooh, a tech guy, must be rich. What did you think of Singapore?"

"Singapore is a great town, great food, clean, diverse. Isn't it?" I said and glared at her.

"So, you KNOW about Asia," she said with presumption.

"Yeah, I guess. I spent ten years there. I like a lot about it—the diversity, languages, and the countries are so different," I gave her my standard thoughts about Asia.

"And, I'm sure you had a lot of fun as a rich, white guy in Asia," she blind-sided me.

"I have fun everywhere," I replied and then excused myself. I didn't stick around after that comment. *Racism comes in many forms,* I thought.

It turned out to be fortuitous because I met others from many different backgrounds. Some were involved in non-profits, focused on marine research and whale shark conservation projects. Others were from Brazil, volunteering with the government on legal structures for businesses, and I teamed up with them for my final ocean safari.

The final night was New Year's Eve, and Fatima's was holding a big party. By the time I arrived right before midnight, the party was in full swing. Walking around aimlessly, I bumped into a light brown-skinned woman who laughed vibrantly and introduced herself as "Cardi—Not B!" before darting off elsewhere. I had this strange feeling that I'd met her before but couldn't pinpoint where—I hadn't, but she'd reappear on the trip again. I meandered outside and found a group dancing to DJ Ganesh's nineties mixes. Several members of the group were Indians visiting from Uganda. They explained that Uganda has a large Indian population that had gradually been returning in the past few years. (It wasn't until my trip to Uganda that I'd find out why the Indians had left.)

As it approached at 2 a.m., I went to my truck and made a bed in the back seat. That night, the hotel kicked me out of my lodge. They'd made a mistake, giving my room to a couple who'd booked before me but didn't let me know until that morning. It wasn't exactly how I'd envisioned my fortieth birthday, sleeping in a truck in the beach village of Tofo, Mozambique. By sun-up at five, I was ready to make the return drive to Maputo.

Getting out of the truck, I looked around and couldn't find my sandals. Someone had swiped them. Dadgummit! Although I did feel fortunate because they were the only thing I'd lost on my entire trip. Then out of the blue, two blond-haired Dutch girls shouted at me. "Hey, is that your truck? Can we get a ride?"

Like duh, of course. I drove them to their hostel, and they invited me in for breakfast and a swim in the hostel pool, which was still half-full of party-goers. When I told them it was my birthday, they kissed me on opposite cheeks. Not a bad way to start the New Year! With a jolt of happiness, I said goodbye and got in the car for the long drive to Maputo.

Just thirty minutes away from Tofo, I stopped in Inhambane to fill up, explore, and take a few photographs. What once appeared to be an attractive town, with many of its Portuguese-inspired buildings, was now a crumbling one with rows of eroding storefronts with chipped paint in blues, greens, and pinks lining the streets. Muslim and Persian traders, including Vasco da Gama, visited Inhambane in the late 1500s. Music from the beautiful Cathedral of Our Lady of the Conception drew me in for mass with a heavenly choir of two dozen singers.

After a long drive on a mostly empty road back to Maputo, I got a speeding ticket. The lady police officer let me off after I showed her on my license that it was my birthday. How humane!

As I arrived at the outskirts of the city, I could see that the beaches were packed with people drinking, listening to music, and swimming. I arrived at the Maputo branch of Fatima's hostel, which was a large two-story tan and red roof house surrounded by palm trees. The inside walls were colorfully painted purple and green, a cozy lounge of colorful seats, and a small bar where tourists—black and white—congregated. Too tired to partake, I checked in, grabbed water, and went straight to my bunk room to crash.

Thirty minutes later, someone climbed down from the bunk next to me. He wore round glasses, a pressed purple polo, and khaki shorts. We introduced ourselves then carried on the conversation in the lounge over a beer. Femi was Nigerian and worked for an IT services company in Lagos, Nigeria, developing websites. He came to South Africa to obtain his Ph.D. in Optical Communications. I immediately noticed his soft voice and polite choice of words. I was unsure if this was just his style or the way all Nigerians spoke.

"So, what brought you here?" I inquired.

"I started my MSC two years ago. I always wanted to be an academic. I enjoy teaching. Now I want to get a Ph.D."

"Why more school? I can't take sitting there all day. My ADHD goes crazy." I said.

"I did startups for six years; I mean, I liked it, we used already developed technologies nothing too innovative."

"I just did seven years at a startup. It was the same; we didn't have any advanced technology per se, but I'm not an engineer."

"I see. Cool. I wanted to do more fundamental work. You know, go deeper into technology. I felt tired of doing the same development day in and day out. It wasn't very intellectual."

"My job in sales wasn't very thoughtful, either. I'm sure coding was much more. What do you mean by fundamental technology?"

"I'd like to know more about the core of technology. Like base network infrastructure so people can build services on it."

"Tell me more."

"Do you know anything about tech infrastructure or optical communications?"

"A little bit." *Like nothing,* I thought.

"Optical communications are about using lasers and lights for data transmission. I'd like to study that."

"So, you just left your job and came here to do that?"

"Yeah, sure. I mean, there is a good program here. Many Nigerians come to study here and everywhere these days. And I like to teach."

"Me too. I'm doing a bit of that in Africa."

"At our company, we didn't have enough money to employ experienced programmers.

So, we would employ people who are rather passionate and train them. That was fulfilling. I want to do more of that. Why did you come to Africa?" He spoke, looked, and carried himself with the confidence of a professor.

"I just wanted to check it out, travel, and backpack. I've traveled a lot and had not been here. Anyway, a lot of business will happen here in the coming decades. Africa is the future, a frontier market, isn't it?"

"Yes, a lot of overseas investors are looking to invest in Nigeria and South Africa. It seems that way."

Exiting the hostel together, we saw a small guy pulled a two-wheeled cart full of pineapples.

"Hey, let's get some of these!" I said.

"Are you sure your stomach can handle that?"

"Sure, my stomach is a rock; it can handle anything. It's just a pineapple. Why?" My rock, stable stomach would be tested later in the trip.

"Ok, O. I thought maybe you would feel it is dirty or something. I can't eat it because I don't have an adventurous stomach." I learned that O at the end of phrases is standard in Nigeria.

"It looks pretty fresh to me. An adventurous stomach? I'll eat anything, and I usually pay the price for it later."

The vendor carved the pineapples and placed them onto sticks making a pineapple shish kabob. We bought one each and a couple for later, pleasing the vendor with a big tip. We strolled around eating our pineapple popsicles and found an Indian restaurant that served sweets where we nutted out a plan to explore the city, the island of Inhaca the following day, and continued our get-to-know discussion.

"Have you been to Nigeria?" he asked.

"No, that's next."

"Oh great, you can meet my partners there."

"That would be awesome and appreciated."

"They can show you their business and show you around."

"That would be a lot of fun. What's Nigeria like?"

"Busy, fast-paced, but good. Lots of business is happening there. Make sure you try the local food like jollof rice and suya."

"That sounds exciting; it sounds like China. Good business and food."

"I want to go to China. There is so much happening there, and they are coming here."

"They are coming everywhere. I saw the influence of Lesotho and Swaziland. It would be worth your time to learn about China and Japan. You must go to Japan; it's the best."

"Really? How so?"

"Clean, great infrastructure, delicious food on every corner, and bullet trains." That was my best summary.

"I need to travel more."

"In some ways, Africa reminds me of China in the late '90s. There are a lot of opportunities here for investment."

"Yes, it seems that way."

"I bet you can use your Ph.D. to study abroad. It's a very technical niche that can take you places. Try Japan, they have programs, and many Africans are studying and working there now. I met a few just before I left."

"Maybe, after the Ph.D."

"How about the US?" I continued.

"My brother lives there in Florida, and I did a bus trip to DC."

"What did you think?"

"It was good, comfortable, but the entertainment system broke. Ha-ha. I saw lots of the country, how people live. It was just like Hollywood movies. Everything I saw was just like the movies."

"Speaking of Hollywood, O. What's a Nollywood movie like?"

"Movies are completed in one week, less complex, and they teach lessons like family structure and romance."

"Oh, you mean people don't shoot each other's brains out?"

"Not really, not much violence."

"What did you think of DC?"

"DC was fascinating. It had a lot of symbolism, monuments, and history. It was meaningful. I liked it. It was also very diverse; many Africans as well. It reminded me of Cape Town. Oh, and people were very busy there. So busy."

"I'm from South Carolina, just a few states down. It's the countryside, and on the coast, there's a pretty beach. Not to mention, it's hot and humid like Mozambique."

"I know; I drove through there. It looked like a pleasant place, and I had a small talk with a few people on the bus. They were quite nice."

"That's cool. Glad you had a nice impression." Except for politicians, we all want people to say our country was friendly, treated them well, and had good food. That's what it comes down to, doesn't it?

"OK. Sorry I have to go now. Let's stay in touch, though."

"Goodnight," I said.

The next day, after a trip to Inhaca Island that lasted one hour plus a two-hour boat ride back and forth, we hung out at the fish market, which was second to none in Asia. But it was then that I learned about the Nigerian bargaining style. He negotiated for everything—boat trips, tickets, fish, cooking—but in a manner that surprised me. With a big smile, he referred to everyone as his "friend," and despite driving a tough bargain, he was always careful about it and even apologized for pushing too hard. I thought it was a smart and useful approach. When I later asked him about it, he replied, "That's the way we do it in Nigeria." *It is the perfect balance of aggression and charm and something I'll use back at home,* I thought.

Femi inspired me to take the time to learn and search for something that would be more fulfilling or stimulating. Taking time to get his Ph.D. could change his trajectory from being just a startup employee to doing something more impactful. He was not only very mindful of himself and his situation but also willing to act on it. He convinced me to let go of my old self and invest in the unknown future, one hopefully more fulfilling. Thank you, Femi. (Femi visited Japan in early 2020 as part of his Ph.D. program.)

200 meter waterfall where I abseiled

The popcorn popper in Swaziland

The scuba diving owners at Africa Dive Adventures;
I'm wearing the contentious soccer jersey.

The beach at Tofo, Mozambique

Chapter 9

LEADING WITH HEART AND HUSTLE IN NIGERIA

*"There was a certain luxury to charity that she could not
identify with and did not have. To take "charity" for granted, to
revel in this charity toward people whom one did not know—
perhaps it came from having had yesterday and having today
and expecting to have tomorrow. She envied them."*
—Chimamanda Ngozi Adichie in *Americanah*

I was becoming calmer and more mindful. When I came across that quote by Nigerian-born writer Chimamanda in her book *Americanah*, *What impression am I giving to others?* I thought. *How do people view me?* Act like a guest. Humility. Clear communication and intent. Politeness. Cultural sensitivity. With this in mind, I walked from the runway into the hectic, hustling, airport in Lagos, Nigeria.

Greeting me at the airport with a big smile was Tobi. Tobi was an energetic and buttoned-up young man whose short stature was more than compensated for by his spunk. "Isn't the airport dangerous?" I asked. Tobi looked surprised. "It's just chaotic, not dangerous," he replied.

As the Human Resource manager at Meltwater, he was helping companies find talent. Meltwater is a digital marketing/media company founded by Jorn

Lyseggen, a Norwegian entrepreneur. Lyseggen committed $1 million per year for ten years to fund the entrepreneurship center in Ghana called MEST; it now extended to Nigeria and other parts of Africa. No return was expected, just making the world a better place by sharing knowledge and giving others an opportunity. *How benevolent,* I thought.

During the daytime, I spent the week meeting new startups. There was a mobile lending finance bank, a video platform for interviews, and a mobile travel service helping Nigerians find cultural experiences in other countries. Composed of teams of two or three, they were trying to get enough traction to apply to incubators—some in the United States. Just recently, YCombinator—the famous US accelerator—had invited Nigerian startups to join, and many of the teams were keen to get in.

Then it hit me. I couldn't offer much help. I was just an Oyinbo—white guy—visiting for a week who knew nothing about Nigeria or how things worked. I needed to reassess my contributions. This experience had taught me to be more prepared, so I decided to make a presentation about what I knew in business development and sales. Then when I'd go to the MEST headquarters in Ghana, I'd have tangible insights to offer. Teaching the acquired general finance, sales, and business development skills certainly can be applied to their entrepreneurial missions.

After my days spent at MEST, I'd hang out with my Airbnb host and a budding entrepreneur—let's call him T-Bone after the nickname of my high school shortstop. Dressed in T-shirts and cut-off jean shorts, he was a low-key guy that smelled of spray-on Axe deodorant—a smell that I'd later adopt myself. He was hard to understand as he mixed languages—Hausa, English, and the local Pidgin dialect.

T-Bone's apartment was situated smack-bang in the middle of Lagos and home to Yabacon Valley, Nigeria's Silicon Valley. His apartment was located on a very crowded, narrow street, behind a massive green gate that you could only pass through by telling the guard the secret password. The password puzzled me because it didn't seem like highly valuable real estate. I'd later see that every apartment had a gated entrance, and any real estate in Lagos was valuable. On the third floor, his apartment had almost nothing but arrangements for guests.

Looking around, I thought *it's quite convenient to have nothing—no dirt, no mess.* There was just a TV, a mattress, and a few crates.

He was a recent returnee from the United States, with (of course) a background in tech product management. A born hustler, he held a full-time job while night lighting at a local company and night lighting his startup. His startup was putting together a company aimed at fixing one of Nigeria's leading causes of death—no, not malaria or crime, but traffic accidents. That was the Nigerian way: everyone had two or three hustles. It reminded me of Shanghai in the early 2000s when everyone was trying to catch a tiger by the tail (i.e., to get rich by joining a fast-growing startup). In China, the boom started with an e-commerce startup called Alibaba (among other web portal companies), and just recently an e-commerce startup in Africa, Jumio, had raised well over $100M (later it would go IPO on the NYSE.) That IPO was enough to excite the startup ecosystem.

T-Bone loved to dive deep into logical business discussions. He explained that there are 33.7 deaths per 100,000 people every year in Nigeria due to vehicle collisions, and his startup aimed to lower insurance prices. The next significant cause of death was misdiagnosed diseases and fake pills that doctors gave patients. Later on, he would tell me the story of his brother who had passed away six months earlier due to a misdiagnosed case of typhoid. T-Bone had returned from the United States to help him, but it was too late. "It's just death, man," T-Bone stated. "It will happen to all of us. But my technology will help people live." This would be the first of many stories I would hear of how fleeting life is in Africa, yet also how it spurred entrepreneurs into action, investing sweat and soul in creating solutions for real-life problems.

We went on a motorcycle ride to check out the town. Yaba is a bustling city packed with street-side stalls and kekenapep (three-wheeled motorbikes) zipping by, not to mention hawkers selling anything and everything from containers balanced on their heads or strapped to the back of bikes. We stopped beside one of the multi-colored umbrellas that shielded stalls from the elements and grabbed some suya (barbecue-grilled meat on a stick), smoked with cayenne pepper, and chopped peanuts sprinkled on top. It reminded me of spicy Malaysian charkweteo but with more zest. Yaba's old roads were riddled with potholes while hundreds of cars, buses, and moto-bikes jostled for space. I could understand how just blinking could result in getting hit by something—or doing the hitting yourself.

As we drove toward central Lagos and Victoria Island—separated by a beautiful bridge over the oil and plastic-polluted water—traffic eased as the apparent wealth of the residents increased. On one side of the bridge stretched one of the biggest and poorest slums in the world—Makoko—while on the other, skyscrapers, office buildings, and apartments. Lagos Island is one of the most expensive real estate markets in the world, rated as high as number three by landlagos.com. Like most places, the wealth sits in the hands of a few. There are either 15,000 or 70,000 millionaires (reported by New World Wealth and AfraAsia Bank, respectively) plus a handful of billionaires in Nigeria. Entrepreneurs wanted a piece of the action. We ended the night at Domino's Pizza and Cold Stone Ice Cream, a treat for the Nigerians who return from overseas and whose kids have acquired a western palate.

Through Femi—whom I had met in Mozambique—we connected with Joba the following day. He worked at an IT services technology firm, XSolve, which he joined after living in the UK for five years off and on and where he studied law. He returned to Nigeria to build a better country with the business idea of creating a legal incubator to educate Nigerian lawyers in Western law. He explained that there was an increasing movement of Nigerian diaspora returning home to affect change—this was happening all across Africa. He was welcoming, polite, and good-spirited, as well as interested in who I was.

Over lunch, Joba took me to a small cafe of local cuisine. It was my first introduction to Nigerian food (aside from street-side barbecues), with chicken stew, a mix of okra, yellow yams, and plantains, as well as a big vat of orange-tinted rice. "That is jollof," Joba explained with a proud smile.

We sat down to eat with a TV behind us, showing footage of Trump. Joba saw my visible sigh.

"Not a Trump fan?" he asked.

"No," I said emphatically.

"He will be good for business, no?"

"Maybe, but business isn't exactly bad."

"He will do more in Africa. Obama couldn't do much here since he was black," he said convincingly.

"Really?"

"Yeah, he couldn't sell African investment to white people."

"I never thought of that." I nodded.

"Africans are positive about Trump. Of course, we have to be," he said with a grin.

"The US has its problems. The economy is lacking in the middle part of the country. Lots of people are suffering too—drugs like opioids, failing education, and more."

"He is better than what most of Africa has."

"That's one way to look at it."

"The U.K. has some of the same problems, but we don't have a lot of drugs in Nigeria. Everyone is just trying to survive; we don't need to complicate our lives. Our President is a military guy, so he keeps things straight, keeps the peace if he can."

"Yeah, I think a heavy hand is good sometimes." So did my dad.

"We have rebels up north, terrorists. They are evil, so he is good for us. Still, we need business. Ghana just elected a businessman as president; there will be more business people in politics."

"The world of trade is pushing that way. Regulators have to understand it. How does

US-Africa work together? How does Africa-China get along? It's necessary for humanity."

"Right! The Chinese are here, too. They are investing a lot in government infrastructure and textiles. Culturally there is some tension." He paused and looked up. "There is always tension. You know that, be it white or Chinese."

"Yeah, that's right. Trade brings tension." I thought back to all of my travels around the world. It did.

"We need more business here to help us grow, so we are open to foreigners."

"Good to know. Let's do some work." The hustle was rubbing off.

"So, how's the food?" Joba asked.

"Great, I love okra. We serve this in the South."

"And the jollof? It's our most famous dish and the best in Africa. When you go to Ghana, they will tell you that their jollof is the best. But ours is better. You tell them Nigeria's is better. OK?" he emphasized, seriously questioning whether I'd heard him.

"I'll do that," I conceded.

"Why are you here, anyway? What are you doing?"

"I like to travel. Africa has been in the news, and I had some time, so why not check it out?"

"An explorer. That's great. We Africans don't even travel Africa like this," he said in awe.

"I'd like to do some humanitarian work, you know, see what it's like in the poorer areas."

"Why? Africa is more than poverty."

"I know. I can see that, but I like to know both sides of the tracks—rich and poor. And it helps to learn about life a bit more."

"You must check out Makoko."

"What's that?"

"The biggest slum in Nigeria, maybe Africa. Fumni will take you. She is my friend and runs a non-profit there for women. She has a golden heart."

"OK, sounds good, and much appreciated."

"It's tough. It will change your life." That was what I was seeking.

"So, are you Yoruba?"

"Yes, it's one of the tribes here. How'd you know?"

"I was reading a bit. What's the culture about?"

"Family first, community second, and then the rest," he replied with no hesitation.

"It's interesting how the community comes as a priority. We have lost a lot of community in the US, especially in big cities. It's ultra-competitive—dog eat dog. The rural areas are more laid back, but politics have divided our communities there."

"Dog eat what?"

"It's a saying—you are out on your own."

"I like that. Dog eat dog. Ha. We had a lot of slaves go over there, so many African Americans are Yoruban, but they probably don't know. If you look closely, though, you may see the big smiles, a bit bigger boned. Yorubans like to eat."

"What kind of food?"

"Yams, cassava, fish stews like these. But we eat a lot. We've also got voodoo."

"Voodoo? What's that?"

"Our old traditional religion. We don't do that stuff anymore. They do it a bit in Benin.

Check it out if you go."

"You mean like, little doll statues, incense smoke, dancing around, wishing people break a leg?"

"Ha. Kind of mate. But usually, it's positive prayers. Just check it out in Benin. Are you Christian?"

"Yes, well, a bit of everything." At this point, I didn't know what I was.

He cracked a smile. "I need to get home to the kids, and we have community meetings too," Joba said, getting up to leave. "Oh, and we will get some Odeku, which is Guinness Extra Stout—African style." He smiled." It gives you a little extra when you need it." He laughed as he walked off. *Another African beer with a punch?* I couldn't believe it.

The next day, I met up with Funmi at a small green building that housed a corner restaurant called Sweet Sensation. It was one of the first fast-food chains in Nigeria, starting with western food before converting to Nigerian. Getting off my bike, I could see a tall lady standing near the entrance dressed in gray work pants and a white ruffled blouse, looking at her phone. As I walked toward her, she looked up, and I stumbled, almost falling flat on my face. She was stunning!

"Are you OK?" she exclaimed in a British-tinged accent with an upward inflection.

"Yes, great . . . fantastic. Sorry, I just tripped on that curb." She looked down, nodded her head, then looked at me.

"Flat curb. You're just fine, let's get some food. Have you had Nigerian food?" she asked.

"I tried a bit here and there, some jollof and suya."

"Great, then, you can go ahead. I'm not too hungry."

Her speaking style was so polite and proper that I became insecure over my grammar and accent. I must have sounded like a dead beat to her. The light made her black skin appear as melted honey, and she was just as sweet. The restaurant seemed to be a local chain, with all the staff dressed in green and orange attire. Nigerian Afrobeat played in the background. I was eating adventurously and wanted to try the local cuisine, so I asked for the fufu.

"Our local dish is efo-riro, not fufu. Fufu is in Ghana. This is a spinach and smoked fish dish native to Nigeria. There is also Ponmo, which is processed cow skin." She spoke casually.

"Processed, what?"

"Ha-ha, yes, you are eating shoes." She pointed at mine.

"Well, looks pretty good to me. Oh, and I'll get some jollof, too."

"Oh, you know the local foods in only a few days. Impressive. Try the moin-moin—bean pudding wrapped in leaves."

"Looks delish."

I quickly grabbed my tray, walked to the table, took a bite, and scarfed down the food.

She looked at me strangely and said, "Haven't eaten in a while?"

"Not since yesterday. This is so good," I mumbled with food in my mouth.

"If you eat like that, you will fit in well around here." Her grin lit up her face. "I'm going to organize a trip to Makoko. Want to join?"

"Absolutely."

"It's the largest floating slum in the world."

"That sounds terrible."

"It *is*," she rolled out the "s" and looked up. "It is a community spread across land and water on the shore of Lagos Lagoon. The one you see when you are on that big bridge. Families of four, five, six people live in single-room wooden shacks held by stilts sunk into the lagoon. Poverty is everywhere; most kids don't go to school; girls get married young."

"Sounds rough."

"Especially for women. So that's why I started Kindle Africa, to help women get or create their jobs. To empower them."

"The women get the brunt in poorer communities, huh?"

"Yes, that is the case. You can see it for yourself tomorrow. I have another friend joining."

"OK, can I bring one too?"

"Let me inform the Chief, so we get security."

"How did you get into this anyway?"

"I came to volunteer with a friend, and I decided to start an organization to help the people here. I wanted to help."

"That's courageous. You had saved up enough?"

"Just a little. People need a lot more help than I do." Her heart and passion for helping others shone through her eyes and smile. She continued, "So I sold my car, got some money from family, and started to build a vocational school for women. The US embassy gave us a grant for twenty-five sewing machines."

"Have you been to the US?"

"I have been. I was a Mandela Fellow."

"What's that?"

"It's a program started by Obama which invites one thousand Africans to the US to stay for four to six weeks with a sponsor, and then we all congregate in DC."

"That sounds great. We need to do more stuff like this in the US, not just for Africa."

"It was a great experience. I'm so thankful for it."

"What did you think of the US? And where did you stay?"

"I was in Rutgers, New Jersey."

"That's cold. Had a friend who went there."

"So cold, and I'm Nigerian! I had to wear two pairs of socks, five camisoles, and two sweaters to go to my first class."

"Camisole?"

"You know, undershirt." Her vocab was better than mine.

"Oh, of course."

"It just seemed like a more organized, nice, and beautiful version of Lagos. Americans, you are always on time, too. Classes start at 9 a.m. sharp."

"Yeah, I guess so. We could learn to chill a bit."

"That's what makes Americans so reliable. And you guys are smiling to everyone. We don't do that here."

"Not recently, not a lot of smiles in bipartisan America." I shook my head back and forth. "So then, how do the women get jobs?" I asked, turning the conversation back to her project.

"That's what we do. We help staff them as cleaners or other low-skilled staff in an organization. It's only about a fifteen-minute walk to get out of the slum."

"That's shocking. A slum right in the backyard!"

"Yes, that's true. There are universities, government buildings, and cities all around it. We get women of all ages and, more recently, young girls with kids. Most are between fourteen and twenty, so now I need to figure out how to help them and educate them."

We finished up lunch, then walked outside to get our transport. Standing in front of the crosswalk, we said our goodbyes. "Hopefully, we get approval to enter. I'll let you know. Watch it; cars don't stop for the zebra crossing." She looked at the cars zooming by.

"Zebra, what?" I asked, looking around for an animal.

"No, the crosswalk. You know, it looks like a zebra. In the US, people obey it. Here they don't."

"Noted. I'll WhatsApp you. Cheerio!"

The next day, we received the approval and met up together with T-Bone, Funmi, and Johan. Under one of Lagos' massive bridges, the slum grew like a tentacle extending down the southwest side to Lagos Island. The bridges in Nigeria were impressive feats of engineering for their sheer length alone—the longest was 11.8 kilometers (7.4 miles).

Johan was a young Dane in his early twenties who worked with Architects Without Borders. Skinny with brown hair and a speckled beard, he wore loose-fitting linen garb picked up in the city. He was living in a slum where he was trying to figure out a better way to build scalable houses in those communities. His idea was to design them so they could be made in hours and stacked next to each other. Armed to take some excellent footage, he carried a DSLR camera, a drone, and an iPhone. Looking at his iPhone, *Apple should build and sell stacked houses in the slums,* I thought.

"So, let me brief you before we go in," said Funmi. "They treat this like a separate village or city if you will."

"It sure looks like one," I said, looking around.

"It's something they can call their home."

"Makes sense to me."

"Be respectful, smile, and just let them know you would like to visit. Nothing more."

"I play tourist all the time; that's easy."

"Good, and don't go acting like you are a white savior."

"White, what? What's that mean, Funmi?"

"White people act like they are going to save a bunch of people in Africa. They end up irritating us. Pictures, selfies online, and so on."

"OK, got it. I'm not saving anyone." Then on second thought, I mumbled, "Well, maybe myself." Then I raised my voice and said, "I'm just exploring and learning."

The right side of her lip curved up, giving me a sense that she thought I knew better already. "That's all you need to tell people," she replied.

A large gate with a sign displaying "Makoko" marked the entrance to the slum and beyond. What surprised me about the slums in Africa was that they were well marked like Japanese Torii gates. Through the gates, we followed a tarred road that led toward the docks and stopped beside a cluster of concrete blocks with tin-awnings and chipped yellow paint that, though small, were sturdily built.

Funmi knocked on the door of one, and we each took off our shoes before entering its small space. A few other people were already seated on the couches, with bloodshot eyes either from the heat, stress, or alcohol—I became accustomed to red eyes in oppressed places like refugee camps and slums. A fan blew across the room toward an older man, upward of eighty, sitting on a ledge. Completely engulfed in a yellow gown, his heading protruded out at the top, and hands rested on a small cane—he was the slum's chief. He greeted us and inquired as to why we had come. To look and learn was our answer. He said we could only stay a short time, and it would cost extra for pictures and videos of both him and the locals. Funmi conversed with him in Yoruba and gave him some naira (the local currency). We all bowed respectfully and left, walking across a swampy area in the direction of her school amidst chickens and half-clothed kids running about freely.

The Kindle Africa school consisted of a wooden building with tin awnings that Funmi had constructed with her own money—and some of it with her own hands. It was painted purple outside, with three rooms and about twenty small desks with legs still attached. There was a chalkboard, no lights, and a small window that daylight poured through. I was devastated, only gazing at the lack of infrastructure, lack of anything. My heart dropped to the floor. On the other hand, Funmi walked around proudly, confident they could build this school and make an impact.

She then announced that she was going to show us the slum. "OMG, this isn't the slum?" I said. "Not exactly, this is the city before the slum," she replied. "We're now going to take a rare boat ride through the real slums of Makoko." The ground became marshier before we arrived at a dock with wooden awnings where people were living. It wasn't a small dock, but one that resembled a grid-like city that spread wide and far, almost out to the bridge a few kilometers away.

The people lived in dire circumstances. We passed a woman giving birth in a hotel, people on their deathbeds in a so-called hospital, and drunks stumbling about in the local tavern, known as the oloboyi in Yoruba. Taverns were looked down upon by the Yoruba people. Kids ran around collecting drinking bottles to fill up water and food for their bloated tummies and asked us for a dollar with a big smile. I didn't resist. Funmi directed us onto a small but burly rowboat where we sat two to a seat while rowing through this massive water village of poverty.

Dozens of fishers rowed in and out with tiny catches. Women smoked the fish over an open fire, laid them in a basket, and hawked them on the docks. Most didn't speak English, only a local dialect and some French. For a highly educated country like Nigeria, this uneducated place was a scar of the Yaba community. Our eyes met those of locals who didn't blink—staring in wonder as to who we were but delighted to see us. They all waved and smiled, holding up their catch and asking us to buy fish about the size of my hand—bony, tarred fish that didn't look like they could even be bait.

We kept on rowing toward the highway bridge and finally stopped next to a large pillar that we climbed upon—the foundations of the bridge. Cars raced overhead as we all took a deep breath and looked at one another in amazement. There was nothing to say as we grappled with emotions that none of us had experienced before—except Funmi. The sun set behind the slum, and looking back, I saw her silhouetted like the angel she was—in awe of her work. We made our way back in to witness its comings and goings one more time, and departed that night to go our separate ways, planning to meet for lunch the following day.

At the time of writing this book, Funmi's non-profit, Kindle Africa, has provided over five-hundred women in the community with education. It also currently sponsors 102 children in primary schools across different slum communities.

The next day, we met up at a small fish grill restaurant outside the E-Center shopping mall, with as much activity taking place outside the mall as within. As we sat there eating grilled fish and watching the African Cup, I got sucked into the game. Johan encouraged me to get a Maltismo—a local malt drink—but I took one sip and spat it out. "This is terrible. Malt in a milkshake, yes. But not like this." He laughed, and we agreed to get beers instead. While chatting about my travel plans, I got a text from Joba asking if we wanted to go to a wedding?! Why not? He even tailored some Nigerian clothes for us. What amazing hospitality!

The wedding was considered small by Nigerian standards—only around three hundred guests!—yet still boasted famous local DJs playing popular Nollywood songs, a mosaic of strobe lights, and the best food I'd had so far on what seemed like a never-ending buffet. He introduced us to his colleagues, and, as I mingled with the guests, I thought how Nigeria had felt much safer and friendlier than expected. People were approachable, trustworthy, and enterprising.

As the wedding party began to die down, Johan looked over and asked me if I wanted to check out Femi Kuta (Fela Kuta's eldest son) at the New Africa Shrine. Joba chimed in "Time for some Guinness Extra!" The party was just beginning. It was time for Femi and the New Africa Shrine—where the music was great and the entertainment excellent. The outdoor venue had music, tables, and colored plastic chairs where you could sit and eat or drink. Local vendors sold a variety of food, and people danced a bit. It was the ideal place to end my time in Nigeria. T-Bone and I were taking a bus to Benin at 4 a.m., so as the night came to a close, I jumped in a taxi back to Yaba. Getting out and walking toward the hotel, a guy looked at me and said,

"What's a white n***** doing walking around?"

"Just getting a bite to eat before going to sleep. What are you doing?" He looked at me surprised by how casually I'd replied to his question.

He clarified, "No white people are walking around here at this time."

"I'm hungry. I'm getting some suya and going to sleep. Want some?" That was the great thing about suya; the shops stayed open all night long.

"Sure," he replied and smiled.

So, I bought extra and dropped him off some wrapped in tin foil.

While eating my suya, I flashbacked to high school—the other time I was called that name. A classmate was so infuriated at me after a pickup game that he was going to whoop me in the locker room. A basketball teammate of mine, about half the size of the angry accuser, glanced at him and said, "One hand on him, and you are mine." I didn't know what power my friend yielded, but I was happy to be on his side. Being called that didn't make me feel good, and it was downright scary—how it must have felt to African Americans.

T-Bone pounded on the door at four o'clock to catch our bus north. We would travel north to Benin, Togo, all the way to Ghana. We walked outside, and I grabbed a shot of coffee from a guy selling Nescafe under an umbrella. They don't sleep on the streets of Nigeria. Half-awake, we grabbed a taxi to the bus depot about an hour from Yaba. It was just as bustling in the wee hours of the morning as it was during the day. Perhaps half the city worked the night shift. A couple of dozen tour buses lined the streets and packed the parking lot while people slept inside the terminal on bags laid out on the floor.

The Nigerian spirit was remarkable: they remain good-humored, work hard, and build a good life for themselves despite a system that seems stacked against them.[6] The generosity they showed me was characteristic of how Nigerians treated foreigners, but, in reverse, foreigners had to earn mutual respect by giving time to understand the Nigerian culture. It was a reciprocal relationship, and I didn't want to come across as just a white guy content on receiving. However, honestly, I didn't know what I could offer in return. Joba, Funmi, and T-Bone gave me a marvelous experience, and I'd have to repay them someday.

Sitting around on the floor of the bus terminal with hundreds of people swarming around, I noted on my phone that I hoped I'd left others with a decent impression. I had told Funmi and Joba I'd help out the best I could, and we'd stay in touch. With my teaching warmup behind me at MEST Nigeria, I was ready for MEST in Ghana. I marveled at how Nigerians formed their missions by following their heart and executed it with relentless hustle. There was little doubt in my mind that they would propel Nigeria to new heights in the coming decades.

Chapter 10

THE CONTRAST BETWEEN BENIN AND TOGO

"Don't Mess with Voodoo"

—KD

Being called a white n***** me of the quote by Chimamanda, "Black people are susceptible to unusual looks, stark comments, and unfair treatment." On the flip side, white people are susceptible to comments and unfair labeling in Africa and even Asia. That experience taught me—to some extent—how it must feel when black people are called such names in the USA.

Benin showed me the worst manifestation of racism in the form of the slave trade. On top of that, the government repressed the people, creating an unhappy society. Togo, on the other hand, was more upbeat, positive, and similar to laid-back island culture. When I discovered this difference, I wanted to figure out how two countries, alike in the population (Togo -8M; Benin -12M), culture, and location, could have such different outlooks.

Over the gospel music playing on the overhead speakers, I heard, "Praise the Lord!" A guy dressed in a dark grey suit and a black top hat was shouting and kneeling in the middle of the aisle. "Amen!" responded a few people next to him as he shook a Bible at them. Southern churches in South Carolina became vivid in the back of my mind, just as money exchanged hands, and the preacher moved back a seat, kneeling then reading a verse from the Bible.

T-Bone took out his earbuds and leaned over. "They are praying for a safe passage. These buses often crash. I told you, a high fatality on the roads. Give him some Naira." He put his earbuds back in, draining out the noise with Afro beats, and I sat there whispering to myself, "Amen, Hallelujah."

My impression of Benin was tainted even before I arrived in the country. The consulate guard had abruptly led me into a dimly lit room. A big man resembling Hollywood actor Samuel Jackson looked out from behind a desk of stacked papers and old encyclopedias. I had researched that the visa cost $25 at the border, but he was trying to charge me four times that. When I questioned him, he just laughed at me and said, "Then you go to the border, and they will send you back to Nigeria." Afterward, I'd gone directly to the Togo embassy nearby to do the same, and an official dressed in a Hawaiian shirt—at least that's how I'd like to remember it—kindly told me that I could get a visa at the border for $25. "Just go," he said. "We aren't like Benin!"

As we approached the border at Seme, the bus stopped, all the curtains were closed, and the bus driver told us not to look out the window. I freaked, thinking it was a terrorist attack. T-Bone laughed. "No, they just don't want people to see what's happening outside. Its Benin's secret."

Two large men dressed in camouflage boarded the bus, with one singling me out and demanding from the bus conductor that he see my passport. I gave it to him; he glanced at it and handed it back. That was weird. Then, a guy seated behind me tapped me on the shoulder and apologized for what he called "racial profiling for money," although I only thought it was funny. I reflected on racial profiling in the United States and the devastating consequences for the victims.

The bus arrived outside Cotonou Stadium, and I disembarked to a lively stream of hustlers. T-Bone and I jumped in a taxi to the Cotonou Guesthouse, situated down a sandy road lined with international embassies. Towering palms gave the area a beach-town feel (albeit without the beach), and our guesthouse was comfortable, although we found it hard to communicate with the French-speaking owners.

We discovered that around 200,000 tourists visit Benin every year (predominantly from Europe), with most coming to learn about West Africa's slave history and medicinal practices and some for business. We met one guy helping Belgium juice makers source pineapples, which I thought was a practical entrepreneurial endeavor. After a breakfast of spaghetti, eggs, and fresh baguettes—one of the benefits of visiting a French colony are the baguettes the locals still make—we drove a few hours to the small town of Ouidah, regarded as the principal center of the trans-Atlantic slave trade up until the mid-1800s.[7]

Local kings were complicit in handing over slaves to the Europeans in exchange for guns and supplies. The slaves walked from Abomey (the capital of the Kingdom of Dahomey) to Ouidah, where they were stuffed into ships like sardines and transported to Brazil, Western Europe, and the United States.

We visited the Ouidah Museum of History, housed within an eighteenth-century Portuguese fort, which detailed the horrors of the slave trade. What was most impactful was following in the footsteps of the slaves along the Slave Route, marked by signs and monuments en route to the Gate of No Return.

It was a seven-step process to export slaves: chained up, branded like cattle, and then herded around the "tree of forgetfulness"—a symbolic spot that washed clean memories of their history, culture, and self-identity. Then they spent three months in dark cells to weed out the weak; those who survived buried their compatriots in a slave cemetery, then circled the tree of ancestors to pay respects. At last, they exited through the "Gate of No Return" to board the slave ships.[8] Today, this was a large white gate on a sandy beach looking onto a crystal blue ocean. Staring through that gate gave me goosebumps all way down my back.

From student mode, we snapped back to tourism mode; we stopped at the Python Temple, overflowing with snakes. Close by was a voodoo ceremony for $100. We passed and decided to catch voodoo elsewhere and headed instead to Abomey to see The National Museum, loaded with more artifacts and history.

On the way back from Abomey, we drove a few hours and looped to the other side of the country towards the capital, Porto Novo. The following day we stopped at churches, mosques, and a few small museums. We visited the Brazilian-inspired Great Mosque (which was first built as a church) and the Musée da Silva that explores Benin's unique Afro-Brazilian culture. Benin exported nearly one-third of all slaves from Africa, and Brazil received about 4.7M or about 25% of all slave exports.[9] Over time, descendants returned to Africa, infusing this new Portuguese culture. In Porto Novo, we also visited the Ethnographic Museum, which details the tribal history of the region, with a traditional collection of primitive masks, clothing, and musical instruments.

Just outside of Porto Novo, Songhai Farm was the most interesting place we visited in Benin. It's a successful agricultural non-profit that educated entrepreneurs and engineers in sustainability. Founded by Father Godfrey Nzamujo, a Nigerian/Dominican priest with an electronics degree from the United States, he came to Benin during the tremendous African famine of 1982 to help the hungry.

From a one-acre farm, it's now state of the art. It consisted of a modern facility with greenhouses, aquaponics, and hydroponics lakes for growing tilapia fish, which in turn provide fertilizer for soil and farms. Their goal was to teach anyone in Benin how to live off the land. Not only do they educate farmers, but they also gave them the resources to get started. As Trevor Noah said, "You can teach a man to fish, but he needs a pole!" Lunch was a testament to the efficacy of the work. We ate the freshest vegetables and fish since coming to Africa. I was amazed and convinced of the importance of natural food and sustainable farming by taste alone.

For our final dinner in Benin, we headed back to the Cotonou Stadium to feast on grilled fish, maize, and rice while soaking up the lively atmosphere watching the Africa Cup. The Africa Cup takes place every two years and is an exciting time, with everyone outside in the streets watching the games and talking football (i.e., American soccer). I'd noticed during my travels in Asia and Europe the unifying force of football and the bond it creates. What I thought was cool was that people would congregate around the stadium, eat outside, and watch the games. The stadiums served as a place for community gathering. Why didn't stadiums back home invite such activity, rather than reserving them for sporting events and concerts? I questioned—what a waste of space and community potential.

We boarded the ABC bus the following day to Togo, and at the border, the contrast hit me in the face. Nicer people. Relaxed atmosphere. Lovely passport stamps of palm trees. Just beyond the border were several wooden fishing boats painted light blue and white, with fishers hauling them in and out of the sea. They were smiling and handing nets filled with fish to people waiting on the sand.

This beach extended to Ghana, interrupted only by a massive port on the outskirts of Lome, which provided an economic boom to West Africa. As we drove toward the capital city, I looked out across the white sands and azure waters of the Atlantic Ocean and felt immediately calm. Motorbikes, fishers, and beach bars scattered the palm-lined route, eventually giving way to a sprawl of vendors and stores as we approached a large Togo port.

Even the taxi drivers were more pleasant. During a pit stop, I waited beside our taxi when another taxi driver approached me. "You look worried and confused. Don't worry, Togo is a safe country with good food." That wasn't the same advice I got from a taxi driver in Benin, who said, "You have to yell to get what you want here."

From Lome, the capital of Togo, we made our way to Airbnb, which to our dismay, was around ten kilometers inland from the beach, though the beach environment and atmosphere didn't change. The sandy roads continued inland as did the vendors with large umbrellas shielding themselves from the sun, selling all types of tropical fruits. Makeshift bars lined the streets screening the African Cup of Nations—the joys of West Africa were starting to grow on me. Our Airbnb appeared like a mansion compared to those nearby.

The following day we hired a local driver to tour the area and then headed down to the beach for a Togolese lunch—pasta, beans, fresh fish, couscous, and spinach. Togo and Benin seemed very similar in size, culture, and heritage. Yet, something was very different. The people in Togo were much happier and positive than those in Benin. But why?

While walking around with T-Bone, we came upon a voodoo market, a large square filled with some creepy artifacts. There were dead animal corpses, skeletons, skulls of all types of species, and dolls—lots of dolls. That's where the shaman was sitting when he said, "Come with me; you have demons." How'd he know? T-Bone looked at me and said that it wasn't for him and he'd wait for me in the square.

The shaman was a young man dressed in a grey robe blotted with red patches, a white rectangular hat with buildings etched into it, and a cane with a small animal's skull on top. He waved to me and said, "Follow me to rid your demons." Thinking this was a good idea, I led the way. I walked into a small hut with two small wooden benches. I sat down in his booth, about three arms lengths each way and covered by black silk. The shaman sat cross-legged in front of me. Drapes shielded all four sides of his little hut, with various types of voodoo paraphernalia hanging on the walls. It smelled of mustiness and a hint of death.

The shaman had a small pot where he burned different things that I smoked through a pipe. He pulled out a series of little, hand-sized dolls, telling me to pick the ones I wanted to burn. Envy, Greed, Anger, and Love were the choices. Why Love? I wondered. He was a witch doctor and knew what killed people's souls. After a small price hassle, he turned off the backlight and went to work.

He hummed and chanted before lighting the fire with a marijuana-like substance. Placing the mini-doll on it, he waved his hands to create a small flame. I sat meditating beside him with closed eyes. A few minutes later, the smoke began to rise, creating a fog inside the small room. I coughed, and the back of my throat salivated as I inhaled, resulting in a burning sensation in the throat, stopping in my lungs, and subsiding down in my feet.

He placed the ashes into a small pipe and handed it over to me. I didn't like smoking anything, much less a foreign substance. Puff. Puff. Puff. I coughed terribly.

Speaking in another African language I hadn't heard, the shaman sensed my fear and laughed out loud. He then stabbed the doll with a small pin in the side twice. He took a big inhale through the pipe, as though it was oxygen at the top of a mountain. He stabbed the doll again, right in the butt, and took another inhale. I sat there for a few more minutes, inhaling the smoke in the room and, in the deafening silence, started to buzz. He then stuck the needle right into the doll's heart and placed it in the small fire.

"No more anger, no more pain. Repeat with me," the shaman said.

"No more anger, no more pain, no more anger, no more pain, no more anger, no more pain," I repeated steadily.

He stood up, started to wave his hands in the smoke, then twirled, touched his toes, and raised his arms over his head. Turning slowly to the black, back curtain, he grabbed it and ripped it open with an "Ahhhh. Look into my eyes!" I looked into the shaman's eyes as the smoke started to clear. Right above him, I saw. I couldn't believe it. My eye focused on the eyes of a full-sized human cranium, staring straight through its sockets to darkness. Humming and smoking and laughing, he kept repeating like a broken record, "No more anger, no more pain, go away."

"Holy Mary!" I was gazing into the dead skull—it wouldn't be the last time in Africa. "Am I next? Oh, I'm next!" I gasped, jumped up, and bolted out of the room. "T-Bone! T-Bone!" I yelled, "Where are you?"

"Yo, man, what's up? You alright?"

"You won't believe this," I panted. "Let's get out of here."

"I told you that it's creepy, man," T-Bone laughed aloud. We ended the evening strolling around the beach, sipping beers to cool my nerves.

The next morning we boarded the bus to Ghana on our long trip, and I kept researching the history and politics of the countries, both of which were politically unstable. The governments evolved a bit differently. Though Togo was family-controlled for fifty years, it created relatively free elections in 2007 and has continued to take steps forward ever since.[10] Just after I left Togo, there were massive protests against the fifty-year father-son regime. On the other hand, the Economist Intelligence Unit rated Benin as a hybrid regime that has electoral frauds, widespread corruption, voter repression, and so forth and so on.

While Togo seemed—and was by GDP measures—more destitute on the first impression, people appeared more self-sufficient, supported by a healthier community, and uplifted by burgeoning commercial activity. A rising economy gave the Togolese hope; perhaps this was why people seemed much happier there. Another may be that a fairer democracy gave people some voice or autonomy, whereas the people of Benin seemed more oppressed.

As it became darker, I no longer wanted to research on my phone. Right when I put it down, I started to feel pricks on my skin. It felt like when the humidity causes the hair on your skin to rise. Then, all of a sudden, I felt a hard poke that jolted me out of my seat. Not once, not twice, but three times in the side. WTF!? T-Bone was dead asleep. I shook him awake. "T-Bone, what the heck, I'm getting a pain in my side like a poke," I said.

He opened one eye and whispered, "Oh, yeah? Three times?"

"How'd you know?" I was puzzled.

"That's voodoo, you idiot. He's just saying goodbye."

Things that entertain me cause me pain, but I don't know why I still do them. That repeated like a broken record during the eight-hour bus ride to Accra, Ghana.

Fishers rowing a boat in Makoko.

T-Bone, Johan, and Funmi in Makoko

Joba and I at the wedding

The Gate of No Return in Benin

Voodoo paraphernalia in Togo

Chapter 11

BUILDING A BETTER WORLD IN GHANA

*"The gift of a new way of seeing. The chance to participate in
the work of building a better world. The ultimate example of
perseverance and faith for each new generation to follow."*
—**President Barack Obama** on the Thirtieth
Anniversary of Mandela's Release from Prison

Waiting to be poked again, I gave up on sleep and felt anxiety rise. *I had
to do something productive and impactful—but what?* I doubted myself.
Ghana showed me several ways to build a better world and taught me
that gifts could come in many forms.

At the Ghana border, two women greeted T-Bone and me with a warm
smile. When I told them that they were the first women I'd met at the borders,
they proclaimed that women have equal rights and opportunities in Ghana,
unlike other parts of Africa. Seeing women with power and equal rights set the
tone for Ghana. In this respect, Ghana was the leader in Africa. On March 6,
1957, Ghana (formerly the Gold Coast) became the first sub-Saharan African
country to gain its independence from European colonization—it was a gift
from Ghana to Africa. In a fantastic historical book about Africa called The
Fate of Africa, Martin Meredith says, "Ghana was seen as a portent watched and

106

admired around the world. No other event in Africa had previously attracted such attention."

The customs ladies escorted me out of the immigration building and stopped under a gate engraved with a Ghana flag. In the middle of the flag was the Lodestar, a bold, black star symbolizing African Freedom and anti-colonialism. She wished us well and warned me about getting ripped off by money exchangers and not to accept any rate under 5:1. Buoyed by this advice, I confidently haggled until I got a fair price, then bought a few mangoes, more guavas, and boarded the bus to Accra.

We arrived in the Ghanaian capital in the middle of the night, and I was relieved by the civility everywhere. We pulled up to a roundabout, lit with traffic lights, where a line of taxis was patiently waiting—no hustling or quarreling. Jumping in the first one, we told the driver where we were going, he turned on the meter and knew precisely where to go. A functional taxi meter and the knowledgeable driver indicated to me that we had entered a new economic zone. I sighed in relief.

Togo and Benin have a per capita GDP of $700-ish while Ghana's is double that at over $1600—and growing. The roads and hotels were in better condition, as were the convenience stores, and there were signs of foreign investment, such as restaurants and malls. This area reminded me of a blog post that Bill Gates wrote in reference to Hans Rosling: "The world is divided into four economic zones—not just the developing and developed world."[11] Classifying the world into different economic levels will help economies receive the right investments.

The taxi dropped us off at the headquarters of MEST, whose small campus comprised four buildings for classes and housing. It was impressive, with a large, two-story classroom that was separated from the living quarters by a mosquito-malaria-infested stream that we crossed along a rope bridge. Expecting to see lights out by the time of our arrival, people were still roaming around the buildings, snacking on food, and working at their computers. I could sense the effervescence of youth and the excitement of entrepreneurship. It seemed similar to the work ethic of a Silicon Valley startup, without pizza, but with the addition of potential malaria.

We were welcomed by "Big Ash" and a few other workers, one of whom directed me to a nearby shopping center. One of the things that I enjoyed most about my time in Accra was sampling the Ghanaian cuisine, especially the stews, known as banku and fufu. They featured ingredients such as okra and plantains. At a local restaurant, I sampled all of their different stews in one sitting, as well as Ghana's version of jollof rice, which everyone presumed I liked more than the Nigerian version. The night scene was happening in Accra: the cool beach bars like Rehab and Cochromite, rooftop bars like Sky, and local music bars would go late into the night.

A week here proved enough time to create some strong bonds with both the faculty and students. The diverse team included Todd, a US tech veteran and musician; Vineet, an Indian entrepreneur; Celine, an energetic French lady who led the fundraising efforts; and Mike, a young American who wanted to learn about Africa, go to a top MBA, and then return and build something big, either with a firm or on his own.

Building on my time in Nigeria, I offered to teach business development and sales class to help out the budding entrepreneurs. The presentation started slowly, and I could see my students' eyes wandering around, so I had to catch their interest. To do this, I outright told them that in my last start-up, I helped to close many deals, including contracts with Microsoft, Apple, and Sony. Their eyes lit up. That's the hook! But how to teach them what I did?

I couldn't precisely articulate it, so I spent hours before and after class in one-on-one meetings explaining the steps. What was apparent to me in Ghana— and later in other parts of Africa—was that selling wasn't a natural skill. Many perceived sales as low-level jobs. The thinkers, designers, and researchers valued themselves higher. The problem many companies had was that they spent their time philosophizing about the product rather than penetrating the market. I convinced them to put that creativity into action in the form of sales and marketing. Their excitement to learn this conveyed that this new skill could be super useful to them. The fire in my belly lit up. Beyond any doubt, I was here to teach these entrepreneurs how to close deals.

From Kenya, South Africa, Nigeria, and Ghana, the entrepreneurs conceptualized a wide variety of businesses: an E-commerce tools businesses for

US consumers (SynCommerce & Kudobuzz), a GPS tracking device for farming equipment (TroTroTractor), a streaming, mobile music/radio service (AfRadio), and (arguably the most successful idea) a church focused content management software company (Asoriba).

I didn't understand Asoriba's potential until I stumbled into a church while walking around on Sunday. I heard singing coming from a small, purple building behind the school and decided to enter. About fifty people came in and out during the sermon (which lasted for around three hours), with a mix of preaching, praying, lots of loud singing and swaying, kneeling and bowing while yelling "Praise the Lord!" The lead priest spoke seriously while the younger priest preached spectacularly. In between sermons, they would request offerings, and the emotional shifts were effective in inspiring people to open their wallets. No doubt, there was money flowing through the church, but I questioned the authenticity and integrity of those receiving it—at least at this one.

Often, when a country or region starts to grow, the first indication is the rise of new financial instruments like China in the mid-2000s, mobile payments took off, and this was happening all across Africa. While attending an event hosted by Village Capital, a large non-profit that helps entrepreneurs in emerging markets, I met Piggybank. Their service was scaling fast. Ghanaians wanted to save, but many didn't have the discipline, or it was just difficult on a meager income. So, for every transaction made, a few cents were deposited into an untouchable savings account. Piggybank had recently struck a deal with a big bank and had several million accounts

It wasn't until I met AfRadio, a mobile phone music streaming company that I could demonstrate my deal closing methods. We set up a plan to speak to local mobile phone carriers—similarly to what I had done in my last company. In a few days only, we contacted the major telecom carriers and set up a meeting with the largest one, inviting them to the facility. The deal didn't close, but I successfully demonstrated the power of proactive sales.

Teaching at MEST reinvigorated me. It rewarded me with time to think through everything experienced in a decade in Silicon Valley. To do this, I had to recall my past and remember the decisions I'd made—all by writing out notes of what I did. The deeper the reflection, the better I was able to recall information, connect the dots, and learn about myself in the process. What it taught me, once again, was that teaching is learning.

After a week in Accra, I planned to fly to the Ivory Coast. That didn't happen. Due to a military uprising and occupation of the airport, the airlines emailed me in French to let me know my flight was canceled. My eight grade French came in handy—along with a bit of Google Translate. With this unlucky—or perhaps lucky—turn of events, I hit up Vineet and asked him what he was doing for the weekend. Vineet was in his late twenties—though he looked nineteen—free-spirited and had the impish grin of a trickster.

"So Vineet, what do you do outside of MEST?" I asked.

"Travel and hike."

"Hike? Like a walk in the park or hike?" I asked, wondering if he was a nature walker or power hiker.

"No, really hike, long hikes." His tone of voice accepted the challenge.

"OK, where do you go? You wanna road trip?"

"Yes, yes. Do you want to see a waterfall? I know this amazing place around four hours from Accra. Want to go?"

"Now you are talking. We can do it at the weekend."

Vineet and I met up at the Madina tro tro (what they call a minibus) terminal, a bustling mini-bus station of small vans that transported people from city to city. There must have been two dozen buses, hundreds of people waiting, and vending goods sold to all. We found the bus that had a wooden sign on the hood, "Ho Hoe," and picked up a few snacks. Sharing the front seat of the min-bus, snacking on nuts and fruit, and listening to our audiobooks, four hours later, we arrived.

"So, you know the people out here?"

"I have been here before. It is such a peaceful place. And really, it is so easy to make friends in this setting."

"I bet; being in nature always relaxes people. Even the science says so: It's soup for the soul."

We alighted the bus on a dirt road around a few buildings with an arrow pointing to the Wli Waterfalls. After a twenty-minute walk in the woods, we arrived at a small campground with a dozen tents and small cooking facility. The manager at the camp, and a few girls approached us. Vineet started chatting with them as though they were some of his closest friends and introduced me to the group.

The lower waterfalls were around forty-five minutes away. They were beautiful and formed a swimming lake at the bottom. We swam a bit and decided to make the trek to the upper waterfall. Energized by our accomplishment, we ran down the dirt trail that led back to the camp where cold beers awaited us.

When I got back, I took a bath in the river while the ladies at the camp were cooking grilled tilapia fish with banku, along with corn and cassava, which was pounded into a paste and typically served with a meat or fish soup. Given an option to choose between roast potatoes and banku, I wanted both, of course.

The food was delicious. How could it not be when cooked in such a pristine environment with a wood fire in the woods of Ghana?

"Amazing food! I think we need a beer before we call it a night," Vineet suggested.

"Great!" I said. We chilled with our beers, listening to the sounds of crickets chirping. Then we started to learn more about each other. "What brings you to Africa? Why did you move to Ghana?" I asked.

"An impulsive decision. I have never lived outside of India and didn't enjoy the corporate environment back home." He looked at the stars.

"Makes two of us. I think we should send anyone who wants to quit a job in Africa."

"Ha-ha. That's funny. When I heard about the opportunity to mentor startups in Ghana, I knew this was something I wanted to do. I applied, got selected, and in two months packed my bags to Ghana."

"Darn, just like that. Impressive."

"I am glad I made this choice. Africa, being the last frontier, will shape the future. Just being around the entrepreneurs from different parts of Africa is amazing."

"You going to stick around?"

"For a couple of years, maybe Kenya next. I was just there a month ago; the startup scene there is vibrant, the country is beautiful, and Mount Kenya is amazing!" He stood up and drifted around.

"Sounds good to me. I'm going there next. If I meet some people, I'll introduce you." I liked connecting people.

"That would be wonderful!"

That afternoon, we bid farewell to our camp hosts and traveled to a Rastafari place in the Volta region. Ghana had a large ecotourism scene that includes hostels run by natural resources and energy. Forests and streams surrounded our lodge. In this eco-menagerie, there was a butterfly forest. Light rays and butterflies showered us in color as we ran the 1.5-mile path. It wasn't the only one; there are many butterfly sanctuaries scattered across Ghana and other parts of West Africa. Every city needs a butterfly farm.

Vineet and I parted ways after a perfect weekend, befriending each other, and building a lasting bond that we'd later rekindle in India. On the way out, I took a picture of a memorable sign at the hostel that read, "Life is not measured by the number of breaths you take, but by the moments in life that take your breath away."

Meeting a carefree, easy-going person like Vineet loosened me up. He came from a very humble home in India and traveled to Africa to give him a different perspective from his own culture. It had nothing to do with charity, business, or impact. It was a simple and unfussy way to live life, and I wanted to find a way to do the same.

I had a few extra days before I needed to fly across the continent, and Vineet suggested that I check out Cape Coast, the home of the slave castles. I didn't think my soul could take more slave history, but I decided to make the trip.

As the bus pulled into Cape Coast, the slave castles grew bigger and bigger. These were massive castles and forts built and occupied by the Dutch, Portuguese, Spanish, and British who fought to hold the region. Around the castles were communities of fishermen who went out to sea by the dozens in their colorful fishing boats.

I spent the following day in the Cape Coast Castle, one of the forty castles on the coast of West Africa. This one was a massive white castle first built by the Portuguese and later taken over by the Swedes. Walking through the dungeon, I stepped over chains, iron balls, shackles, and other metal tortures scattered there. But "The Point of No Return" was my when my soul cried. I stared at the small doorway in the concrete wall—what looked like it should be for a little person, not a man. It led to a stream where wooden boats would line up, waiting to load with slaves. These boats would then take the chained-up men to bigger boats and packed up like sardines in a can. Only a quarter of them would live to make it to their destination; the others would be thrown out to sea. Tears rolled down my eyes, looking at the blurry plaque that was unveiled by Barack Obama when he visited in July 2009.

Many of these slaves, a reported 400,000, had landed in the Southeast of the US and specifically, South Carolina, where I grew up.[12] To understand where many of my fellow South Carolinians came from touched me deeply. Psychologists say that trauma lasts six to seven generations. No wonder African Americans still have mental scars in the United States. Their lives had been a constant struggle, and to see this, to understand where they started from, then tie that into what they overcame in the United States during segregation and the Jim Crow laws, ripped a hole in my heart. I wondered what's the best way the USA could help its African American citizens, many of whom still haven't overcome the scars.

That night outside my small, beachfront hostel, I walked around feeling the sand in between my toes and sipping beer. Living' the good life. A white lady dressed in a colorful red and yellow Ghanaian skirt approached me. I struck up a conversation complimenting her skirt. She said it'd made locally at a women's focused non-profit called Global Mamas, where she was volunteering. There, they made batik fashion skirts, shirts, and more. She offered to show me the facility the next day.

The three-story facility housed hundreds of women who were busy dying, drying, and dividing material—some inside and some outside in the neighborhood. By building a supply chain of batik production throughout Ghana, they employed over 600 women making colorfully designed shirts and blouses. The clothes received the Fair Trade Certification, which ensured they get a fair price for their products sold overseas. A reasonable price sustained the operations. On the way out at the exit, the operations manager showed me a picture of the founder, a young white American lady who first came to Ghana with the Peace Corps. "Where is she now?" I asked. She replied, "She passed away." But she never found out what happened. That entrepreneur left a thriving, enduring organization.

That evening the friendship continued. She'd worked in marketing for years but needed time away from Australia and discovered this non-profit. Her volunteer work turned into a modest paying job and a few trips to Ghana. She said that Africa invigorated her and gave her new energy. We spoke a little about life's tumultuous twists and turns, which seemed trivial compared to people's difficulties in Africa

As the night wore down, I took it easy. "Let her make a move. Don't be the aggressive one," I coached myself. Then after we finished a few Castle lagers, she looked at me in the eye and said, "I think I should go." I nodded.

Then she stared straight into my eyes and said, "Does it make sense?"

"Whatever makes sense for you?" I replied. "Well, we just met. Let's stay in touch; maybe we will meet again." I thought *I'll let the universe decide my fate.* And, it did.

She hugged me and kissed me on the cheek, turned, and vanished in the dark. I plopped down on my plastic chair struck by the moon, light glow of the waves rolling in and out. OMG, did I miss her cue?

A rooster's crow awoke me sometime between 4 and 5 a.m. I jumped out of my chair, grabbed my bag in the room, and boarded an early bus straight to the airport to catch my flight to Uganda. On the way out, I looked back to get a final glimpse of the slave castles; I didn't want ever to forget that sight and the feeling it left inside of me.

"What gift would I leave the world with?" I pondered on the long bus ride to the airport. Like MEST's mission, everything I did, didn't have to have a return on investment. Like Vineet's outlook, life didn't have to be a fuss or have a purpose in everything. Like Global Mamas, I wanted something that would endure past my time. I commiserated over the Peace Corps woman who died after founding Global Mamas. Ghana gave Africa the gift of independence, and it gave me the gift of wanting to do something for its own sake, to make the world a better place.

The team at Meltwater

Vineet and I about to start a hike.

The Cape Coast Slave Castle

A point of no return inside the castle

Chapter 12

DISCOVERING A LAYER DEEPER

"Forget Safety. Live where you fear to live."
—Rumi

E n route to Nairobi. My senses soothed, my patience prolonged, and my anxieties atrophied. Rhythm was the African's rhyme, and mine was becoming a slow, calm pace. Moving around by bus; eating maize, plantains, and fried greens; taking—more often than not—cold showers with limited water, and sometimes filling up buckets. Life was not in a rush, because just living was enough. Just living in the moment without lots of distractions settled me. While Africa didn't have so many luxuries or options, the West offered, life here was simpler and less stressful; there was no scorecard to keep track of or soul to impress.

In some ways, I was softening up. What I meant was I listening better, receiving others' opinions more openly, and just thoroughly adapting to a new environment—empathy in action.

Father Paul greeted me at the Entebbe Airport with a spiritual twinkle in his eye. We, first, stopped at Kampala, a metropolis sitting at the valley of rolling hills. Kampala was a bustling city full of banks, stores, universities, restaurants, and lots of people. Father Paul stopped at the bank, and I entertained myself at a local bookstore picking up *A State of Blood* by Henry Kyemba, which detailed the reign of Idi Amin in Uganda. A military dictator, Idi Amin killed hundreds of thousands—many in the Karamoja region where we headed.

Quiet gospel music played in the car as we drove toward Karamoja. We continued through Jinja—home to the source of the Nile and a white-water rafting adventure hub—to pick up some snacks at a local store, whose owner had a lighter shade of brown than the other Ugandans. He was Somalian, and Father Paul explained that they usually have a lighter skin color, and many came to Uganda for business. For centuries, Somalia was a major trading hub between Africa and the Middle East/Asia, which fostered an environment of trade and enterprise. Coy and savvy, Somali entrepreneurs set up businesses across East Africa—even in refugee camps, I'd come to find out.

Continuing, we passed the one ostrich farm I was looking out for—it had as many armed guards as ostriches. I approached the ostriches, gazing at the armed guards, then Father yelled, "Don't get too close, they will run over you!" I was worried about the guns; he was concerned about the ostriches—the irony. When I asked about the guns, Father Paul explained that the region had been cleared of firearms by the government. They launched a campaign to buyback each weapon for $1,000. It had made Uganda a much safer place.

We met the Innovation Africa team at mBale and then continued by 4x4 to Nakapiripiri in the Karamoja desert. The boss, Sivan, was a highly energetic entrepreneur who desired to strengthen the ties between Israel and Uganda. Uganda had supported a Jewish state after the 1976 Israeli counter-terrorist hostage-rescue mission called "Operation Entebbe." Sivan's energy kept us going. Her mission was to provide solar and water well innovations to rural Ugandan and African villages. The large water pumps and solar energy generators were monitored over the air by telecom networks and satellites that routed back to Israel, ensuring that everything worked properly.

We spent the first few days scoping out new sites, implementing solar solutions on the roof of a hospital then checking on existing implementations. The work was hands-on, practical, and it was nice to touch technology and not just play with software.

Kids walked about half-clothed begging for plastic water bottles, which they used to fill with any water they could scoop up. One young lad wanted to build a farm for his village. One older man who'd studied in the United Kingdom and had dreams of being a professor just wanted irrigation pipes. After returning to Uganda, he'd gotten trapped during the revolution and now was in hiding in the villages. End of the dream.

Unprepared to witness the harsh environment and abject poverty they endured, I spiraled downward into depression. Emotions swung from dismay to hope with the anticipation of playing a role to help empower these people. Who am I to help anyone? This question sent me into a dark space, alone, sitting on my hostel bed with a mosquito net draped over me, gazing at the ceiling.

All of a sudden, my roommate, Ron, came storming into the room.

"This makes you appreciate everything we have, doesn't it?" He flipped on the light.

"Tell me about it."

"We're born in the USA, got irrigation systems, lights don't shut off, and plastic bottles for all."

"We have so much, too much." I kept looking down.

"Yes, we do. Anyway, did you hydrate? You have to drink water, buddy. You look pale." He put his hand on my shoulder.

"Oh, I'm bad at that. I haven't had much water. I blame Chimamanda." I looked up.

"Who?"

"She wrote the book *Americanah*. She joked that Americans freak out when they don't drink two liters of water per day."

"You crazy? It's blazing hot here. You should drink double that." Handing me a bottle of water, he added, "Learned this in the military. Take care of yourself first. No shortcuts."

"Thanks." I flashbacked to the line from the Biloxi Blues movie and said, "It never got this hot in Brooklyn. This is like Africa hot; Tarzan couldn't take this kind of hot." We both laughed. "So, how'd you like the military?"

"Loved it. I loved the people, the purpose, the mission. I wanted to stay, but my Hebrew wasn't up to par."

"Sorry, but now you can do things like this," I reassured him.

"Yes, I love Africa. Lots to do here, and the people are so pleasant."

"There are so many things we can do. Where to even start? It's so hard to see people like this. It makes you question our lives and meaning," I remarked.

"Yes, but we can't dwell on it. We are here to help, learn, and execute. I'm going for a workout to make me feel better. Get the endorphins going." He spoke with the wisdom of a rabbi.

"Good idea, I'm with you."

"Bring it. You do bear crawls?"

"Bear crawls? No, but I eat them."

"I can tell." He pointed to my stomach. "It will keep you young. Do you know what they say in Israel? Tight butt, a clean shave, and smooth hands will keep you looking young." That served as motivation for me, now in my forties.

With a short brown hair cut, slim profile, and smile magnifying his stature, Ron was in his early twenties and had just finished two years with the Israeli Defense Forces (IDF). Although he was an American and raised in the Northeastern USA, his parents were from Israel, so he moved there and served in the military. Like many young Israelis who had completed their two years of mandatory service, he took time off to travel. Israelis viewed travel as part of their education after service to their country. I'd met many young IDF members in Southeast Asia, usually in groups of three or four, hiking mountains, scuba diving, and pursuing whatever adventures they could find. Close in proximity and growing in global and Middle Eastern influence, Africa had become a spot many wanted to understand.

Over the next few days, we visited different villages and tribes who welcomed us with anticipation. In one community, the women wore beautiful and colorful gowns, and the men wore traditional skirts. After the water spigot turned on, they sang and danced for hours. While the women spun and shook, the men jumped as though it were a high jumping contest. Shortly after, we were approached by a dozen members from a neighboring village who had walked miles to ask when they, too, would get a water well. Other villages needed what IA had to offer, but IA only had so much to give without money and resources.

On our final day in the field, we spent a lot of time driving around and looking out the window. It dawned on me. Just looking out the window was how I experienced the world of problems, poverty, and despair. Whether in India, South East Asia, or even in the United States, I didn't do much to help others or get my hands dirty. My perspective began to shift as I was doing something for others. I put myself in their shoes and, once I did, the pity left giving way to compassion. These people weren't depressed or unhappy. They just got on with life while immensely appreciating our help. Getting a glimpse into their world, speaking to them, and eating with them, we connected on a deeper level of humanity. I felt our souls connect at a deeper layer of empathy and compassion.

After five days in the desert, I rode back to Mbale with Father Paul. He could see that I was grappling with a lot of emotions. How can I help make the world a better place? No answers, just nothingness in my mind—*if only I could meditate that well,* I thought. He saw my unease and said, "Stay on your journey and be patient. Your time will come to figure it out."

Father Paul left me at the Jinja Nile Rivers Explorers, a dormitory-like lodge with a bar overlooking the Nile where white water rafting trips happened. Walking through the gate, I peered into the Nile, which was flowing in the broad valley below. Then, I crossed paths with an auburn-haired lady with freckles, dressed in a flowing reddish gown—white girls in African clothes. Scintillating. Sensual. Sultry.

"Pardon me, is this where to sign up for the rafting?" I said with a twinge of my new

African-British like accent.

"Yes, over there. What brings you here?"

"Just stopping by from Mbale and wanted to do some rafting."

"Oh, I see. You are just stopping by from Mbale as if that is commonplace for tourists. What's there?" she asked.

"Just a non-profit I was volunteering with," I said nonchalantly.

"Interesting. Tell me more, but not yet. I have to go to my room. Meet me in the bar in an hour? I'm Jenny, by the way."

It was one of those rare times when the magnetism was so strong that I could feel static in the air. She skipped—or at least that's what I imagined—back to the hostel dorm.

Her freckles made her look young, and she had an outdoorsy style that indicated she'd climb any mountain. I sat down at the bar and ordered the local beer, Nile Special Draft—while awaiting her return. The sun setting behind the Nile was magnificent, yet my eyes didn't fixate on the sunset, but on one fisherman wading his small raft across the river. I imagined what it would be like to be him. Before my daydream ended, she returned smelling like she scrubbed down with bar soap and a tint of the African wilderness.

"I'll have the Nile, too." She smiled at the bartender. "So where did we leave off? Oh yes, why are you here?"

"Just checking out Africa." Be cool, I said to myself.

"Nah, it can't be that simple, never is." She turned her head slightly to learn more.

"No. I like to travel, and Africa is going to develop a lot in the coming decades."

"So, it's all about money?"

"No, not all. That's why I'm volunteering and such."

"Like what?"

"I worked with Innovation Africa. They are building a lot of wells in the region—Israeli connections." Showing her the website on my phone, our hands touched, breaking the touch barrier.

"Oh, let me see," she looked at the link. "That looks cool. It's worthwhile work too."

"So, what do you do?"

"I work for a small non-profit helping with women's needs—hygiene and sexual training."

"You like it?" I asked.

"It's gratifying. I'm on a one-year program then back to Oregon. Are you planning to find other places to volunteer?"

"Yes, I hope to teach more with entrepreneurs as I did in Ghana. I'd also like to do more humanitarian work."

"You'll find your soul if you do that." She stared in my eyes, searching for mine.

"Really? I've heard this before. Tell me more."

"Every day, it reminds me we are all the same—minds, bodies, and souls."

"That's deep." I fixed my unblinking gaze into her brown eyes, which had a softness most didn't.

"Anyway, don't try to be a white savior." She broke our gaze, perhaps not finding anything.

"Yeah, I've heard that before." I nodded.

"There are a lot of people who come here, trying to do things that they don't have experience with, acting like they can save Africa."

"Africa seems fine to me. That's not me, but it's good to know."

"There is even an organization called No White Saviors dot org."

"Crazy. How can people be so upset for others helping out?"

"They aren't upset about helping out, but ex-pats come here thinking that their experience at home will be useful. What the country needs is expertise young adults can't provide during their three-week mission trip. And they shouldn't act like heroes."

"Ahh, I can understand why locals dislike that."

"Might be good if you let others know your intent and who you are so they don't look at you skeptically. Some people glorify what they are doing here and overreaching their capabilities. Locals are sensitive to that."

"I get it, thanks for the heads-up."

She kept my phone and flipped to my music to see my list, something a millennial would do to check your coolness.

"Country music? I'm a country girl at heart." My heart skipped a beat.

"Trade songs then? I'll send you a few songs to listen to. You know what they say, people learn to love country music when they either are falling in love or breaking up."

"So who are you breaking up with?"

"Ha-ha! No one at the moment, thankfully."

"You aren't running from anything?"

"I'm running from the craziness of America, but that's a long story."

"Tell me about it. It's a crazy country at the moment. I think they should come to visit Africa and see how good they have it at home." She scrolled to the contacts and started to punch in her name and number.

"Maybe I don't want your number?" I teased.

"Then, I'll delete it, and you'll never see me again." She touched her name on the contact list and went to the delete button, calling my bluff.

"Don't do that. Don't do that." I took the phone back.

"So, send me a song you like." She touched my shoulder.

"Here is one of my favorites, 'Heads Carolina Tails California,' by Jo Dee Messina. Those are my two most favorite places in the world."

"So, where else are you going?"

"Rwanda next, maybe Congo, then doing an overland trip with a bus—like that one out front—from Victoria Falls to South Africa."

"Rwanda . . . that's Africa-lite. The infrastructure is better there. Many call it the Singapore of Africa."

"That sounds comfortable. I love Singapore."

"Never been, what's it like?"

"A massively clean, high tech, clinical, and organized Asian city in the middle of a tropical rain forest."

"It sounds amazing. Rwanda doesn't have the high tech and large buildings, but other stuff seems right on."

"Can't wait to check it out."

"How long is the bus trip?"

"About three or four weeks."

"Oh goodness, I can't imagine being on a bus for three weeks with the same tourists. Sounds miserable."

"I can always get off the bus in the middle, around Namibia."

"In the middle of Namibia—ha!"

"Oh, it's the desert out there?"

"Yeah. A big one with rocks, off-roads, flat tires, and very little in between cities. Better stay on that bus." She laughed, "But Congo seems fascinating, I've wanted to go but worried about the rebels out there, outside of Goma."

"Rebels?"

"You don't know? How can you not research a place like Congo, are you crazy?!"

"Some people read instructions, others don't." I winked at her.

"My goodness, where are you from?"

"South Carolina."

"Everyone like you from down there?"

"Nah, well maybe, You know the famous last words of a redneck?"

"What's that?"

"Hold my beer and watch this," I said, handing her the beer, running towards the cliff of the Nile.

"Too funny! Oh, did you sign up for the whitewater rafting tomorrow? You better go now if you didn't."

"Aren't you going?"

"No, I have to get up early tomorrow for a three-day program out in the desert."

"Sounds intense. Why'd you come here then?" I liked intense ladies because I'm so laid back.

"I was just dropping off something to my friend who works here. She helps me out. I don't typically hang with tourists, but I made an exception for you." She squinted her eyes as if she hadn't figured me out.

"Of course, you wouldn't. We are too bland, too much like home."

"Just kidding. I like to have a chat now and then; it lessens the culture shock when I return home. You know what I mean."

"I get it. It helps keep the mind sane. Re-entry must be tough. I'm not sure how I'm going to handle it and how it will be different than returning from Asia. How do you stay sane out here all this time?"

"It'll be very different. You'll see. America is a wasteful culture, so don't get annoyed when it hits you. Like anything, you get used to it. The mind and body gradually adapt after a bit of time. It becomes your new life. I don't think much about it anymore."

"I can feel that, too. I'm in a pretty good flow at the moment."

"Hungry? Wanna rolex?"

"A rolex—a watch?"

"No, you goofball, a rolled egg chapati. Rolled Eggs said fast is rolex. Let me show you." *I just love it when a woman calls me a goofball,* I thought.

She got up and walked over to the lobby. After I signed up for the rafting trip, we strolled out of the hostel and to a small Rolex vendor. Rolex was the staple, the dish, the delicacy of Uganda. Made of eggs and fresh veggies of your choice, it was cooked within a few minutes on a hot plate then rolled up into a chapati wrapped up like a burrito. Fast. Flavorful. Filling. Fast food to perfection.

According to Blanche D'Souza's book *Harnessing the Trade Winds*, maritime trade with West India brought the chapati to Africa centuries ago.[13] Even when trade stopped, the Indian population prospered and contributed to Uganda's economic growth. During the Idi Amin massacres of the early 1970s, some Indians had been spared and given 48 hours to leave the country—or else. In the 1990s, the Indian population started coming back as did the chapati and one street vendor started to roll it with eggs. That experiment started a food revolution.[14]

It was getting late, so we parted ways. She gave me a hug and a long kiss. "Let's meet again, somewhere in Africa." The connection was more than lustful and made think *maybe there are soul mates; maybe they do exist.*

The next day, I went out on the Nile River Explorers, one of the best-reviewed whitewater rafting trips in Africa, then headed back to Kampala. Through a friend on the Couch Surfing App, I met Paul, who had over 100 favorable reviews. We met in Kabalagala—nicknamed the pancake district. (I just loved saying the name. Kabalagala. Try it. Ka-ba-la-ga-la.) Smashed in between the business district and five significant universities attended by East Africans from all over, it was filled with restaurants, offices, and pubs. By day, Paul imported and sold Chinese electronics and anti-theft car tracking systems. By night, he enjoyed the nightlife while hustling; he burnt the candle on both ends. Similar to others in Africa, he used the profits to help others much less fortunate than he. His community project was building a mango tree farm in impoverished areas.

Crashing with me at Paul's was an Israeli couple who just graduated from the military service and an Argentinian named Santiago. We roamed around the fish market, restaurants, and other parts of Kampala. It's worth describing Santiago's remarkable travel style. Santiago was a Ph.D. student in economics who was skinny with longish hair and somewhat resembled pictures of Jesus—perhaps that was just how I pictured him after hearing his stories. He wore a tank top, sandals, brown shorts, and carried two satchels: one with three thick, academic philosophy books and his DSLR camera, while the other contained his pauper-like clothes. His tales amazed me. He spent a month walking across Rwanda. Locals took him in, shared stories about the genocide and how they dined with neighbors who had once fought and killed their family members. Crossing the border from Mozambique into Tanzania, he had crossed a crocodile-infested river by canoe, getting his customs to stamp by one guy sitting on a tree stump. Santiago even lived with an Ethiopian tribe for a month in their mud huts. My new travel hero, he summarized his philosophy from Rumi: "Forget safety. Live where you fear to live." He added, "Only then will you understand the people in every land."

After two days, I had to keep moving to cover ground before the overland trip, so the next day I headed to Rwanda. Outside Paul's apartment, I hailed a beat-up taxi with missing hub caps, driven by an older man with one eye half-open. I jumped in the front seat while throwing my stuff in the back. Down the road, unsettled by the oncoming traffic and honking horns, I snapped a bit, asking him to drive safely. He turned his head so he could stare at me with his left eye. "It's my mission."

"My two daughters—aged nine and eleven—have been killed in a bus accident a few months ago. A large truck hit the school van. They all died." With a tear rolling down his cheek, he looked over to me and asked, "Do you have a mission?"

Choked up, I said, "No . . . not yet." But it didn't seem to matter at that moment. Everyone is searching for meaning; maybe that is the meaning of life. We all find it in different places: some right at home with family and kids, some in community, and others in grander schemes like business, politics, or non-profits. Others, sadly, find it after a tragedy. In all of those places, humankind looks for it—whether they know it or not. *Perhaps, that's what the soul is saying to each of us: find meaning.*

The Innovation Africa trip threw me, mentally unequipped, into an impoverished region. That experience evolved my empathy into compassion. No longer was I just the "guy looking out the window"; now I was the "guy getting his hands dirty." The missions of Sivan, Jenny, Paul, and my driver were inspiring and authentic. Out of the corner of my eye, I saw the glint of a tear stream down his cheek. Epiphanies blurred over the backdrop of Lake Victoria. *What is my soul searching for?*

Chapter 13

LEARNING TO MOVE ON IN RWANDA

"This is about our past and our futures;
Nightmare and our dreams;
Our fear and our hope;
Which is why we begin where we end . . .
With the country we love."
Quote at Rwanda Genocide Museum

eaving Uganda, I was thinking about what my mission might be, but before I'd figure that out, I had to learn about moving on in life. I knew Rwanda, like Uganda, had its genocide in the 1990s, which was still etched in people's minds. Other travelers had told me positive things about how Rwanda had rebuilt and moved forward. Jenny had described Rwanda as the "Singapore of Africa," and when Googling it, I learned that the same city planners who'd designed Kigali hailed from Singapore.

The first surprise came at customs upon arrival at the small, clean, and organized Kigali Airport. An official checked my luggage and glanced at the plastic bag full of goodies I was carrying. Then he said, "No plastic bags in Rwanda, Sir." Wow, no plastic bags?! I replaced it with one of the cloth bags next to the customs counter. Was I entering Singapore or the Nordics?

Everything seemed organized and structured with a standard of living a step up from Uganda. A taxi driver welcomed me to Rwanda in an accent that blended French and British, then stated his price. I turned to buy a SIM, seeing if he would begin negotiating lower, but he held firm. It appeared the taxis were fixed-rate, saving tourists the hassle of bargaining for a ride—another sign of a more advanced economy. Perhaps this was the Singapore of Africa.

Rolling hills blanketed in agricultural fields stretched in both directions. Now I understood why it was called the "land of a thousand hills." Hills rolled over the top of hills, growing onto hills, disappearing into hills. The lush greenery gradually became dotted with patches of ochre as the residential houses of Kigali came into view.

I stayed at a hostel called the Discover Rwanda Youth Hostel that brought together people from around the globe. It was a full house. I met a Swazi guy studying his MBA in Kigali, an Aussie hiker about to head off trekking in the Rwenzori Mountains, three sisters from Colombia on a girls' trip, and a few non-profit workers.

That first night had a festive atmosphere as people chatted, trying to figure out each other's stories. The Aussie hiker was the type of guy you'd see hanging upside down at a climbing gym. He had traveled across the northern border of the Congo—still occupied by rebels who held his friend at gunpoint, stripped him down to his boxers and left him on the road. He reassured me, however, that Goma would be safe.

The Colombian sisters had already booked a trip to the Congo to see the mountain gorillas and go volcano hiking. They gave me a contact. It was also in that circle that I met Kendra from Seattle, who was part of a project at ReapLifeDig. It had been founded in Atlanta, Georgia, by a Peace Corps alumnus. We chatted about what was involved, and when I asked if I could volunteer, she helped me apply.

One of the benefits of staying in hostels over hotels was the connections and information flow between travelers. It was there that I learned—through a Japanese girl—about the Ntarama Genocide Memorial, which lies about an hour's bus drive from Kigali and marks the spot of a horrific massacre. We grabbed a matatu (white minibus) and traveled there together, visiting the burial grounds and church filled with skulls and bones, all marked as 'unknown.' It was there that I walked into the church, staring eye to eye socket, once again, with several skulls.

Being unknown in Africa was common, unknown parents, birthdays, and sometimes given names were the norm. Africa was full of unknowns, and these people who died during the genocide lived lives unknown, all the way through to death.

Leaving the small memorial, I walked back to the gardens that led up a hill and into a forest behind the mortuary. Sadness had given way to a sense of peace as flowers blossomed and birds sang. I felt the spirits roaming free amidst the birds soaring in circles above us. Death is so peaceful. The souls spoke to us.

Later that evening, I had dinner with Claudine and her family, who had been introduced to me by a student in Ghana. They came together on Sundays to feast on sweet potatoes (ibijumba), rice (umuceli), vegetables (imboga, courgette, carrots, red eggs), and chicken (inkoko). They explained that, according to their beliefs, there is new life after death, so we must "fight to live again," no matter how hard it might seem. *They were so mentally tough*, I thought. I wanted to learn more about this mental toughness; the next day, I would.

The family also introduced me to Umuganda, a national unity day that occurs the last Saturday of every month. Almost everyone participates in community activities like cleaning up streets, trimming forestry, or building houses for the poor. It's a program by the government to unite the country with shared activities and a shared mission to move forward together.

The following day, I went for a run and stopped into a beautiful church on the hillside holding a Sunday mass. It was lovely, and several people waved to me, including a little girl who came over to say hello and give me a pamphlet. That day I also met Norbert, who was introduced to me by Brett, an old friend in Hong Kong. Brett, whom I was planning to reconnect with later in the trip, now lived in Uganda.

Norbert and I met at Pili Pili, a happening spot in Kigali, similar to a swanky bar you'd see in Shanghai. It overlooked the city, had a swimming pool and several bars, and hosted a young, vibrant scene.

"Something you'd see in the Shang?" I said.

"Similar, isn't it? Replace the forest with the Shanghai Bay. The Chinese are coming here to Rwanda." He said, looking over the valley, drinking half his beer.

"How so?"

"That's my business. I help the Chinese and Rwanda government build out special projects, and right now, we are working on a massive business complex. It's just a start. Multi-million-dollar megaplex."

"How's your Mandarin?" I inquired.

"Fluent. You need a beer?"

"Of course. Like, how fluent?"

"I do everything in Mandarin. I lived there for thirteen years. Even got thirty-sixth out of 100,000 in a Mandarin-speaking contest. You?"

"I only studied about 1000 words. "

"Not bad, ready for intermediate now!" He teased as he flagged the waiter for a beer.

Between a teddy and grizzly bear, Norbert was a very likable guy who was determined to put Rwanda on the map of the world. He chitchatted about Rwanda's comeback and the leadership of President Kagame, who led the rebellion to end the civil war—a genocide in 1994 that saw 800,000 people massacred in a feud between the two tribes Tutsi and Hutus. Seared with terrible memories and scars, only twenty years later, Rwandans overcame these and created a better society.

"Norbert, I'd like to ask a sensitive question. How did you move on from the genocide? I can't even imagine anything like this."

"The entire country was affected; everyone lost family and friends. In some ways, that made it in a way more acceptable to all of us. But we had to move on; there was no choice."

"Really? How do you move on when neighbors kill each other?"

"My neighbors killed my aunt and uncle. Families had perpetrators and victims. There were no psychologists left in the country, so people simply started sharing their stories, and the more you heard, the less pain you felt. You realized that you were lucky to be alive, and that had a huge psychological impact."

"I'm lucky to be alive," I said my thoughts under my breath.

"What have you been doing—to be lucky to be alive?"

"Just moving around too much, little this, little that, checking out places."

"Ha-ha! Well, don't kill yourself, please." He put his arm on my shoulder.

"I guess I can see what you are saying, but don't people hold a grudge?"

"If we wanted a better country, we had to get on with it. That's what Kagame made us realize. He told us that we are all accountable, and we must stay together and think big about the future."

"Wow, that's great. That's real leadership."

"Very much. First, he removed ethnic mentions in the identity cards to unite us—a small detail, big deal."

"I noticed no plastic bags allowed in the country at the airport."

"Right, even little things like that get us excited to be unique, to be different in Africa. We want to be known as environmentally friendly—set the trends for Africa."

"That's so cool. How do you unite people, though?"

"History. We had to rediscover our history and the relationships between the tribes of Hutu, Tutsi, and Twa; they had lived together in peace for more than a thousand years. There were substantial media around that, letting people know we lived together in peace before and can do it again."

"What's the difference among the groups?"

"These three ethnic groups are not ethnic groups, as they share the same language, same culture, same religion, and nowhere in the country was a Tutsi region or a Hutu region. They were more of a social construct, one cultivating the land, another raising cows, and another living off the forests and pottery."

"So, what happened?"

"Colonialism. The Germans and Belgium separated us and made it a divide and conquer mentality. Post-independence in 1961, we started to fight, and then it finally erupted."

"Colonialism was bad for Africa."

"Bad for everyone."

"How about the Chinese then?" I was skeptical.

"I don't think they are colonizing; they are investing resources to build it up and trying to make a profit. There are some cultural flares, but that's why I'm here."

"But what about the debt trap?"

"We'll see, but Rwanda can pay it back."

"What a time to be bilingual in Mandarin and Africa! You can help so much. America has to wake up and get over here."

"Yes, I agree. Where are the American companies?"

"I don't know, but it's such a great time to invest and get their piece," I said, lightly using slang.

"Oh no, we aren't giving up anything to anyone. No one will control Africa but Africans."

"Sorry, I didn't mean it like that. Of course, I don't mean that. I mean, American companies should invest in the economic benefit of all. America brings in know-how, innovation, and capital."

"Yes, I agree. So how do we get them here? Trump likes business, and he has been talking about Africa."

"He speaks out of both sides of his mouth."

"Ha! That's funny. It doesn't matter. We will progress, move forward, with or without the USA," he said with conviction, courage, and confidence.

"But Norbert, one last question. I mean, how mentally do you tell yourself to move on? I mean, people must get depressed or want revenge."

"Oh yes, we do . . . but we tell each other to move on. If we want a better country for our family, friends, and children, we just MOVE ON. No questions asked." He pounded the table with his fist and stared at me.

And just like that, it hit me. It was sheer mental toughness, fortitude, and rational acceptance of what is done is done, and that's that—like wrestling a bull to the ground. That's the way to treat the mind at times. That's what Kagame taught the Rwandans to do: control their mind, push away the evil thoughts, and move on peacefully.

As we chatted, I told him I was thinking about going to Congo, to which he replied, "It's crazy there, you shouldn't go. Just one bad incident, and it's all over. Not worth the risk. Just watch the gorillas and the guerillas on YouTube."

"The reward is to see the gorillas and to hike a volcano—which could explode. And, I heard the rebels are camping on the other side of the volcano," I explained, but then started to agree.

"You want to take those risks just to see some gorillas, which could break your neck? Or the other guerillas who will behead you?" he prodded.

"Maybe I should think about it more." He had a point. There wasn't much upside to going to Congo, other than it was a dream since I read the Heart of Darkness. A chance to fulfill a dream. *I'm going*, I said to myself.

On that note, we ended the night, both agreeing to stay in touch and work on some projects together. I thanked him for the time. In those few hours, I learned more than from a museum or a book.

Early the next morning, I grabbed a bus to Gisenyi, the border crossing to Congo, and once again found myself focused on the green, flowing hills. The mountains gradually became dotted with patches of ochre as the residential houses and villages appeared then disappeared. Villages had a reasonable quality of infrastructure, school buildings, and small shopping centers. Outside of the city, the communities seemed organized and relatively clean, with a standard of living a step or two higher than in Uganda. Kids played in the streets. I spoke to a salesman on the bus who was selling building materials, happy to have work. Perhaps this was why Rwanda was referred to as the Singapore of Africa: employment, a priority for people's well-being, and a tidy infrastructure. A society that worked for all was the incentive to move on together, united in a shared purpose to lift each other's souls.

Chapter 14

KEEPING CALM IN CHAOTIC CONGO

"But his soul was mad. Being alone in the wilderness, it had
looked within itself and, by heavens I tell you, it had gone mad."
—Joseph Conrad

R ight before I entered the Congo, Jenny texted me to stay safe and not get too close to the rebels. She was looking forward to seeing me again. I was happy to hear that, but I wasn't going to play it that safe.

The thoughts of the Democratic Republic of Congo (herein, the Congo) had crossed my mind every few years since reading *The Heart of Darkness* by Joseph Conrad while in high school. I didn't anticipate walking into that book's world. While African borders were chaotic, the Congolese border—specifically the Congo side—won the prize for grimness. One man had a white bubble the size of a softball on his arm that needed medical assistance. Another lady's face had swollen to the size of a small pumpkin. I had just gotten rid of my internal madman and now this. Was this the land of darkness and death? I could feel my toes and fingers tingle as I arrived at the beautiful shores of Lake Kivu, a spectacular lake on the border with Congo.

I was met on the other side of immigration by two trekking guides who spoke French with high-pitched accents. Their priority was to change my US dollars into Congolese Francs. I negotiated with a man holding a stack of bills wrapped in cellophane about two feet high. Banks didn't exchange money, but the hawkers, loaded with bills and guns, did.

The seemingly never-ending war in Congo and the rebel uprising near Goma had left me feeling concerned. Yet the opportunity to see mountain gorillas in the wild and trek to one of Congo's volcanic peaks was something I couldn't miss.

The people of the Congo didn't sleep—and wasn't going to let me, either. We rolled up to a small two-story hotel that looked like it would crumble with a light breeze. Here I would spend the night. A steady stream of people came in and out from the hotel's buffet while stores were selling French baguettes clustered in the surroundings. A bar across the street played African dance music from sundown to sunup, and the road was a constant flow of voices and traffic.

Congo was a colorful nation in so many ways. The following morning, we drove through the outskirts of town, weaving down muddy roads and passing UN tanks and soldiers. (I'd later meet a UN soldier from Uruguay on a boat cruise in Zambia who spoke about how vital the United Nations' presence was to maintain stability, and I couldn't agree more.) People sat outside cooking food and wandering the streets, all of them wearing graphic outfits that sometimes clashed with equally vibrant, multi-hued buildings. Music blasted from discotheques on alternating corner.

During the ride to our guide's office, I met a group of Belgium travelers when our 4x4s stopped at a United Nations roadblock. They had come to do some research and attend an annual music concert that was being sponsored by the Belgium Government. One was researching the fashions and styles of the Congo and how it enhanced their happiness—the men and women here certainly knew how to dress.

They explained to me Congo's tumultuous history with Belgium. Like many African countries, the Congo had been colonized by Europeans, in this case, King Leopold II of Belgium who was an "ambitious, greedy, and devious monarch . . ."[15] His rule was particularly brutal—historians estimate that eight to ten million Congolese were killed under slave conditions while extracting resources that would be shipped abroad. Today, the relationship is still tense, although the Belgian Prime Minister Charles Michel (from

2014 to 2019) has issued a formal apology and wants to "move forward" and support the Congo.[16]

Our trek to see the mountain gorillas began in a field, winding between houses where kids were running around fertilizing the crops carrying cans of pesticides. It was chilly, with lingering mist above the tree line creating an aura of mystery. Just ahead, the farms blended into the hills and the mountains, painting a picture of rich jungle-like vegetation.

Escorted by guides carrying guns and large machetes, we hiked into the forest. The trees changed from palm to mahogany and ebony. Pushing away large, green-yellow leaves the size of our bodies, right then, we entered the world of the gorillas. Getting up close to these primates was breathtaking, not because of the sheer size and strength but the way they looked at you. The sight of the silverback made the hair on my neck rise. Every move of his was powerful, graceful, measured. With one swoop of his arm, he could have swept us all off our feet. Instead, he looked just as fearful of us as we were of him. Coming from behind only 10 feet away, one caught me off guard when, in a flash, the guide jumped between us, but not before the silverback, and I connected eye to eye. He wasn't scared, only curious—as if he wanted to know who I was. After about thirty minutes with the gorillas, we returned along the trail we had come, humbled by the experience of our kin.

The following day, I teamed up with a small group to hike the 3,500-meter (11,500 feet) peak of Mount Nyiragongo, with a lava lake at the top that merits rave reviews from travelers. My guide assured me that the rebels didn't access these paths, but, just in case, I devised an escape route around the far western side. From a tree-lined trail, the landscape transformed with giant green succulents reminding me of the film, Avatar. These then gave way to sparsely vegetated volcanic rocks, with a handful of wooden huts built at the top. We spent the evening taking photos of the lava flow and staring at its red-yellow-blue kaleidoscope. It was a meditative experience.

During the night on top of the volcano, I met a French Ph.D. student, Aurore, who researched economic empowerment for refugees. I asked her if it would be possible to visit a refugee camp. She said, "Absolutely," and that she would introduce me to her host in Kakuma. That would set the stage for my trip to the refugee camp. The next morning we hiked down through the mist and rain; it was a setting I'd never forget.

The third day ended my trip to the Congo, and the guides drove me to the border, somewhat wondering why I was in a rush to leave. I appreciated their hospitality as well as their pride in Congo's progress. They had a talented knack of making me feel at ease in what was a hectic country. Despite the madness, I yearned for more. To ride a boat down the Congo River as Kurtz did and visit the Pygmy communities would be thrilling. When I asked my guide about the feasibility, he joked, "Yes, we can when you come back, but it's not safe now. Besides, they might eat you!"

Congo was as mysterious, disheartening, and corrupt as it was upbeat, cheery, and vivacious. I crossed the border back to Rwanda. Even with the madness of the Congo, somehow, I remained remarkably calm and collected. My mercurial disposition was stabilizing into a softer, steadier state.

Building a solar power well with Innovation Africa

Dancing with the villagers

Carrying water home from the wells

The top of the Mt. Nyiragongo Volcano

A landscape shot of where the gorillas live

Chapter 15

ENJOYING THE JOURNEY FROM ZAMBIA TO SOUTH AFRICA

"I create my journey, change it, adjust it, and make
a new one whenever I want. The only rule is to enjoy
the journey, the moment, no matter what happens."
—Zen Master Toto

On the flight to Livingstone, I remained collected, yet something was amiss. I still felt rushed and not fulfilled with what I was doing—hopping from country to country with little purpose, the only privilege. Inside, I was seeking more—a more defined mission. Why can't I just relax, go with the flow? I switched on some country music, turning on Alabama again, "I'm in a Hurry (And Don't Know Why)."

The host of my next tour was a German named Toto who moved around Africa doing whatever exciting, entrepreneurial endeavors that popped into his mind. I connected with Toto through a shared Facebook post from a friend at the Vipassana retreat in Myanmar, who followed my travels. The Facebook pictures of Toto reminded me of something out of LA: a fusion of a yogi, '80s cover band singer, and Crocodile Dundee, all with a saintly aura—*would he too have a Vipassana connection?* I wondered. This project was to host a dozen so-called digital nomads—i.e., technology professionals—in a van around Southern Africa for thirty days. This excursion wasn't his first crazy idea. Toto had built a non-profit school and orphanage in Kenya, organized sunset silent disco parties, and hosted a reality TV series (thrivors.tv) as an offshoot to our trip. According to him, everything was a learning experience, and he loved every minute of every excursion.

"Kurty, Kurty, Kurty" was how he greeted me at the new Livingstone Airport baggage claim—a significant upgrade from the wooden house that Gerry and I arrived at almost two decades ago. With long, brown curly hair, a bean-stalk skinny and erect figure, surfing swim trunks and a tank top, he had the swagger of Hollywood. "So glad you made it. Tell me, how was Congo?"

"Oh, I haven't digested it all yet. I can only say it was something I'd never experienced. It felt like a different world."

"I haven't been yet; you'll have to tell me everything about it."

"Colorful clothes, music all night, gorillas, and an active volcano and . . . hmmm . . . rebels—all in three days. A very mysterious place."

"Yes, it sounds like my kind of adventure."

Looking at his outfit, I agreed. "You'd like it."

"Where else have you—" Then a loud vibration rang, and he stopped right in his tracks. He had face-planted straight into a glass door.

"What on earth!? Why is there a clear glass door at the entrance of the airport? Are you OK?"

"What the ....? I didn't even see it!" He grabbed his nose.

"Who built this . . . right in the middle?"

"Chinese, of course, like the rest of Africa," he responded.

We chitchatted about the upcoming trip on the car ride to the backpackers' lodge. I wanted him to know my concerns about hanging out with a dozen others for thirty days.

"You know, I'm a bit reluctant to join this trip. I don't know if I can hang out with so many people for so long."

"Why's that?" He didn't seem surprised.

"I just like my own space. Traveling alone. I like to do my thing."

"That's cool. Just do what you need to do. You can leave anytime; we'll figure it out."

"Alrighty." I liked his easy-going attitude.

"Either way, it's good that you joined. It is quite difficult to visit Namibia and Botswana alone."

"Why?"

"It's a lot of nothing; you would need to rent a car and would probably blow a few tires all alone in the heat and end up eating dust. You'll see. Where else have you been?"

Counting on my fingers, "Four countries in Southern Africa, then four in west Africa, then Uganda, Rwanda, Congo . . . so that makes eleven." I said.

"This trip will make it fifteen: Zambia, Zimbabwe, Botswana, and Namibia, then you can visit me in Kenya to make it sixteen." He winked. "But you have to make it out of here first."

We rolled up to the Jolly Boys Backpackers, one of the favorites for young backpackers in Livingstone. "We are over in this hut, which you'll share with me." We walked to a small hut/house with western toiletries inside, and he said, "We'll be roomies for most of the trip!"

"Cool."

"We'll find time to chat about Silicon Valley."

"I can tell you plenty," I said as my voice waned, dismissive of a past growing ever smaller in my rearview mirror.

The embodiment of the digital nomad, Toto was a curious cat, an entrepreneur, interested in any culture or place, all with the desire to help others. Most of all, he liked people, and they loved him.

Ranging in age from twenty-one to seventy-one, we were an eclectic bunch, and it was evident from the outset—our only trait in common was the desire to not be in an office and a belief that the future rested in a remote workforce.

Toto got us together, made a quick introduction then gave us an itinerary. Our first expedition was the well-known Victoria Falls, the awe-inspiring natural wonder that's known locally as "the smoke that thunders." There were plenty of adventurous activities to do here, including the famous sit-on-top-of-the-falls, hold-a-rope-and-take-a-picture scene. What was interesting, though, was a bike ride around the city to see how locals lived, buy honey and nuts at the market, and visit a small elementary school that had been built by our cycling tour operator.

For twenty years he had been conducting bike tours around the area and, little by little, built up the school with his own hard-earned money. Just before I turned to leave, I had déjà vu, sat down for a bit, and let the sun bake on my bald head. I'd been there before; I could sense it. Yes, I had because I never—and I mean never—forget a face. It was my superpower. I had met the bike tour operator the last time I was here with Gerry in 2002.

Since then, Livingstone had changed from a rural village into a lively commercial tourist hub. Fifteen years ago, it was a small town of dirt roads, few hotels, and a little city with only three stores in the shopping plaza: a Shop-Rite (supermarket), Bi-Rite (supplies), and a Dance-Rite (disco). It also wasn't safe. There had been a problem with rebels crossing the border between Zimbabwe and Zambia. We had been warned by the hostel owner not to stay out after dark. One night we didn't heed her warnings—busy arm-wrestling, playing pool, and drinking beers at Dance-Rite. Before the tick of midnight, she turned up in a minivan and drove us back to the hostel. Along the way, we passed two trucks filled with rebels holding guns. "Get your heads down. They're looking for you," she stated grimly. She booked us on the first flight out at 7 a.m.

Unlike then, Livingstone had become a very tourist-friendly city with lots of hostels and a handful of upmarket hotels. There was a large and modern Shop-Rite replacing the old warehouse and bar. I hardly recognized the place and wanted to know how it came to be, so I went in search of answers.

The next morning, I toured the Livingstone museum. The city was named after the famous British doctor and Christian missionary, David Livingstone; he spent a lifetime exploring Africa with the hope of convincing his compatriots back home to abolish the slave trade. The museum had a disinterested description of what westerners brought to the continent. Legal structures, infrastructure, commercial activity, and faith were positives; slavery, exploitation of resources not shared with locals, and artillery were the negatives. Portrayed by text, pictures, and artifacts, Livingstone was held with high esteem, though most were not.

Just beside the museum was the local government office where I met Harold, a local government employee. He explained that they'd received money from the UN World Tourism Organization and the UN General Assembly to develop their tourism services to ensure safety and ease of travel. He suggested that we recruit an American hotel chain to invest and lure more Americans to visit since most of the travelers were from Europe and China. Chinese hotels had been popping up there and also in Zimbabwe.

The following day, our guides rolled up to the hostel in a large white bus with off-road wheels, typical of the overlanding vehicles used across Southern and East Africa. It could seat about thirty people, with a small built-in fridge and storage for tents, food, and more. The driver was a Zambian named Pride who, like many others, had picked an English name with a meaning similar to his native name. Other examples were Trust, Honor, and Innocent. When a female guide appeared, I felt like I'd met her before but couldn't quite place where.

"Hello Everyone, I'm Cardi, and this is Pride. He will drive, and I will cook. If you annoy me, no one gets food!" she laughed out loud at her joke, but we couldn't help joining in. "And I make great food, especially when traveling in the bush." She said with a grand smile, which I mirrored.

"Let's pack up the bags, everyone!" Toto said with a small satchel on his back.

"That's all you got?" I asked, looking at his bag.

"That's all I need. And you've been carrying those two big bags around Africa?" He frowned, from either surprise or disappointment. "Doesn't your back hurt?"

"Actually, it does. I have an old-man back problem. I've electronics in this bag in the other, warm weather clothes."

"Really? You think it's going to get cold?!" He looked up to the sky. "It'll rain, but it won't snow," he said, laughing. He continued, "Look here. Toothbrush, two shorts, two shirts, two underwear, and these flipflops. Let me know if you need to borrow a shirt." He winked.

"Maybe I should downsize . . ." I mumbled, but I didn't think I could be as frugal as he.

"Yeah, just give some clothes away on the way. Get down to one bag; you'll be happier. Less stuff, more happiness. Trust me."

We took off from Livingstone to the border, which wasn't a far drive. At the customs gate, we had to walk across the border into Zimbabwe—where the drizzle started, then day after day for fifteen days, the rains continued, more torrential each day. It was as if the weather had just heard the song, "Rains Down in Africa," which, by the way, Toto did play it on repeat every day.

After checking the falls on the Zimbabwe side—they were less exciting than Zambia and with more Chinese hotels—we continued to Botswana, passing through the dense forested, rich vegetation, and swampy wildlife-rich Caprivi Strip. The 20-mile panhandle was an extension of the borders of Angola, Namibia, Botswana, and Zimbabwe. Part of the old German colony, the colonists had raised cattle, fished, hunted, and farmed corn, cereals, melons, and cassava. David Livingstone often stayed here to recuperate between excursions.

Each day we drove at least five hours in the rain, and the others complained about the lack of cellular reception. What on earth were they thinking? That this was going to be gigabit internet? I kept my head down, kindle lit, and indulged in a several books. At the dinner stop in a small game park, I hopped out of the truck and decided I'd help cook.

Cardi needed help, so I volunteered to be her sous chef to learn a thing or two.

"I'm cooking a mashed potato vegetable casserole and peri-peri chicken on the grill."

"Don't you need an oven?" I questioned, looking around.

"Nope, we make an oven." She had an answer for everything. "Cover this up with tin foil put in on the fire and voila! So, you mash the potatoes now and then add in the veggies when you are ready."

"OK. Where are you from?"

"Port Elizabeth. I'm colored, so here that means I'm mixed race—white and black." She said with a bit of pizazz.

"Oh yes, like Trevor Noah."

"Isn't he amazing and so cute, I just love him."

"Yeah, pretty cool guy," I said with a bit of envy.

"But you don't have colored people in the US. I mean, Obama was colored or mixed. But Americans call him black when he is half white? So strange." Her voice dropped.

"Yeah. Americans have to label everything. Black, white, Republican, Democrat—it's marketing. They can't even have a gray area."

"And Trump? You like him?"

"No, I don't like his style. I can understand some of his ideas, but I don't like him."

"Thank God, or I would have kicked you off the bus. But it's better than what most of Africa gets."

"That seems like a low bar."

"It's the bar. We get used to it. Just move on with our lives and be happy. You can't let politics ruin your happiness." She said, hopping from one task to the next. "Please cut these asparagus. Anyways, what did you do for the holidays?"

"I went to Mozambique."

"Really? Me, too, where?"

"Tofo." And that's when it clicked. "Wait, we met. I knew we had met before." I said in shock.

"No, you are kidding, I don't remember." She stared at me.

"Yes, you were at the Fatima's New Year's party and walked by me and said I'm Cardi—not B—and said I'd meet you later."

"Oh, goodness!" She laughed. "I always say that."

"It was after midnight, and you were running around."

"That's me! Running around! So crazy! Sorry, I don't remember you, though."

"No worries, I never forget a face." I winked. Toto's style was rubbing off.

From there, Cardi and I hit it off, and I helped her cook and pack daily, which helped me learn new dishes and camping tips. Especially learning the grilled chicken recipe with peri-peri, pepper, and butter marinade made it all worth it. Thanks, Cardi!

Our first wildlife experience was a cruise along the Chobe River, followed by a game drive through Chobe National Park. Then we went to the Okavango Delta, exploring first in traditional mokoro canoes while learning about the curing capabilities of native trees. That night, it stormed ferociously, testing our ability to withstand the wilds of Africa. The sound of rain intertwined with growling, howling, and yelping animals was a bit scary. The military-grade tents were blown black and forth so violently that we snuggled together to embrace the fear. Toto and I struck up a conversation.

"Man, this is a bit scary," I said.

"Nah, TIA—This is Africa, bro; it rains a lot in Africa." TIA was often used from one traveler to another, insinuating 'get used to it' to help normalize a situation.

"I guess so. You'd know with a name like Toto."

He grinned. "Are you OK, brother?"

"It's all good. I just don't like the nitpicking and complaining. What did the others think, this was a cruise ship with a buffet?"

"That's funny; it's all good—that's an American saying, isn't it?!"

"Yeah it is, we say it like, 'It's ALLLLL good.'"

"I like it. I'll say it that way." He seemed excited to have a new cultural saying in his repertoire.

"How do you stay so calm?" I asked, leaning in a bit, wanting to know his secret.

"I guess I'm just not taking stuff too seriously. TIA, remember?" he shrugged. "For me, it's like the wild west where adventure is part of everyday life. Ridiculous things happen here all the time, and over the years—I just got used to it. And it's fun. "

"That's a good attitude."

"Yeah, just enjoy the journey. Focus on what you want and think about the crazy stories you'll have to tell. Life is what you make it, brother."

I like telling crazy stories. It was my last thought as the pitter-patter on the tent put us to sleep that night. The rooster's crows woke us up, so I went out for a run down the muddy path before the others got up.

That morning the boat ride was quite exhilarating, hovering above rhinos and crocodiles only a stone's throw away. The highlight was when the young German girl meditated on the front bow of a small motorboat in front of a crocodile; when the crocodile sprung into the water, I screeched and jumped into the arms of Toto.

Then our guide yelled at her, "That's why all the Germans get eaten—it's true!" He explained, "Just last month a German was dragged and killed in the river by a croc because he got too close. Americans like you always scream like little kids!"

The best thing about the following day's sightseeing was the scenic helicopter ride of this watery wonderland. It was pretty spectacular to gaze down at the mosaic of islands and marshy wetlands of the Okavango Delta as herds of elephants, rhinos, and giraffes traversed this UNESCO World Heritage-listed landscape. It was one of the best sightseeing activities I'd ever done.

Our next stop was Namibia. It was on the way to Namibia that Cardi lost her wits. She stopped the truck, got out, and said she was leaving. What was going on? She couldn't take the badgering and complaining that she was getting from an older Australian fellow who spent most of the trip talking about rugby and drinking beer. It was her or him. We had to pick. After an hour's delay, Cardi got in her seat, and I rode shotgun much of the rest of the way to act as a buffer for her, which gave us time to keep chatting.

"What a jerk," she said.

"He'll settle down. I'll make him talk to me so he can't speak to you."

"He is just a bitter old man with no love. That's the problem today—no love and no respect for each other, regardless of where you come from," she philosophized.

"That's certainly one way to look at it," I replied, then paused. "I think you have done a great job and are quite good at this. I've learned a lot from you. Thank you." I boosted her up a bit. "Anyway, what will you do after working here?"

"Start my own business, my tour one day." Her voice rose in anticipation.

"You should; you'd be great at it."

"I need to save up, spend a few more years gaining experience."

"How much does one of these vans cost?" I asked.

"About $50K up to $100K."

"Wow, that's a lot of cash up front."

"Yeah, getting the investment is hard, but getting the people is easy. So many people these days are looking for tours."

"What would you name it?"

"Ubuntu Adventures! And Ubuntu is all about humanity. It's the spirit of seeing the other person as a human first."

"Ah yes, I learned that at the school I taught at in South Africa. The founder, John, often talked of Ubuntu."

"That's great. You know about shared living and learning."

"I sure do! When you start your new company, let me know, please!"

"I will, and you can invest your big money."

"Maybe not big, but I'll help out."

"We are getting close to the border. Namibia is my favorite country! The terrain is rougher, but it's fun. You can get some good runs in the desert here."

Of all the countries we visited, Namibia was the highlight. With the landscape of Utah, the heat of a desert, the culture of Germany, and country music at every rest stop, how could anyone not love it?

At the first Namibian camp in Etosha, I caught Toto meditating outside the tent. We started to chat later that night in our tent.

"You meditate?" I asked.

"Yeah, I noticed that you do it on the bus sometimes, too."

"It helps me to focus, if anything. My ADHD doesn't make it easy to focus for a long time."

"Have you tried Vipassana?" he asked.

"I just did a few months back. It rocked my world." The small world of Dhamma it was.

"Then you ended up in Africa. No surprise there. I did it last year, and it was during the Vipassana, that I received the vision to create my Africa trip. I love how the dots connect." The Vipassana experience was so deep-rooted that when meeting someone else who made it through the ten days, there was an immediate connection.

"It helped me with a few things emotionally and mentally," I said.

"Like what?" He raised his eyebrows.

"It calmed me for sure and helped me control my mind." I looked down.

"Interesting . . . for me it's more about letting go of the mind."

"I think that's one way to do it, but I control it, re-focus it—kind of try to outthink it."

"And who is the one out thinking it?" He was smirking at me.

"Good point," I said quietly.

"I feel life is much simpler than our minds think it is," Toto said.

"Is that why you live the life you do?"

"Yeah, I learned to follow my heart, my intuition. That's how I left Germany in 2012. Back then, I had this feeling that there had to be more to life. I'm glad I trusted it. It was the best decision of my life, made me who I am today."

"And did you come straight to Africa?" I asked.

"Actually, yes. Like a real German, I made this two-year plan for my travels around the world, and my first country happened to be Kenya. It's a long story but coming to Africa changed everything for me. Within three weeks, I had to let go of all my plans and learn to trust the flow. I had planned to reach Cape Town within three months, and eventually, it took me a year and a half."

"Wow, that's crazy!" I exclaimed.

"Yeah, it is . . ." Toto said, deep in thought.

"And what do you like so much about Africa?" I wondered out loud.

"I don't know . . . it just has this special heartbeat. There are so much freedom and potential here. Every day I am reminded of how little we need to be happy."

"I see the potential. The future is here. There is no doubt about that. Not to mention that the world can learn a lot from Africa."

"People are so busy in Germany, work so hard, and yet many are so unhappy. I wish everyone would experience Vipassana at least once. Happiness is a choice."

"Exactly. Be friggin' happy! I wish people could also experience Africa."

"Right on! People in Africa don't have much, so they know how to be happy—friends, family, food, and love. Kind of simple, right?"

"But true. I overcomplicate things. Too many things are going on."

"I can tell; your mind is always racing with ideas."

"You see that?" I wondered what made it so obvious.

"It's kind of obvious. Just a glance at you, and I can tell you are scheming something—not even looking at the animals."

"To be honest, we've seen so many. What I'm thinking right now is how we can build a game park in the USA!"

"Ha! That'll never be the same. Here we are inside their world, not the other way around. That's what makes it special."

"Just kidding, man, just half kidding." I winked.

Toto was a Zen-master throughout our trip. He never showed an ounce of negative emotion and kept everyone upbeat. The last days in Etosha National Park, there were few animals because of the rain. We only saw a few roaming wildebeest—which is, perhaps, the ugliest creature on earth. It resembled an over-sized insect with chicken legs, no butt, and a sizeable beady-eyed head. The rains flooded the salt pans, making for an incredible scene that even the locals said they'd never experienced. We walked around the pans as though we were wading on the shores of Mozambique. Then there was Toto, with hands spread wide yelling, "TIA—this is Africa. Amazing Africa!"

It was at this point that the clouds cleared, and the stars emerged as though they were speaking to us. Without tents, we rolled out on our mats on the desert floor or fell asleep on the roof of the truck. As we became more accustomed to our environment, we also became less concerned with the fears—lions, snakes, honey badgers, and spiders. And I didn't fear mosquitos because I'd only got bitten once so far on the trip. Mosquitos didn't like my blood.

We stopped in the capital, Windhoek, for a hot minute. Here I caught up with three Namibian ladies I'd met in Mozambique. We met at Joe's Beerhouse—an open-air brewery serving game meat. We checked out some museums and learned about German colonization. Namibia had retained many of the European influences brought during that time, including German foods, beer gardens, flat white coffee, the architecture of houses and churches, and some automobiles. After WWI, Germany transferred Namibia to South Africa. Finally, Namibia gained its independence in 1990 after several battles.

On our way out of Windhoek, it became more apparent what an unforgiving country this was, covered by vast swathes of the barren landscape and treacherous dirt roads that resulted in plenty of flat tires along the way. It wasn't long before we had come across several. The ultra-German-inspired town of Swakopmund had good Italian food and plenty of adventure travel tours—it was a traveler's paradise.

We then continued to Sossusvlei—my favorite adventure spot in Namibia and, ironically, my low point in the trip. My travel mates left me for the vultures circulating the one tree in sight. Drenched with sweat, dog tired, downright enervated, I sat in dismay under the tree's shadow, shaped like a witch's hand. If it weren't for a security guard, I would have been dinner for those birds—and they were African size.

What happened was that I decided to run up the "Big Daddy" dune in the over-40-degree heat and was, not surprisingly, the only one up at the top. I'd agreed to be back at the truck by noon, but upon descending at 12:30, I discovered I was the only person around. I was sitting by myself under a tree for about thirty minutes when a white pick-up truck pulled up. The guard yelled, "What are you doing out here?" He gave me a ride to the nearest café and continued to lecture me about how fragile life is and how I could have been dead meat in the heat. When the bus arrived to pick me up at a gas station, I hopped out only to be reprimanded again by one of the young ladies.

Aside from Cardi—there were three other ladies on the bus—two young ones in their early twenties and a forty-some-year-old marketing executive. They had voted to leave and were perfectly fine if I had never been found. How could hardly any tardiness be deemed deserving of a death sentence?

I desperately needed some support, so I texted Jenny and told her the situation. She told me to have a few drinks and open up to the ladies. "Tell them some secrets," was her advice. So with that in mind, I tried to make some new friends. Crossing into South Africa, our first stop was Fish River Canyon, where we finally had an opportunity to release some of the stress that had been building up. I cracked open a few more beers and got a buzz going, which opened me up to bond with the ladies and shared with them my emotional voyage. That's what they wanted—a real heart to heart—and they applauded my ability to become vulnerable with them. I laid my soul bare.

On the final leg of our trip, we headed into the Karoo National Park and spent a couple of days helping to build a Tree of Life Camp at the Afrika Burn site. This was South Africa's version of Burning Man and was to be held just a week after our visit. We spent that night having a few more beers and some laughs about the trip. I dozed off on a mat looking up at heavens when out of the clear sky, a thunder roared. I opened my eyes to the night flashes of lightning, then I heard it again, a loud yell, and felt a big "thump" rock the desert floor. I jumped off my green mat and walked to the other side of the bus, where Cardi stood over the Australian, kicking his dead body.

"Cardi, you didn't?!"

"He had it coming. Payback time." She yelled, dressed in a cowboy hat and boots.

"You can't do that. We are all accomplices." I was freaking out.

"TIA baby. This is Africa! I'll burn and bury him right here!" She proclaimed to the high skies with lightning and thunder.

I turned to run but had a hard time moving in the sand. Mosquitos buzzed around my face, and I caught a glimpse of the others gathering around the bus one by one laughing hysterically and pointing at him. Smacking myself in the side of the head, I awoke, trying to get rid of mosquitos. I thought *she killed him*. I really did. Glad it was just a dream, I fell back asleep.

Up early and out of the burn site, our last nature stop was at the Platbos Forest planting trees with Greenpop, a non-profit mission to counteract global warming and revive people's souls. It was here that I first experienced the healing and rejuvenating culture of South Africans. After planting trees during the day with a few hundred other volunteers, everyone attended different gatherings at night, from yoga to meditation, spiritual trance dancing, and even a few TEDx talks. Of all the things we'd done as a group, this was where we bonded the most. Planting trees is a great team bonding exercise.

After some nearby wine tasting, we stopped at the beautiful coastal town of Hermanus for whale watching and fresh fish. We continued to the Cape Peninsula, stopping to see the penguins in Simonstown and the lighthouse at Cape Point before ending the trip. At the farewell dinner, we each wrote down on a piece of paper one positive thing we'd learned about each other and one positive experience. It was the perfect way to remember each other and savor our memories.

In our last night as roomies, Toto and I had a final chat over a beer.

"How'z it?" Toto looked at the clouds.

"The beer?" I looked at my hand holding the beer.

"Anything."

"It was good, even with the ups and downs, I enjoyed it. Guess I have to think about where to go next. What's next for you?"

"You made it to the end, so congratulations! For me? I'm not sure, but I don't think this is for me. I learned a lot, and it was amazing, but I feel called to do other things that help people who need it." His sad face turned determined.

I nodded. "Do you like going from project to project? Seems unsteady."

"I just learn and change as I go. And somehow, I just love to do several things at the same time. The crazier, the better."

"No script, huh?" I said, stating the obvious. "You just do it. How interesting. It's opposite of what everyone tells you: Just stick to one thing."

"You know, I see every human as the author of their own story. It's in your hands to create each chapter the way you wish, and only you have the power to choose which side of your story, you tell. Moment by moment, you decide if you see the glass as half empty or half full."

That is the advice of a Zen Master, I thought.

"How's your non-profit? It's called Better Me Kenya. Correct?"

"Yes. It's doing great. Our team is incredible, and we're now supporting over three hundred children and youth. We are also welcoming lots of volunteers from across the world—even Americans."

"I'd like to check it out."

"We'd love to have you. Let me know when you are in Kenya. I'll stay in Cape Town a bit longer for Africa Burn."

"Absolutely. I don't know when, though," I said. "What's in Cape Town?"

"Beautiful city, good people, food, nature. Great place to re-invigorate the spirit and the soul."

"I could use some of that after this trip."

"I think everyone can!"

Then we passed out.

Chapter 16

SOUTH AFRICA: STAY OR GO?

"I'm pretty fly for a white guy."
—The Offspring

C ape Town nestles between the coast and the flat-topped peak of Table Mountain, with yacht-filled harbors and an air of wealth in its affluent residential areas. A majestic city. After this last boondoggle, I needed to meditate, and the beautiful coastline of paved beach paths would be the place to lose myself in a run. While running full pace down the beach path, I noticed a car slowly following me, so I sped up. Fear followed. The car honked once, then twice. Peaking back over my shoulder, I saw someone hanging out the window waving at me.

"KD! KD!" It was Jeremiah, one of the teachers at my Team4Tech project in Joburg. He pulled into the parking lot, and when I asked him how he knew it was me, he responded, "You aren't a normal white guy!" *I guess he meant I am "fly for a white guy,"* I thought. He was in town with Dawn and Paul for a new project. The timing was perfect.

We caught up over a meal at a Malaysian restaurant in a train caboose right across from the parking lot. There he invited me to join their ongoing project in Philippi, one of Cape Town's large townships. From the owner of the restaurant, we learned Cape Malays first brought Islam to South Africa. He proudly mentioned the country is home to churches, synagogues, and mosques, and South Africans are proud to share their support for freedom of worship. With a full stomach and new knowledge, Jeremiah and I parted ways, saying we'd meet up later at the school.

A timely message came in from Tessa that afternoon.

"I haven't heard from you in a while."

"Yes, the internet was spotty; I didn't top up my SIM while traveling. It was calming to cut off everyone."

"It is. To be off technology is what we all need. How do you feel?" She asked.

"Good, much calmer at the moment. I love Cape Town. Beautiful here."

"Oh, I know, I wish I were back."

"I am pretty tired, thinking of coming back, you know . . . start a job."

"That's ridiculous; you haven't seen the entire continent yet!"

"I've been to fifteen countries. That's enough."

"How many countries are there . . . forty-eight on the continent, six islands, so fifty-four total. Keep going until you can't go anymore. See it all!" I couldn't believe she was telling me to go, just go.

"Maybe, I could keep going. But I want to do something."

"Then find something to do there for a while. America is here. We'll be here whenever you return."

"Very true."

"How's your health?"

"Good, working out, and my mind is pretty calm."

"Fantastic. If it's working, don't fix it. Get to know Cape Town a bit and send me a picture or two. It's the most beautiful city in the world!" She may be right.

I decided to take a tour led by an Indian South African through the markets that cluster around the main bus terminal. The disparity in wealth was startling. Most of the stall owners had no other means to generate an income or access capital, and tensions were mounting as more people moved from the townships into the city. My guide explained that the money had been consolidated by a few wealthy South Africans who controlled the steel and oil industries without reinvesting much into the local communities. Instead, the capital went abroad. As a result, the income and opportunity divide within the country created anger and resentment.

Despite the friction in the air, I found many Capetonians to be concerned about their society and willing to address the pains of the past. They organized community events—even something as simple as planting a tree brought new life and positive energy. Through my discussions with locals, I realized that healing is a natural process and something needed to go through if their society would come to a peaceful resolution.

The next day, I spent a day at the Philippi Western Cape Township, where I worked with a group of local students, alongside my Team4Tech colleagues, Dawn and Paul. The three of us went out to dinner, and they urged me to stay the course. Paul wrapped it up in one statement, "Dude, you are traveling Africa—almost the entire thing. This is legendary. Few people travel in Africa like this." *I like the sound of being called a legend.* But I thought what Paul and Dawn did was legendary. What they made me realize was that we could all make our contributions—perhaps not of the same magnitude as a Bill Gates—but we could do something.

I took a picture of a Desmond Tutu quote that said, "Do your little bit of good where you are; it's those little bits of good put together that changed the world." But what? I didn't know yet. I *did* know that I needed to decide whether or not to continue the journey. Paul and Tessa said to keep going while my Mom—who had just sent me an email—said to come back to our country, asserting that I'd seen enough. The indecision made me mentally drained and physically tired. I decided to sleep on it.

The next morning, a friend, Michael Morales, sent me an email saying that he'd been reading my mass email updates and wanted to introduce me to his good friend, Jay Chikobe, who worked in DC but was from Zambia. Jay suggested to meet up with Bongohive, an entrepreneurship hub in Lusaka, Zambia. They were looking for teachers/visitors with real-world experience. That's interesting. I can build on my experience in Ghana and teach my Silicon Valley experiences to more entrepreneurs. The universe was speaking to me. It would give me the mission to continue the trip.

A few emails later, I hooked up with Simunza and Emma at Bonghohive. Abra Kadabra! With a stipend from the US Consulate and a plane ticket to Lusaka, I pinged Fred, whose wedding I was supposed to attend in a few weeks, telling him I had a change of plans. He said, "Don't worry, no single ladies will come to the wedding anyway." It didn't matter because Jenny, Jenny just couldn't get my mind.

The overland route in Namibia (Drone shot by Niklas Faralisch)

The overland bus and team in the flooded salt pans (Taken by Niklas)

The team on the sand dunes

That is me taking a jump sandboarding.

Toto and the team—TIA = This is Afrika!(Taken by Niklas)

The sunset at Spitzkoppe, Namibia

A picture of Cape Town

Chapter 17

ZAMBIA: PURPOSE IN COMMUNITY ENTREPRENEURSHIP

"God Made Beer So Zambians Wouldn't Rule the World."
—Random Sign in an Irish Pub in Zambia

ow no longer doubting my purpose, I was enthusiastic about continuing. As Goenka said in his Vipassana discourse, "Start again, start again, patiently and persistently." Contrary to me, the Zambians seemed to remain eternally optimistic. They did this by creating purpose in the community through entrepreneurship, and I was about to learn all about it.

My host in Zambia was Wilcliff, a professional who worked at the American Consulate, looked about my age and dressed in a sharp style. Being greeted by Wilcliff was like opening a car door, then having a gust of cold wind hit you smack in the face. With his big smile, endearing British accent, and loads of energy, he just wanted to get stuff done and have fun. Each day, he picked me up bright and early for presentations at Bongohive, the American Chamber of Commerce, and WeCreate, followed by evenings spent drinking Guinness Extra at a local Irish pub and checking out Lusaka's discos. He kept a schedule as tight as working at a startup.

Lusaka had mushroomed in the middle of grasslands, with plenty of new hotels, two large shopping malls, and a newly built, magnificent American embassy. The new open economic policies were visibly attracting overseas investment, particularly from the United Kingdom, both as an opportunity and repatriation. The United Kingdom had a long-established relationship in the region ever since colonial days and has continued to foster development through investments since pulling out of the region. It was immediately apparent from the infrastructure, the development of malls, and businesses that capital was freely flowing into the country. However, the pitfall to this economic boom was that those left behind needed cash to survive. Around some of the neighborhoods and backpacker spots, working women came out after dusk.

Along with the roosters, Wilcliff jolted me out of bed at the crack of dawn. The first person I met at Bongohive was Emma, a young and spicy Brit. She was on top of things both organizationally and socially, introducing me to plenty of ex-pat non-profit workers and local entrepreneurs. Although I told her I was here to teach, she was adamant that I was going to have fun. (By the way, it was here that I recognized Zambians' uniquely, spoken form of British English. They spoke with sophisticated politeness and straightforwardness, without the British pompousness. I soon found myself unconsciously replicating their accent. I spoke like this for the rest of the trip.)

The local incubator was run by three smart, charismatic, and driven men: Simunza, Lukonga, and Silumesii. They provided coaching, space, and help for entrepreneurs in industries ranging from clothing and furniture design to ride-sharing and mobile messaging services. Impressively, over half of the entrepreneurs were women. Like any emerging country, raising capital was challenging. A combination of investments from foreign governments and the Zambian diaspora was the only means of funding.

Njavwa, a well-dressed and charismatic entrepreneur, led one of the highest potential projects. He started a logistics company called Musanga, hiring just three motorbikes to deliver packages. Building the local economy fueled his fire. Since launching it, he'd raised money from several overseas investors, non-profits, and other Zambian diaspora based in NYC. Later, he would visit the United States as part of the Mandela Fellowship and attend meetings in Silicon

Valley with companies like Uber. Since this writing, he has now joined forces with Lori—a well-funded logistics startup in Kenya.

One of Bongohive's female entrepreneurs was Ruth, who dressed exotically and acted as a mother to all; she created interior design goods and furniture featuring African colors, much like those in the Congo. With that talent, she started My Perfect Stitch with only two sewing machines and now operated with ten. Another project was led by Linda, who'd recently returned from the United Kingdom, where she'd studied computer science. She was now building telecom connections for mobile messaging and marketing, and her business had grown throughout Southern Africa.

When I worked with the entrepreneurs, the one thing they echoed was that they wanted to help their community and employ people. The most salient example was a group that began an after-school program for students, teaching them music, dance, computer skills, and art. The students needed activities to keep them busy and out of trouble while also learning practical skills. Supportive of these ideas, thousands of parents signed them up. Even though these businesses were on financial life support, a greater meaning pulled these entrepreneurs along—the vision to make their lives and society better. To stay steadfast to this vision, the entrepreneurs supported each other emotionally and the surrounding community. They had group get-togethers and outings, shared knowledge, and sustained a constant flow of encouragement among each other. For them, entrepreneurship was community.

The next experience was at WeCreate, a Hillary Clinton initiative for women's entrepreneurship operated around the world. Simply put, this redefined my take on entrepreneurship. I worked with women who ran small shops selling eggs, fruit, and fashion. These women told me stories of men stealing their money and products; some men even destroyed their stores. Other men were flat-out told not to do business with women. I had no response to this but to tell them what I knew. I taught them the basics of economics and that the power of women working together to create scale could give them leverage over their male competitors. However, getting them to work together was also a challenge in what was an untrustworthy environment.

Working with them impacted me profoundly. If the women hadn't created stores, they had no means of income, and the community had limited access to these goods. They acted with whatever resources they had and made the best of it. *Back home, entrepreneurship was a choice or a luxury; here, it's a necessity.* I didn't expect that women selling eggs and fruit would teach me such a lesson, but they certainly did.

Once the day's work was over, we had a lot of fun hanging out. Led by Emma, the ladies were particularly friendly and always poking fun, asking questions about why I wasn't married and if I wanted an African wife. We spent one evening shopping at a mall, dancing at Latitude 15, smoking Hukkah, and carrying on our conversation. They taught me a lot about society, government, and just day-to-day life as a Zambian. Emma caught me texting with Jenny, and she quietly joked, "Maybe she wants one of her own." *I certainly hope so,* I thought.

It was during one of these late-night sessions at a local bar that I learned that HIV was still a big issue in Zambia having an HIV infection rate of 15 percent. The availability of affordable antiretrovirals prolonged many people's lives but also exacerbated the problem. Many people wrongly thought HIV was no longer a big deal as the drugs made it possible to live a normal life. Dating was dangerous. People would sometimes lie about not having the disease or just be willing to play the game of roulette, not worrying if their partner had been tested or not. *Glad I wasn't single in Zambia.*

It's worth noting that some Americans started interesting projects in Zambia, as well. During the week, I met Brian, a thirty-something American, who built and financed a fish farm and a motorcycle lending company, Yalelo. Bored with the idea of working consulting and private equity in the US, he became excited by the opportunities in Africa. I also met Gritcube, a group organized by Jennifer Shen, that introduces overseas mentors to Zambian entrepreneurs. I'd later team up with them, Jay in DC and Bongohive to form a project called Southern Africa Venture Partners (www.savp.co). In particular, the relatively clear legal infrastructure, overseas investment, and some of copper/mining investments up north were spawning the future growth of the economy. Hopefully, Zambia will continue to welcome ex-pats and foreigners to invest, as it will help catalyze the country's economic development and growth.

My positivity increased when Jenny texted me.

"Hey, how's the teaching going?"

"Great, I'm having a blast here. Zambians are fun."

"Yeah, I heard they have a good vibe."

"Positive and upbeat. Lots of potential here."

"That's encouraging. When am I going to see you? Want to rendezvous in Mozambique?"

"Nah, I have to stay the course, and I've already been there."

"OK. Visit me in Uganda soon?"

"Sure, any fun things to do?" I couldn't remember when a lady ever invited me to visit her.

"I'm running the Ugandan Half Marathon. Want to do that?"

"Perfect. Sounds awesome. I'm in. You rock." I liked to say that as a compliment.

"You aren't bad yourself."

It was all on the up and up: Jenny was ready to see me again, Zambia had great vibes, and the community-focused entrepreneurship was eye-opening. Though it was all very uplifting, it was about to crash in Zimbabwe.

Chapter 18

THE INDOMITABLE SPIRITS OF ZIMBABWEANS

"With whatever you do, take with you
the indomitable spirit of a Zimbabwean"
—KD

About half-way through my Zimbabwe trip, I met Vuyo. Vuyo graduated from high school in 2016. He had a glimmer in his eyes as if he could do anything he wanted. He didn't just have a dream; he had a plan and an indomitable spirit like no one I'd ever met. After finishing my sales presentation with a group of enthusiastic, young entrepreneurs at the American Corner—a small library in Bulawayo with old Western history, math, and computer science books—I felt a bit exhausted and went outside to look for a cup of coffee.

"Hi Kurt, my name is Vuyo. I'm the intern here."

"Hi buddy, how are you?"

"I'm fine, thanks, and you?" replied Vuyo.

"Not so great. I need some coffee. I couldn't find one anywhere. See what I'm drinking? Milk tea, again." I sighed.

Vuyo smiled a little and said, "We like tea here."

"That's British. I'm American. I need coffee," I said. I was getting sick of the British influence around me.

"I see. You mentioned that you're from California, right?"

"Yeah, that's right. I'm from San Francisco. You know of it?" He seemed on top of things, but I was making sure.

"Yes! Of course. It's Silicon Valley. I'm raising money for a coding boot camp there in the summer."

"Really? Tell me more."

"I got accepted for the Make School Summer Academy. So I'll spend two months learning how to build iPhone apps and exploring the Bay Area."

"So you are an engineer? Must be clever."

Vuyo smiled and said, "Yes, I like to make things. But there's a catch."

I frowned a little, "And?"

"I have to raise $10,000 by June to get to Silicon Valley."

"Ten thousand dollars?! That's a lot of money for a short trip."

"Yes, it's taxing. I have to pay $7,000 for tuition, buy a new laptop, and the rest is for transport and accommodation."

"My goodness! It's 7K to attend school?"

"I will make it to Silicon Valley," said Vuyo.

"Try it for sure," I said, not believing it for a second.

"I can get the $10,000 through grants and donations from GoFundMe."

"I'm happy to help you find a place once you confirm you can raise the money. Maybe you should start a company, too, and make some money?"

"Like what?" He said.

"Sell 5000 cups of coffee for $1 each. I could be your first customer."

"Five thousand? In a month and a half. Yeah, I can do it!"

"You do that, and I'll send $1K more."

"Deal. Let's do that!"

And he did it. The indomitable spirit of young Vuyo, had visited the American Corner, joined the United States Achiever Program (USAP), taught himself to code at Zimcode, and raised the money to join Make School in Berkeley in 2017 (right after I got home). He embodied the indomitable spirit of the Zimbabweans—a spirit of positivity, hope, resourcefulness, and resilience. Sadly, all this remains repressed by the government at hand. Mugabe still held the highest office, but his wife had just announced she would be taking over if something were to happen to him. *Fingers crossed that wouldn't be while I am here,* crossed my mind.

The airport seemed relatively normal, albeit a little small and ran down. It was the first indication that the Zimbabweans didn't keep up or improve the legacy of the European colonial infrastructure. My host, Marisa, greeted me at the airport; her cheery smile immediately allayed my anxieties of the authoritarian regime. She had a sister in the United States, so she was accustomed to the American culture. She set up a busy schedule of meetings for me not only in Harare but also Bulawayo—a city that reminded me of the American West.

Driving through Harare, I felt that *I could have been in a midwestern city like Cleveland or Detroit (before its recent uptick).* Much of the infrastructure had been built up and expanded decades prior, only to be left to deteriorate during the recent tumult. The old Sheraton, once the largest hotel in Africa, lavishly built with gold and copper-plated interior, was now a run-down haunt filled with dust where you could only get a stale bologna sandwich.

As we drove around the city, I noticed how grim it was. The only places where there were people were the banks and grocery stores—long lines of hundreds hoping they could get their necessities. People would line up at banks for 24 hours to get cash before they opened—which was once a week; they slept outside for days so that they'd be able to buy bread and milk. A reprieve from the chaos had come in the form of Ecocash mobile money, which allowed people to pay for goods. The problem was getting money into the account in the first place.

Once the sun went down, the ghost town that was Harare by day transformed into a vibrant black market where hawkers sold everything from clothing to homewares. Taxis, people shopping, and food vendors packed the streets—a shocking contrast to daytime.

How did this country get to this point? During British colonization, Harare was the capital of what the British called Rhodesia, considered the Jewel of Africa due to its natural resources. I'd heard some people in my travels mention that the British extracted minerals and resources in the north (present-day Malawi and Zambia), then transported to Harare to build its infrastructure. Zimbabwe benefitted, while Malawi and Zambia suffered.

In 1965, the white minority, due to several factors, declared Rhodesia independent. Rhodesia was their name for the independent colony encompassing the three nations today. The declaration of independence led to battles for over 15 years between the ruling white party and the black nationalists led by Mugabe. After the black nationalists won, Mugabe came to power and promised to make amends with the opposing white party.[17] Instead, Mugabe stripped them of their farmlands and businesses. Then he gave these businesses to locals who had no skills or training, and that left the country without a stable food supply and an economy precipitously declining until today. That's the short version of this country's tumultuous history. Later in my trip, I'd learn more from white farmers.

Marisa showed me all facets of Harare, from the decent hotel (for ex-pats) where I was staying to the poverty-ridden slums and impressive art galleries. We feasted on traditional Zimbabwean fish beneath a tent and attended an English class where locals were being taught the fineries of speaking like an American. We ate lunch of fish and sadza—what they called their maize dish. The staple food across Southern Africa was mashed corn, called maize. Eaten by hand, it reminded me of slightly hardened grits, without the butter, bacon, and shrimp. Malawians called it nsima; Zambians called it nshima; South Africans called it mielie pap. With a hand full of it, I noticed some golfers walking over a crosswalk; I asked Marisa if she played golf. She didn't hesitate, "I love golf; we love golf in Zimbabwe!" I was surprised, even though I didn't play a lot of golf—it hurt my back.

She was excited about her work at a local incubator called Stimulus. We met with different entrepreneurs at both this incubator and a co-working space where I found the engineering capabilities to be much advanced than in other parts of Africa. Companies in surrounding countries often hired Zimbabwean engineers because of their skills.

The startups created innovative applications including an e-commerce marketplace, a bitcoin app, an insurance app, and a shipping and logistical platform. It was here that I learned the power of cryptocurrencies. One entrepreneur named Tawanda founded a bitcoin trading platform called Golix, and people used it to store money since the Kwacha—Zimbabwean currency—suffered so much instability and hyperinflation. Those who used the platform to buy bitcoin used it to purchase goods overseas, primarily in China and Japan. Zimbabwean car buyers converted cash to bitcoin to send money to Japanese used car exporters. The Japanese exported used cars all around the world and recently targeted Africa because of the massive opportunity. The largest investor in his platform was also Japanese.

The Zimbabwean entrepreneurs were "nuts and bolts." They were also humble and soft-spoken. Because of the political and economic issues, they seem to keep a pretty low profile. I felt as if no one really wanted to say too much about their companies. It was clear that people had their hands tied behind their backs in fear of government autocracy.

From Harare, I took a bus to Bulawayo, passing neglected farms overrun with weeds that hadn't been maintained. As we approached the city, empty water towers bumped up against shopping malls with barred up doors and windows. The open stores had few daily necessities available to purchase.

My host at Techvillage, Lydia, picked me up, and we chatted about the region and its difficulties. I was about to learn about a lot more than just that. She was about five feet, shy, and curious about my story—why was I here, and what could I teach? Lydia wasn't familiar with the United States and had never left Zimbabwe but was grateful for the American Consulate's support. She had a calm demeanor, one filled with hope. Her favorite quote was, "This too will pass," referring to the political dissent. It reminded me of Vipassana meditation: the pain will pass, everything is impermanent. She had already figured it out on her own.

Sans cowboys, the last Wild West city in the world, Bulawayo, was an old industrial city with colonial red and green buildings. There was a large empty water tower in the middle of town, carved out by streets that reminded me a little of Austin, Texas. While Bulawayo had an organized, grid-like street system and grand churches, everything was in decay. The buildings were crumbling and vacant, potholes lined the streets, and paint was peeling off the walls. The solemnness deepened. *What a lively Bulawayo must have been once and what it could be now*, I thought.

That evening I had dinner with a few entrepreneurs who took me to the darn near best steak house I'd ever eaten at, called The Cattleman. It had full Western aesthetics of bullheads and cowboy clothes decorating the walls. While we ate, the entrepreneurs told me that Zimbabwe had the best steak in the world; I countered with second only to Japan. We chatted about their startups, and they inquired about financing. I had to politely decline and let them know I wasn't in Africa to make investments but to learn about the continent. They understood, and we agreed to meet the next day.

Later into the night at a different restaurant and dance floor underneath a large white tent—a common practice in Zimbabwe—Lydia and her friend Lily took me for an Amarula, my new favorite drink to kill stomach bacteria. These two were partners in crime; two girls equally pretty as bright who probably broke plenty of hearts. They mentioned a large food festival up the road, and I offered to road trip with them. The next day we drove to a food festival in Matobo, a city around 30 miles west. Though a small food festival, the cuisine was unique. I tried a local beer called Chibuku, which tasted like yeast in a bottle, as well as a variety of millets, maize, sorghums, and sugarcane that were eaten by hand. After drinking a beer, I still wasn't buzzed enough to try the fried caterpillars and insects.

The Matobo region featured rocks stacked up like Legos that lined the hills as far as the eye could see. I stared in wonder at these natural formations, having never seen anything like them. Striking up a conversation with some locals, I asked if it was possible to venture there. To see the 6,000-year-old rock art, tour guides were required. "If you go," one of the men began, "the rocks may speak to you." Locals believed that this land was very spiritual; many dead roamed the area from past tribal wars. It was my introduction to the mysticism of Zimbabwe.

The next day, we visited the Great Zimbabwe National Monument, a small fortress of rocks left over from what was a thriving city between the eleventh and fifteenth centuries. It was once home to around 20,000 cattle-herders who turned their skills into metalworking with copper and gold. The ruins are the largest of their kind on the Zimbabwe Plateau. One archaeologist had described them as exhibiting "an architecture that is unparalleled elsewhere in Africa or beyond."[18]

When my trip with Lydia and Lily was over, I had come to appreciate their friendship. Lily was reserved but tough—just like Lydia—and had recently been accepted into the Mandela Fellowship Program, so that made two people I'd meet in the fall in DC. Upon departing, they joked, be careful, and don't let the spirits get you.

The following day, I headed east across Zimbabwe by bus to Mutare, a small city close to the Mozambique border. I booked to stay in an Airbnb in the suburbs, run by an elderly white couple who'd had their farm and all its equipment seized a few years prior. Many people had been killed during the tumult. Those who lacked any agricultural training took over the farms. The results had been devastating for Zimbabwean society. Even recently, the government confiscated more of their land and several tractors. Once a several hundred-acre farm was now a one-acre yard with a tractor and a horse. But this was their home, and they were determined to outlast these setbacks. I awed at their loyalty and commitment.

The next day I continued on my way to the mysterious highlands of Nyanga, a national park that encompassed rugged mountains and sparkling streams near the Mozambique border. Upon arrival, a guide escorted each visitor because people frequently disappeared or became stranded at night—or so that's what they said at the entrance gate. Just recently, two young boys had disappeared while swimming in the lake after purportedly being attacked by a mermaid. Another group had vanished in the mountains during a cloudy night; the locals said they could hear their voices for miles and blamed the wild and free spirits. Mermaids and ghosts? No way.

An eeriness followed the car as we drove through the park gate. The guards were the only visible souls, and the roads deteriorated, posing a challenge in our old Toyota Corolla. My mind was racing: a mermaid-haunted park, clouds on the horizon, no one in sight, and the chance of a flat tire. Though somewhat spooked, I was emboldened by the confidence of my driver as we headed into the vast wilderness where mountains rippled as far as the eye could see. A hovering fog persisted. I could feel that the spirits knew we were here. My driver explained that tribal wars had been fought in these mountains, and the souls of the deceased roamed free—*maybe ghosts roamed all over Zimbabwe,* I thought.

Closer to Mount Nyangani, the driver offered a story: on the other side of the mountain, there was a lake that turned red whenever the stillness broke.

He explained that many had committed suicide there, and more had died there during the wars. Their blood was said to have dripped to the bottom of the lake. Looking up at the quickly approaching clouds, I nudged him to turn around.

After a few hours, my car driver stopped at a bus terminus, letting me off. It was an eerily peaceful ride back to Harare. I checked into a colonial-style mansion that had transformed into a hotel frequented by business elites. I safely retreated into the world of a tourist, protected from the turmoil of the outside reality.

The mysticism of the park was bewildering; the black markets, disheartening. Cruel dictators and corruption tore apart a society that could be thriving. I get it, "Life isn't fair. Move on." Still, it put me in a very dark, deep place.

To climb out of that trance, I needed some company, so I texted Marisa and Tawanda. They came to the hotel for dinner. "One day, we will bounce back," said Tawanda. "When is the last time you saw magic?" Then he pulled out a deck of cards and played some card tricks. The best way to change a situation is to amaze people and make them laugh, and he did just that over a few beers.

The people and entrepreneurs of Zimbabwe had a spirit of ingenuity and perseverance. It was indomitable even in the face of a despotic government. I hoped to take that indomitable spirit—frightening visions of mermaids and ghosts and all—with me wherever I may go.

The team at Bongohive

The rocks that speak outside of Bulawayo

The food festival outside of Bulawayo

Hiking with Lydia and Lily

The magical, mystical mountains close to Mozambique

The night market in Harare.

Chapter 19

MALAWI: SPEAKING SOFTLY IN THE WARM HEART OF AFRICA

"People who are soft-spoken and truthful are loved by all."
—Rigveda

S trolling through the Harare Airport, I heard someone shout my name: "Kurt!"

What on earth? I thought.

Someone was approaching with his hand up. "I'm Vincent from mHub (Malawi's first tech hub)," he introduced himself. "It looks like we're on the same flight to Lilongwe. You look just like your picture!"

"You mean a balding white guy?"

"Yes, just like that." His smile indicated he was teasing, and we began a lengthy discussion on the way to Malawi.

"Tell me, what's Malawi like?"

"It's kind of like here, a little less infrastructure." He was so soft-spoken I had to lean in to hear him.

"More farms?"

"Yeah, the country is mostly agriculture, besides Lilongwe and Blantyre."

"How is the government situation?"

"Not as bad as Zimbabwe, but not that good."

"Somewhere in the middle, you say?"

"Sure. We do the best with what we got." You could tell that he didn't put too much pressure on things he couldn't control.

"Poorer than Zimbabwe?" I asked, not sure if I should.

"You like to ask questions." He smiled. "Sadly, it's very poor still." He had a glaze over his eyes and changed the subject. "You have gone to many places in Africa, that's great to see."

"I've been fortunate to see so much."

"Even Africans don't see that much."

"Have you been to the US?"

"Not yet, but I'll be there for the Mandela Program."

"Right on, buddy! You are the third person I've met going. I'll see you there!"

"Great, then we can meet again."

"What are the fun things to do in Malawi?"

"Fun? You mean for tourists?" He responded as if there would be a clear difference between fun for locals and tourists.

"Yes, yes, I am a tourist but prefer local ideas."

"Lake Malawi, of course, is beautiful; there is hiking down south and a nice game reserve up north. If you have time, you should go, but it's Easter, so it will be busy."

"So what about mHub center, your business center? Is it on vacation, or are you still working?"

"Now we are working, but we will have some days off at the end of the week. You could teach some now, then go on vacation. Did you bring the certificates?" Vincent had asked me to make certificates to formalize my class—KDAlive Sales Certificates.

"I made them but haven't printed them."

"No problem, we can do that here."

"OK, so I'll cram the sessions in a few days then, take off to Lake Malawi and return. It's like a short vacation within my big African vacation," I joked.

"Ha-ha, yes. A Malawi vacation. The lake is beautiful."

"Is it close?"

"About four hours from Lilongwe, but traffic can be heavy, so you never know."

"Yup, never know, TIA—this is Africa."

"Yes, this is Africa."

During our flight, we chatted, showed pictures, and learned about the country. He was curious, sincere, and exceedingly warm—all confirming what other travelers had told me about the kindest people on earth, Malawians.

After touching down in Lilongwe, the drive from the airport provided the first glimpse of Malawi, a former British colony and one of Africa's poorest countries. Lilongwe was a suburban-like city, with a small downtown area clustered with a few British banks and South African supermarkets, as well as shops with local restaurants serving fish from Lake Malawi interspersed throughout. It was a quaint and quiet town with potential, I remembered thinking.

Receiving a small amount of funding from the United States and the United Kingdom, mHub was another business incubator that worked with local entrepreneurs to create innovative solutions for life's necessities. The entrepreneurs were thoughtful and listened intently. I spent a few hours chatting with an entrepreneur, James, about his insurance-selling scheme and how to make it competitive.

James offered to drive me back to my hostel at the end of the day, asking on the ride why I was roaming around Africa and not married. "I don't know. I just like to explore," I replied.

"My wife and kids are my life . . . there is so much love there," he explained. "Without them, I have nothing. I know you people in the West have different values, but nothing beats a family. When you go back, you should at least try."

I appreciated his thoughts, and, to some degree, I thought he was right. Perhaps I had valued my freedom, experiences, and my career pursuits more than romantic relationships. To my defense, though, every time I tried to have a relationship, I felt like I had to compete with my girlfriend's career, her friend's husband's stellar career, and whatever else she could compare me to in Silicon Valley. Satisfying a lady in today's career-focused world seemed nearly impossible. So it was just easier to do my own thing, be myself, and let women come and go as they pleased. No strings attached. I fell asleep under the mosquito net, with the light on looking at the ceiling at the Mabuya Camp Hostel. Alone.

Malaria had four major strands and infected over 200M people annually with over 400,000 deaths.[19] I was about to learn that the one in Malawi wasn't the innocuous one that resided in other parts of Africa. At the crack of dawn, I awoke to go for a run and, right before exiting the hostel, approached upon two men who the night before were selling clothes at the entrance. Working out with no rest in between sets and dripping sweat on the dirt, they had only two pairs of dumbbells and a pull-up bar above them. Over the next thirty minutes, I joined them doing pull-ups, bicep curls, and shoulder presses until I dropped, well before they did. When I asked why they worked out this intensely, they responded: "It's anti-malarial. If you get bitten, you won't feel it so much." So much for taking pills. I'll just keep working out and sleeping under nets.

Later that day, I joined a rugby group who was teaching rugby in Africa with the non-profit Rugby in Africa. It was great to see them building community through sport in the region. I hadn't worked out that much in one day since college and was ready to eat a feast. Over dinner at the hostel, I joined other hostel members eating nsima (the local maize mash) and vegetables. They were traveling and volunteering at local schools. During dinner, they were discussing the rare strand of malaria in the vicinity. More dangerous than in other parts of Africa, it could attack the host's brain and, within days, disable or kill someone. "Oh no, I haven't been taking my pills." I panicked, jumped out of my seat, and ran to my room where I took two pills, hoping that would shorten the time to get them into my system—bad idea.

Walking out to the hostel lobby, I noticed three ladies hanging out at the bar—ooh-la-la. I sat down at the counter and introduced myself to the nearest one. She was from Puerto Rico, worked at the Peace Corps in Zambia, and was on vacation in Malawi, where she met up with the other two, an African American and a 'colored' American—if I may use that term now. Until now, those two were the first African Americans I'd met on my trip. Over a few beers, they mentioned they were going to Lake Malawi. I leaned in, waiting for the invite but got nothing except, "Have a good night." With hopes dashed and my second Carlsberg polished off, I called it a night.

It didn't take long for the dreams to start. Vivid. Lucid. Neon. Animals grazed outside my window and, approaching my room, beat down the door and windows. Sweat soaked through my clothes and sheets. One by one, the animals turned into giant mosquitos that flew directly into my ears. Punching myself in the side of my face and ear, I jolted awake with church bells ringing. But it wasn't light outside yet, so it couldn't be the church. It was still the middle of the night. Unable to go back to sleep, I went back to the closed bar, found a cooler, had another beer, and passed out on the couch. Never again would I mix alcohol and anti-malarial meds.

Upon waking hours later, I realized that it was only a few days to Easter, and I still had not figured out my mini-vacation. I walked by the ladies' tents and over to the hostel's gym. After a few sets, I returned to help them disassemble the tents when—surprise, surprise—one of them invited me to Lake Malawi. Mission successful.

Next thing I knew, I was on a jam-packed, eight-hour bus trip heading in the direction of Cape Maclear on Lake Malawi and was being slammed against the windscreen at every turn. I kept the bus driver company at the door. The standing-room ticket gave me a perspective of the vendors and the people getting in and out of the bus. With a clear view of the road with my nose pressed against the glass, I couldn't have bought a better movie ticket. I could hear someone reading Bible verses out loud and praying for a safe trip. Sitting right next to a preacher, I found myself repeating and throwing my hands up, "Amen, Amen." After all, it *was* Easter.

We drove through the countryside dotted with palm trees and destitute villages. Over 25 percent of the population lived on less than $1.90/day—the United Nations cutoff wage for abject poverty—while another 50 percent lived on amounts just above that.[20] But whatever they lacked in money, they made up in warmth and love. On one occasion, we stopped behind an Easter vigil where hundreds of people dressed in purple and white gowns following a man carrying a cross resembling that of Jesus. We stopped, and they came on the bus to give us blessings.

The bus took breaks and allowed vendors on, selling small plastic bands of peanuts, nuts, and fruit, and dozens of fish hanging on a large metal wire. Young people approached me with a wave and a smile, and I couldn't resist buying enough snacks to pass around to others. Vendors competed, but after one scored a victory, he shared it with the others. I noticed one young man sharing the money I gave him with four other children.

Alighting from the bus, I didn't feel the chaos that had appeared through the window. The politeness of the Malawian people created calming energy. Malawians never hassled or asked for money—another stark difference from other countries. It was when we bundled into a small, white, and rundown station-wagon with a sofa loaded onto its roof that I understood the true nature of a Malawian. While negotiating a price, the driver commented, "We have four people; what's fair for you?" I pushed a little. His calm response was, "Please, I apologize if you think I'm cheating you. We don't cheat people here in Malawi. It's not our custom; as you can see, we are all poor. I'm not giving you an unreasonable price; it is a long drive, and our car already has a sofa on top. If you don't accept it, it's OK." He said it so nicely and calmly I gave him not only his price but also a large tip.

Bumping down a dirt road, one of the most beautiful lakes I'd ever seen came into view. It reminded me of this quote by William Kamkwamba in *The Boy Who Harnessed the Wind.* "Lake Malawi is one of the biggest in the world and nearly covers the entire eastern half of the country. It's so vast it has waves like an ocean . . . I stood out on the banks and looked out across its endless looking water. My heart was filled with great love for my country."

Thatched roof hostels and campgrounds lined the lakeshore. Small stores and street vendors selling art, clothing, and food set up outside tourist destinations. Getting out of the car, I noticed a small stand grilling fish, called chambo—a staple white fish served with a spicy sauce known as kachumbari. It reminded me of the white fish served in Israel on the Mediterranean Sea.

Walking around and looking up at the clear, blue sky speckled with cotton-wool clouds, I felt something exceptional about this place. Or maybe it was something about the people of Malawi. They were the most 'at ease' people in the world, and, for the first time in a long time, I didn't feel anxious, stressed, or in need of doing something. I was simply there, completely in the moment. *There is nothing more calming than fully appreciating the moment,* I thought.

Our hostel, the Malambe Camp, was chill compared to a few others on the strip; it was a sandy tent ground right on the lake, occupied mostly of locals and foreign travelers. The strip had just a few beachfront bars that turned into dance and karaoke parties. I enjoyed hanging out with my new Peace Corps friends. The most memorable quote was from one Puerto Rican who said she was impressed that I wasn't a complaining white boy on the bus ride. "People are not always what you think," I winked at her, quoting Chimamanda, who'd written about a white business guy from Tennessee who adopted a black daughter in *Americanah*. I'd later meet a business partner from Tennessee who did just that.

The next few days were spent lounging, talking, and reading. The lake was renowned for its cichlids, tiny fish that appeared like small silver/blue flashes in what was incredibly clear waters. On a scuba trip, rather than taking the small wooden fisherman boat back, I decided to swim the kilometer back to shore. As I approached the beach, many locals bathed and rinsed buckets of water. Walking out of the water, I was approached by a white lady tourist who said, "You shouldn't swim in there, the schistosomiasis is bad. If you get a stomachache, go and get some pills immediately." I didn't even know what she'd said. So I looked it up on Google. Schistosomiasis was also called bilharzia, and, if it wasn't tough to pronounce, it was even worse to read about.

In layman's term, it was called "snail fever." Tiny little snails penetrate the body through the skin then lodge onto the liver and kidneys, creating offspring in the shape of worms. The worms go everywhere and create stomach issues, cold-like symptoms, skin rash, and, if not treated, can get into your brain, causing severe neurological disease. Like Malaria, roughly 200M people suffer from this in Africa.[21] I had just swum a kilometer through the lake of death. How could that be? The water was so crystal clear, and I doubted there could there be anything harmful in there.

In the evenings, we would sing karaoke and dance at the Gecko Lounge. One night the festivities were hosted by my scuba guide, who was raising money for a non-profit that was lobbying the government to stop oil drilling in Lake Malawi. The drilling would kill tourism in the area, and the mercenaries had no plans to share profits with those who needed it most. Profits prioritized over people.

The last day, I parted ways with my Peace Corps friends who were adventurous, positive, and always uplifting. One of them told me, "You learn so much every day by just traveling here, seeing the people, and doing new things. That in and of itself is mental strain. Give yourself credit for that." I'd never thought that just being in a new environment is a mental challenge before.

After our goodbyes, I started looking for a ride south and met some British doctors who just happened to have a seat in their car. In return for gas and lunch, they gave me a ride to Blantyre, a city in Southern Malawi. There, I'd meet another entrepreneurship center.

Blantyre was much smaller than Lilongwe. I bunked down at a hotel within walking distance of both the tech accelerator and the university. I worked alongside Dineo, a super positive and upbeat South African lady who was establishing a local incubator called Dzuka Africa, and Arthur, a young entrepreneur with chutzpah trying to get an incubator called Incube8 off the ground.

It just so happened that Ron, the young friend I met in Uganda, was now in Malawi, and he wanted to hike Mount Mulanje on a three-day excursion. The hike was challenging with a few technical parts, but still doable for non-rock climbers. It was a great way to end my mini-vacation.

I headed back to Lilongwe for a few days and reconnected with Vincent at a famous Korean restaurant.

"Vincent, why is this Korean restaurant here?"

"It's been here a long time. The politicians eat here." He spoke in a soft, soothing voice.

"So, I guess we will eat here again one day," I said.

"Ha-ha. Maybe."

"I was thinking, why not work with the other incubators in Zambia and Zimbabwe?"

"It's a good idea, and we all know each other. But it's difficult to work across borders."

"I can understand that. It's just an idea, and if we can do something, let me know." I wanted to help out.

"Thank you so much for your ideas and time. I really appreciate it." He was always courteous.

"It's no problem. I didn't do much, but I'd like to do something with you. What you do is an inspiration."

"Thank you. We just do our best with what we have."

"You do what you love." Vincent loved entrepreneurship as a way to empower others.

"Yes, mHub loves entrepreneurship, and I'm so grateful I do this."

"Even in a difficult economic environment, you just keep on. That's impressive."

"We can't change the economy; we can only help it. Thanks to the US Embassy for the funds as well."

"How much do they fund you if I may ask?"

"Oh, it's not much, maybe $10,000 for one year." He replied.

"That's not much to fund a business center of a hundred people."

"No, but it's enough to do what we love, and for the small profits we make, we're grateful." His comment reminded me of the quote in The Boy Who Harnessed the Wind, "Our profit is that we live."

"So, we will meet again?"

"Yes, let's meet in DC at the end of the Mandela program. We will all gather there for a week."

"What will you do there?"

"Not sure of the schedule except that we take part in workshops centered around creating opportunities in Africa and networking."

"Sounds like a place I should go." I liked networking and meeting people, or at least I used to.

"Please join me. I'll let you know the schedule." He was the third person I'd met going.

"Thank you."

"Zikomo." That meant "no problem; take it easy." We discussed the idea of working together alongside startups in Zambia or Zimbabwe. If we created a broader market opportunity, maybe we might entice more investors. The idea resonated and formed the beginning of Southern Africa Venture Partners with the other business incubators in Zimbabwe and Zambia. I was so excited to have a project and a reason to return to Africa.

That was the last night I spent in Malawi—relaxed and calm. Despite being one of the most impoverished countries in the world, they struck me as one of the richest in compassion, warmth, and soul. I vowed to emulate their soft-spoken, an overly polite voice in all my relationships going forward.

An Easter procession on the way to Lake Malawi

Lake Mulawi from a mountain top

Mount Mulanje in Malawi

Chapter 20

UGANDA: SEEING PEOPLE AS SOULS

*"If you never looked in the mirror, there would be
nothing to fear, nor feelings that needed care . . ."*
—KD

'll admit this wasn't exactly how the trip went as I had a quick stop in Kenya before heading to Uganda again. For the sake of ease, I'll just start quickly back in Rwanda, where I grabbed a bus to Uganda and work my way back east. I was excited to go back to Uganda because I had loved the kindness and gentleness of the people there. It left a deep impression on my first visit. This trip would prove even more impactful: It brought closure on my thoughts on racism and another closure with Jenny. First, I was bound for the western hills of Uganda to fulfill my work at ReapLifeDig.

Jenny and I had been WhatsApping.

"Are you ready to run?"

"Not really. If drinking beers on the lake is training, then yes."

"Get in shape; you only have a week." She liked to push.

"I either got it now, or I don't," I remarked.

"You can make progress in a week; anyway, let me know when you will arrive in mBale."

"Sweet."

"Why do you want to see me, anyway?" she pried.

"I like you. I think you are interesting and different."

"Oh, is that it? I'm sure you think that way of many."

"Cute, too. I want to kiss you on the neck." I sent a voice memo.

"Stop it. This isn't getting you anywhere."

"OK. OK. We can spend some time together and get to know each other better."

"That's better; now, I'm listening."

It was as if she was teaching me a game of "How to get the girl." At the sprawling and hectic Kigali bus depot in Rwanda, I met Kendra, who I'd met in Rwanda at the hostel. She had invited me to volunteer at ReapLifeDig in the west of Uganda. An American from Boston, she had dirty, blonde-red hair, blue eyes, and a determined look on her face. We crammed into the taxi with a few others and passed through Eastern Rwanda's lush Rift Valley to the Ugandan frontier. I was keen for a rolex—and nobody makes rolex (rolled-eggs, remember?) better than a Ugandan. I knew it would be waiting on the other side of the border and made a beeline to the nearest stall as soon as we were across.

Kendra was not unlike many Peace Corp women I'd met. Tough. Smart. Fit. Equally beautiful inside as outside. She was always on the lookout: nothing could rattle her, no one could get one by her, and nothing made her madder than not to pay the local price. After I paid $1 for a $.20 rolex, she flipped out on me telling me I got the mzungu (white person) price, and now she'd have to pay the same. I wasn't allowed to negotiate anymore, and we continued to our destination, Kisoro. I felt like she was rubbing in my poor negotiation skills, which I already knew I had from negotiating my employment contracts.

The following morning, Kendra and I jumped on a motorbike and made our way along the winding roads, stopping only for a quick milk tea. Then we continued to Lake Bunyonyi. A lake that floated amidst emerald green hills patch-worked with agricultural fields. Magnificent was not the word. This lake was a pristine, serene, and seemingly untouched part of the world.

ReapLifeDig sought to improve the nutrition and health of HIV-affected and at-risk people in the Batwa community through sustainable gardening.

The Uganda government chased the Batwa people from the national parks in 1990 for conservation purposes—that is to say, to sell carbon credits to China. A carbon credit is a tradable certificate representing the right to emit one ton of carbon dioxide. These people and their lives were the side of the carbon credit market that you'd never heard about. They lived in clusters of small families and had no farming background; previously, they'd hunted, gathered fruit, and harvested other forest products like bamboo for income. ReapLifeDig's mission was to teach these former hunters to be farmers.

Kendra was driven and energetic, motivating people to get to work preparing the soil, planting crops, and using soap as a pesticide. She was not only a determined leader but also a caring host, ensuring we had enough to eat every day and that coffee was ready in the morning. She also trained me in the art of bucket showers or I should say she said, "You do know how to take bucket showers, don't you?" *Of course I did, cough cough.* First, I needed to fetch some water and boil it. How do we do that? She noticed that I didn't have much of an appetite. I told her I was struggling with a brick in my stomach. Her response was, "TIA—this is Africa, tough it out."

I shook it off and went for a run. Each evening, I trained for the upcoming Uganda marathon. Locals would sometimes join me on long runs into the bucolic hills. One day I ran up the mountain that rose behind the village with kids trailing me all the way. After a scramble over rocks and past a small waterfall, I finally reached a pass where there were incredible views across what seemed like growing mountains below. These were the rough crags of the Rwenzori Mountains, the highest in Africa, rising into the horizon. In this vast landscape of green, I could imagine dinosaurs sauntering below, a scene I would never forget. As I sat in awe, a kid tagged my arm and pointed at the sun, just wavering above the distant hills. It was time to go home.

Half-way down, I stopped to say goodbye, but the kids wanted to see my phone and watch. Right when I took a selfie, their eyes lit up in amazement and screamed. I didn't know what was happening. They touched the screen on their faces and smiled. Imagine that. These kids had never seen their faces.

I ran down the hill faster and faster until I got to the house. Back in my room, I sat on the exposed couch springs and typed:

If you never looked in the mirror
There would be nothing to fear
Nor feelings that needed care
If you never saw your face
True loved ones would be simple to trace
And strangers would have no race
If you did not think about your features
Helping others could be your teacher
And we'd have respect for every creature

The week of my arrival was also the first week for Kendra's new director, Chris Festo. He was educated in Kampala and, shortly after I met him, he received a scholarship to study plant agribusiness in North Dakota. He invited me to his home and explained the history of the village, as well as how rich people from Kampala were building vacation homes to show off their wealth.

As we walked around, we'd stop to watch a soccer game, visit a school, and even attended a funeral once. Compared to the grim funerals, funeral homes, and religious ceremonies in the West, this was a celebratory community gathering of singing and prayer. Instead of crying, people rejoiced in life, drinking beer and wine, even slaughtering animals. In the evenings, they held a night vigil where neighbors were required to come. Chris told me that family members fined those who didn't show up. In many ways, this was the developed world, far ahead of what we perceived as progress in the United States and Europe. Attending a funeral can calm the soul. In the end, we all end up in the same place.

One evening at the house, the village chief arrived quite upset—and visibly drunk—complaining that I didn't have permission to be there.

"You are a madman!" he shouted at me, "You are running all over the place and up in the mountains. The people think you are crazy. We don't run up the mountains in Uganda; only crazy people run around like you."

"I'm kind of crazy." I replied, "It's true, but I'm training for a marathon. What's the big deal?"

He looked aghast at Kendra, maintaining his position, "He even admits he is crazy. We don't run in Africa like that, and we don't go up in the mountains.

So please act normal." After a long conversation, Kendra finally subdued him and paid him off.

He was dead wrong about one thing: Africans can run. Just over the eastern border in Kenya was home to the Kenyan marathoners, some of the most accomplished distance runners in the world—yet another example of just how different each African country can be. I'd recently learned that there was even a High Altitude Training Centre in Iten, located in the Rift Valley of Western Kenya. It was on my list.

On my final day with ReapLifeDig, I wrapped up my time with Chris and Kendra and was thankful for all that I had learned about farming. Who would have thought that soap on plants could keep the bugs away?

After returning to Kisoro, I decided to hike Mount Muhabura, an extinct volcano in the Virunga Mountains that rose to 4,127 meters (13,540 feet). It took me about four hours to summit, arriving at a crater lake surrounded by large succulents and with a light fog blanketing the peak. I meditated for a while and snacked on an apple as it was the only thing I could digest—it was strange because, on a hike like that, I usually could scarf down anything.

The next day I was so sore I had to walk lightly because my quads were so painful. I hadn't climbed that much in one day since climbing Mount Rinjani in Indonesia. And after this rest day, I'd be running a half marathon. I wasn't worried, but I wasn't ready either. Getting on the bus to Masaka, I enjoyed how the tiredness in my body calmed my mind. The bus ride was about eight or ten hours, and I arrived at about two o'clock in the morning. Forget being in Africa. Getting off a bus anywhere in the middle of the night was worrisome. *Dial up high alert*, I thought.

I walked out of the bus and glanced around, surveying the situation. The bus stop was somewhat busy, with a few dozen people hanging around on motorbikes, chatting, or what it seemed like playing games on the street. I wasn't sure who to trust. A few bikers approached me. They gently asked me if I needed a ride. That's when a ton of bricks dropped square on top of my head. I sat down, lifted a finger indicating I needed a minute, and held my head in my hands. Seeing that I was dehydrated, one responded, "Take your time," and went to get me a bottle of water.

Out of the darkness, an epiphany struck: voices spoke to me, "What on Earth are these souls doing in the middle of the night?" It struck me that I had not said "black" or "African" or whatever. I'd said, "souls." When I'd said that, fear had vanished because what I saw in that person was that they were a person just like me and that, to them, I was just a soul who needed a ride and a water bottle. That was it! It was one of the most magical moments in Uganda. To this day, I no longer see a person first. I see a soul.

In my euphoric state, I jumped on the back of someone's bike, and he whisked me down the dirt road. After fifteen minutes, I saw a gigantic light reflecting off large tin foil structures that were at least 10 meters (30 feet high). I honestly thought it was some top-secret alien spacecraft. The closer we got, the louder the screeches, and the more I was hit by bugs in my face and shoulder. I caught an insect on my shirt, grabbed it; opening my hand, I saw it was a cricket. OMG! It was a cricket and grasshopper farm. They were catching them to sell and eat.

The next morning at Hotel Brovad's swimming pool, I finally met Jenny again. She was wearing a bikini top with a flowing blue-yellow beach sarong. When our eyes met, my heart melted. She gave me a long hug and a kiss like we were lost lovers. We hung around that afternoon, chatted, swam, and relaxed before the half marathon. The Uganda marathon was a week-long charity event where people came, volunteered, soaked in the local culture, and then celebrated at the end by running a marathon.

Breakfast was a regular hotel buffet with, of course, rolex. Then we warmed up for the marathon, making hip-hop-inspired moves. While warming-up, I met a black guy about my age from Atlanta who used to play American college football and was built like a defensive end. He told me that he traveled around the globe and ran marathons for charity. "People suffer, so I suffer," was his explanation. We paced together for the first five miles through the undulating dirt roads passing through tiny villages where crowds gathered to cheer us along. I finished with a time of around 2 hours and 30 minutes—not bad, even with a quarter-mile ascent towards the end. It was brutal in the heat, and I was knackered.

Jenny and I caught up that night at the hotel. We decided to share a room to keep costs down, of course. After showers, we sat on the bed, just looking at each other.

"That was fun, wasn't it?" Jenny finally broke the silence.

"It was awesome, but hot out there. I don't know how anyone could bear the heat after the half and continue on the full. No way."

Jenny nodded. "That guy you were talking to ran the full marathon. He looked like he was going to die when I saw him pass the half marathon point."

"'People suffer, so he suffers,' he said. I guess that's one way to make an impact."

"I only ran 5K, but that was enough, and I could use a massage."

"Turn around; I'm a master." My fingers pressed into her back and her shoulder.

"That's a bit too hard, mister." She moved away.

"Sorry I like deep tissue. The more pain, the better."

"I know you are masochistic. So why aren't you married and all that?"

Working my ten fingers down to the small of her back, I felt excitement tingle through my fingers. "Honestly, it's because I'm a madman."

"To me, you seem pretty normal, easy to get along with."

"Yeah, that's a façade. There is nothing easy to get along with here."

"Like what?"

"I work, travel, and love challenges and new things. I have a novelty gene. I'm always trying to find the next thing, the newest thing." I put my right hand on her shoulder, tugging her ever so gently closer to me.

"That could be a problem. Why do you stay so busy?"

I felt the warmth of her hand on my leg through my entire body. "I don't know. I guess we all want to change the world, right?"

"Maybe you need to make yourself happy before you try to do that?"

"Yeah, I'm working on it. This trip certainly has given me a different perspective."

"You seem a little calmer than when I met you last. You know, few people change the world," she said softly.

Calm was not how I would have described myself at the moment.

"I know. I'm just saying I'd like to help out. Haven't done much till now," I opined.

"It's not like you are a bad person. Hopefully, Africa taught you not to put too much pressure on yourself."

"Yes, I'm definitely more relaxed."

"I'm getting more relaxed." She responded by turning her head toward me. I tenderly traced the line of her cheekbone and her jaw. "I guess I'd like to get to know why you want to change the world at some point, but not right now." She leaned closer to me.

"Then, when."

"Shut up and kiss me."

There was nothing like the use of lingering endorphins in the bedroom. We passed out delightfully and knowingly. The next morning we took a car back to Kampala, and I kept playing the country song, "Body Like a Back Road," by Sam Hunt on repeat until we found a decent hotel to celebrate our run and budding relationship. There, we'd have more time to get to know each other.

Chapter 21

VENTURING WITH VALUES, VIGOR, AND VERVE

"The entrepreneurs are driven to build systems that can eventually sustain
themselves and, ultimately, serve a wide swath of the population."
—**Jacqueline Novogratz** in The Blue Sweater

J enny and I spent the days in Kampala flirting and enjoying our new
romance. In the mornings, we lounged around the hotel, while she worked,
writing on a non-profit grant. In the afternoons, we went to open-aired
bars to have a few drinks and talk the afternoon away. Sadly, we had only a few
days before I headed to Kenya to hike Mount Kilimanjaro. *Always on the move,*
I thought.

One afternoon, Jenny and I connected with Brett via an introduction from
Jeremy, who would later join me to hike Kilimanjaro. Brett was tallish, with a
full head of short hair, a lean stature, and a deceptively youthful appearance. He
didn't let the ups and downs of international life and business get him down; he
used them as fuel (along with daily yoga and cocktails). He also had a knack for
languages (French and Chinese), and a curious mind that was an asset in his line
of work. He had an equally adventurous and enterprising wife, Rosa, who shared
his commitment to making the world a better place. Hanging out with them

made me think that sharing the same, unique path in life might be a recipe for a successful relationship.

I first met Brett around 2001 in Hong Kong, where I was working at GE Asia Pacific Capital in a finance role looking at investments around the Asia Pacific region. He was also in the venture investment business, running his early stage, technology accelerator business. Since the dot-bomb days, as he said, he had completely changed his path. Most recently, he and his family had moved to Uganda, where he founded the World Food Program's Global Post-Harvest Knowledge and Operations Centre. I was curious about how he arrived here and wanted to learn more about the World Food Program (WFP) and its mission to solve world hunger.

We met up at Que Pasa, a Mexican restaurant with Rosa, who had also been a tech executive in Hong Kong and China, and their two daughters, Margaux and Océane. After dinner, we went to Bush Pig, a backpacker's hostel that had great mojitos. I did not know this before I visited Kampala, but it was one of the nightlife capitals of Africa—if not the entire world. It also became clear throughout the evening that this was one of the reasons why Brett and Rosa enjoyed Kampala so much. All restaurants were alfresco, as were most of the endless nightclubs.

"Brett, I can't believe we met so long ago when you were a venture investor."

"I remember you vaguely; in fact, look here. Your old business card." He could pull up any business card of anyone he'd met. He even knew I was a rather good Japanese speaker. Come on, who does that!?

"Holy cow! That's amazing. So tell me. How'd you get from there to here?"

"Post-tech-bubble crash, I decided to get into working on big world problems, not just tech stuff. It took a long time to convince anyone that I could make a difference but finally found a way. Never could have done it without the support—emotional and financial—offered by Rosa."

"How'd you make the transition?" Seeing as I was in a transition, I wanted to know more.

"The first step—and in hindsight, one of the most important—was becoming a stay-home dad. Those years with Margaux, born in 2003, were and remain incredibly valuable. When I think of the nature of the world's problems, and the lack of empathy and compassion, much of it can be traced back to the failure of parenting. To be able to dedicate time to Margaux, family, and my development as a human being was an incredible luxury."

During that period, Brett told me he also created Overseas Vote to help voters register for US elections wherever they are in the world. It is now one of the most substantial overseas lobby organizations. Through Overseas Vote Foundation, Brett caught the Pentagon blocking voter registration for Americans in twenty-six countries and played a crucial role in forcing the US government to rescind the ban.

Brett continued. "Then, as serendipity happens, a close friend sat down at a wedding next to someone from the WFP, and I ended up joining them in 2005 to launch their private sector initiatives in Asia. They had never worked extensively with the private sector, and they asked me to kick off those activities."

"Amazing. I've been stuck in technology ever since Hong Kong. I can't take it anymore. It's soulless and ruthless."

"There is nothing wrong with being in tech or the private sector. It's the private sector where things really will change for the world's poor. It's the creation of steady jobs that will change the world, not the NGOs (non-profits that operate independently of government) and the United Nations." He paused and took a sip of his margarita. "That being said, our fund Incubasia was a failure—no debate there. It was bad timing. I was working with great people, but most of the ideas were five to ten years before their prime time. We had similar concepts as Airbnb, Expedia, Bayesian Statistical Analysis, but we were way too early in the marketplace."

"Timing, so much is timing," I said, trying to muster some words of wisdom.

"That's true. When the money dried up, and the world changed post 9-11, I wanted to do my part to help. It's always been part of the values my parents instilled in me—and still keep reminding me of."

"Awesome, to just shift like that. I looked at ways to do things but never thought I could. Never knew how to get involved."

Brett's values had propelled his life's mission. How powerful.

"It was not easy. No one wanted a private sector person in their organization. It took me two and a half years to finally breakthrough. The irony is that the moment WFP agreed to give me a try, I got calls every week from other NGOs and UN organizations. Anyway, what did you do in tech?"

"Finance and sales stuff," I lowered my voice.

"Today non-profits love business people who can raise money. They are always looking for that. So that's something to consider as you look around. How's your Chinese?"

"Not great, but I can converse at the dinner table. You know, better than taxi talk but not to the level of business."

"Lots of Chinese money is contributing to the non-profit world. We just closed on some funding from Tencent—you know Wechat, right? My Chinese came in handy there. We set a Guinness World Record for the greatest number of donors in 24 hours, thanks to a Wechat collaboration."

"That's good to know. It's nice to see the Chinese giving back, as well. Where is the funding going?"

"The World Food Program at the United Nations. We raise money and work to prevent post-harvest losses. Farmers across Africa lose 30 to 40 percent of their harvests within months, as they have no safe way to store food. But there are simple ways to almost completely stop these losses—grain that is well dried can be stored for years in hermetic (airtight) storage. The insects suffocate on their CO_2. And these airtight storage bags and silos work for all grains."

"That's amazing. How's it going?"

"The numbers may sound big: we reached 650,000 farming families in just over three years in sixteen countries, but there are over 200 million smallholder families who would benefit in Africa's fifty-five countries. So honestly, we are just getting started."

"Sounds like you are making progress. Start small, as they say in Silicon Valley."

"This simple intervention—airtight storage—changes the game for Africa's smallholder farming families. We empower the local farmers and store owners to buy and sell the bags at a discount. They will sustain the project. So yes, the entrepreneurs have the opportunity to solve their challenges—Nobel Peace Prizes will be awarded for this one day."

"Entrepreneurship seems to be the key to empowerment and sustainment. I've come to realize this during my travels as well." I looked over at his kids and said, "You have some cool parents. Be thankful."

Margaux, the eldest in her early teens, smiled.

"How many countries you been to?" I asked.

"Fifty-ish and a refugee camp."

"You are fourteen and been to fifty countries." I couldn't believe it. "When I was your age, I'd only been to a few states and Canada and Cancun, Mexico."

"That's not a bad thing either," Brett chimed in.

"Ha-ha. I'm just saying. That little bit made me the explorer I am today. You are the future, young lady, but don't forget us, little people. What was the refugee camp like, and how'd you get there?"

"My mom and I went to work with a small non-profit. It was really sad." She responded.

"Oh, I can imagine. I'm planning to go to one in Kakuma. Have any tips?"

"Bring lots of water. Wear suntan lotion. Just be nice to people and smile. Oh, and bring an open mind." She already knew the keys to travel. A smile breaks down all cultural barriers a friend once told me, and an open mind allows for learning about other cultures.

"It's mind-blowing. Check it out. Makes you appreciate even more what you have," said Brett.

Brett's conversation rekindled a thought: how could I make a life in Africa? I wondered if it would be for me. He and Rosa had worked hard for many years and invested wisely, so they'd had the latitude to make the shift to the non-profit world. Would I ever squirrel away enough wealth to do the same? *Screw it; I don't need to,* I thought. *Start now, start small.* Vibrations magnified that night; I could feel them ripple throughout my body. (Brett has recently launched Harvest Solutions—a social enterprise focused on reducing the post-harvest loss for the 200M smallholder families. Contact Brett if you'd like to help.[22])

As our time was running out, I wanted to ask Jenny to come with me to Nairobi.

"Want to come to Nairobi?" I asked.

"I have to get back; I have six more months before my contract is up," she said super matter-of-fact.

"Oh. Well, it was great getting to know you."

"You know, you aren't so bad to hang out with. Don't tell yourself little lies." She was boosting me up.

"Aw . . . thanks, I appreciate it." I blushed.

"We should stay in touch and meet back in the States."

"Yes, we should, but . . . umm."

"What? Umm, what? You know I like you, and I want to see where this can go." I gave her the sales push.

"Maybe, but I think we should stay friends," she pushed back.

"Friends? Like, really? Did I do something wrong?"

"No, not at all. You did everything right—even your sweet kisses."

"So, what's the problem?"

"I'm kinda married—am taking a break right now."

"Kinda married?!" I got dizzy, hands sweaty, and lights were blinking in my eyes.

"I don't know what to say. Sorry, I didn't tell you, but I didn't think it mattered. Right, you must have women everywhere."

"Uh no, not really . . . not." I swallowed hard. *Why do I always give women that impression?* I thought.

"Well, look, give yourself a break. You have a kind heart, and your experience here is solidifying that further. Don't lose that. I should get going." She kissed and hugged me, holding it for a minute.

And that was it. Give myself a break? *She is the married one,* I thought. I hopped in my taxi, and she, on her boda boda motorbike. For some reason, I wasn't depressed nor angry—only shocked. Strangely, it felt right to let it go. I don't know why; maybe it wasn't meant for me, or perhaps I had learned to deprioritize my wants. The Buddha said, "In the end, only three things mattered: How much you loved, how gently you lived, and how gracefully you let go of things not meant for you."

But this didn't just hold for interpersonal relationships and how one interacts with the other. Perhaps it was symbolic of moving on from old careers, old relationships in companies and love, and whatever holds us down. The ego wants to hold onto things, keep things, and bring Jenny back. When the ego disappeared, the universe can take its course; it's a much better way to live.

On the way to Nairobi, I received a text from Tessa: "How are you doing? Where are you?"

"Leaving Uganda and heading to Kenya to go to a refugee camp then to hike Mt. Kilimanjaro."

"Is it safe there?"

"Yes, I have a host, and they assured me it is fine. I'm more worried about my stomach, though. I can't settle it."

"Go see a doctor if you aren't well."

"I'll keep tabs on it."

"OK, keep me informed and send pictures of the hiking."

Chapter 22

KEEPING PACE WITH THE KENYANS

"Train Hard, Win Easy when you come to the race in your singlet, you'll fly."
—Kenyan Marathon Runners

t was as if this journey had trained me to handle anything that Africa could throw at me. By now, Africa felt like home: chaotically organized, fearfully fun, and forever novel. Many things were coming full circle. I had lost my old identity and started to discover more meaningful paths. Besides, I had learned much about history, slavery, and even faced racism myself, only to find out that first impressions aren't everything: people are souls first. With a recent dose of good loving from Jenny—dumping aside—I was confident I could take on anything. The plan was to teach at a local business accelerator, then meet Toto at his non-profit in Kisumu on the west side of Kenya. Other than that, it was an open schedule.

At first, I stayed at the Manyatta Backpackers Hostel, which was located in the heart of the city, close to Uhuru park. A few travelers from different countries were bouncing in and out from Mount Kenya, Mombasa, and the Maasai Mara. It all sounded interesting but didn't tickle me. It didn't take me long to catch up with my Congo hiking buddy, Aurore. With her Ph.D. assignment complete, she was about to return to France but took the time to introduce me to some of her local friends. She'd suggested I visit Kakuma Refugee Camp and assured me it was safe but warned me I'd be sleeping on a dirt floor during my visit. She connected me with Innocent, one of the leaders in the camp.

A few days later, Innocent and I had a Skype call. He was adamant that I needed to bring something useful to teach those in the camp. That was easy— entrepreneurship was my game—and he was super excited to learn from a so-called Silicon Valley executive. He assured me everything was great and asked me to bring certificates to give out to people. That would make it official and entice them to join my class. He made it sound like it was easy to get there. After traveling with Toto, I would catch a flight to Lodwar and a quick taxi to Kakuma.

As I settled into the rhythm of life in Nairobi, I decided to enroll in a Kiswahili class with a local language school, the Language School of Nairobi. It offered me a place to stay in an apartment building that was located in Kilimani. The area was alive with activity: Chinese hotels and casinos, upscale shopping centers, movie theaters, and fruit vendors all competed for space on its heavily-trafficked streets. It was also here that Andela was based—Mark Zuckerberg had invested $24 million into this education center for engineers. Just down the road was Mama Oliech, a famous fish eatery. Kilimani was also home to several tech startups like M-Kopa, a company founded by a British American team financed by overseas technology investors.

At that time, I started some basic one-on-one sales sessions with companies and volunteered at iHub, where I met great entrepreneurial minds trying to build companies in Nairobi. During one session, I met Jael Amara, an established entrepreneur who was more interested in who I was than what I was saying.

She stared at my oversized Garmin watch.

"You a runner?" she asked.

"Yeah," I replied.

"Well, let's go for a run then." Jael was as sharp as she was fast on her feet. She was curious, trusting, and welcoming, but sprinkled enough skepticism on top to keep you at arm's length. I wouldn't race her nor arm wrestle her, but I would go into business with her.

Even though I felt weaker than usual, I agreed to go running. That day also happened to be the day that Kipchoge Keino was trying to break the two-hour marathon record. We decided to reconvene at Java Kileleshwa, a local coffee chain, and watch him live on YouTube. We'd run after coffee if the weather permitted. Keino ended up achieving a time of two hours and one minute— easily beating my half marathon time. On another attempt a year or so later, Keino would break the record. Just watching him fueled my desire to run with Kenyans.

Dressed in our running clothes while sipping on caramel lattes, we chatted.

"So, let's talk about what you are doing in Kenya." She played with her phone to get the race live. In reality, it was less exciting to watch than it appeared to be. Really what it was one guy running next to a car with a film crew.

"I'm just learning about it. I like to travel and such, checking it out."

"You are a traveler? Where else?"

"Lived in Asia for ten years. China and Japan."

"I lived in China, too, when I was younger. My father was a diplomat." I was excited to learn that she, too, was a citizen of the world.

"Cool, so you've been around?"

"Mostly everywhere. I spend some time in NYC, too; my boyfriend is there. So why are you going around all of Africa?"

"To know the continent you have to see the different parts. It's like Asia. You can get a small taste in one spot, but the countries are so different. It's the same in Africa, too."

"I get it. What do you want to do here in Kenya?"

"Make friends and check out startups. Kenya seems like an innovation and investment hub. It's exciting here."

"Yes, it is. But still challenging. There is no fast money here."

"I doubt there is anywhere."

"Silicon Valley?"

"I didn't find it, but that's the impression everyone gets. Anyway, I'd like to see other parts of Kenya. I will go to Kisumu," I said.

"Kisumu? That's my hometown. Why?"

"My friend, Toto, has a non-profit there."

"Toby?"

"No, Toto? Who is Toby?"

"He is an American who built the largest children's non-profit in East Africa. Big runner, too."

"I'd love to meet him. Why all the runners here?" I asked.

"We are the home of the world's greatest marathoners. They train in Iten, which is close by Eldoret, where Toby is located. You should go. You can run with them."

"That would be friggin' awesome. Run with the Kenyans!"

"Yes, you must do it. There are many places to stay like at Lornah—a training center for athletes." She paused. "Look, you seem like a good guy. You can crash at my place and also meet my sister, Mercy. Since you are in and out, just make like home with us."

"That's the nicest thing ever. Sure, I'll do it."

"And let's eat BBQ from Kenya. It's called Nyama Choma."

"Sounds good to me."

We went around town a bit, and she introduced me to her sister, Mercy. Mercy was a bit shorter and more petite than Jael but no less mighty. Both of them worked out every morning—running and lifting. Mercy coached field hockey and had the arms to show for it. They were women who had many shoes in their closets—high heels, running shoes, boxing shoes, and field hockey cleats. They were warm, kind, and compassionate, embodying the Kenyan spirit of "hard work, perseverance, and hustle"—all with a strong desire to improve Kenya and their surroundings. On several nights, they hosted feasts with their fellow lady Kenyans while discussing projects and community events. As far as I could see, these women were the spirit of the town.

It was around this time that I noticed my energy levels drop off significantly. I wanted to go and work out with them, but the brick in my stomach kept me from it. Even worse, I also wasn't able to concentrate on language studies as much as I'd hoped. I attributed it to the weariness of life on the road and pushed it to the back of my mind as I made plans to leave Nairobi.

Aside from the crazy traffic jams in the morning and evening rush hours, I realized that getting around Nairobi wasn't as complicated as I had assumed.

Public service vehicles (locally known as matatus) swarmed the streets and were easy to jump off and on. Although buses seemed to be the most popular mode of transport, motorbikes were also common—albeit a bit dangerous. Like most major cities, the Kenyan capital also had cheap Uber rides and several other taxi apps, including Little Cabs and Bolt.

Hopping from one place to another, I noticed that Nairobi enjoyed a high level of diversity in terms of economic development. A city with cranes and construction, shopping malls, and hotels with casinos—primarily targeted at Chinese overseas workers—and university after university. There were also enormous slums such as Kibera, where tens of thousands of people lived in impoverished and downtrodden conditions. While Nairobi was a hub for East Africa's investment and economic development, once again, the divide between the rich and the poor was vivid. I started to think it's everywhere—even in the USA—if you just care to look.

At the bus terminal in Nairobi, I watched the graffiti-clad painted buses roll in and out. They depicted scenes from near and far—Obama, Mandela, rock 'n' roll bands, NBA players, and even fire-flaming baseballs. It was an artistic expression at its best. This entertainment geared me to up hop on board and see more of Kenya.

Around four hours' drive west of Nairobi, I ended up in Nakuru. There weren't too many cars on the road since it was the weekend. We stopped a few times along the way to get beetroot, mango, and avocado smoothies—the best thing EVER. There we stopped into a local orphanage called Melon Mission established by a local family. Joyce Ciru recruited other foreigners and me to visit and experience working in an orphanage and school. They are in the process of building a better school, so check it out and donate.

The next day, I hopped another bus to Kisumu to meet with Toto. It was great to see a familiar face. He picked me up in a white minivan spotted brown with mud and with a few folks from his team. On the drive, I listened as he narrated how he'd raised enough money to build a volunteer dorm and a care center where he'd once couch surfed. The woman, Mama Dolfine, who founded the center, had asked for his help, and he'd made it his mission to support this place. Downright amazing!

He told me the story. "I wanted to help and thought the best way was to bring more helping hands to the center. I thought if we built this crazy yellow dome home, we'd get media attention, and volunteers would come and experience the work Mama Dolfine was doing for the children. They'd connect with the center just like I did when I first came in 2012. And it all happened just like that!"

Getting a dose of Toto's thoughts was like reading an entire philosophy book. However, I couldn't help but think of the white savior complex I kept hearing about on my trip.

"And what do you think about the white savior complex?" I asked.

"It's a pretty real thing. There are lots of stories where white people come to Africa, see the misery from their perspective, and run to help. They all have good intentions, but often no one asked for help, and they didn't ask if help was invited."

"And what about you?"

"Well, here's the difference. This care center was started by Mama Dolfine, a local widow from this community. She knows each and every family, and they know her. So, she knows best what is needed here. All I do is help her."

"How do you help?"

"Basically, I started this as a three-month project to bring volunteers to the center and help with resources. But now it has become its own thing—a foundation that sponsors high school education and runs mentorship programs beyond school holiday camps. It's called the Better Me Foundation."

"So why the name?"

"A better world starts with a better me. I've had a long spiritual journey that led me to the realization that everything starts within. I felt called to share this wisdom with others. It's a lesson in life, a deeper perspective, a focus on giving."

"That's really deep."

"Ha yea . . . you know me. I'm not a shallow guy! We are almost there. You'll see, there is another group that is visiting us too."

"Who is that?"

"The Ripple Effect Project. They are families from Maine who have been coming for a few years to help out with the school. They are good, kind people."

Today, the school assists more than 350 orphaned and vulnerable children, some of whom have HIV but no place to call home. There wasn't much to the original rundown, wooden house, and iron-sheet structures, but Toto managed to build a large yellow sustainable dome home, as he calls it, to house overseas guests. Behind the house was a small school featuring four rooms split into eleven classrooms where the students attend lessons. It was the most make-shift school I'd ever seen, but it didn't matter because the students loved it. Today, a new solid-state school building stands.

What amazed me was Toto's unrivaled ability to recruit people to visit, help, and donate to this charitable organization. A visionary coupled with incredible sales skills, he made me realize that you can do anything if you want to make a difference, and it's as simple as responding to someone's "Can you help me?"

Next, I made my way up to Eldoret, where I was looking forward to meeting Toby, a friend of Jael's. Jael told me that he was a crazy and amazing American guy who'd built the largest children's hospital in Africa, Shoe4Africa. Toby was tall, lanky in stature, and bounded like a deer when he walked, which came from his running habit of clocking around 40 miles per week. He took me to the hospital, which—true to Jael's description—was massive, like any other hospital in the west. He'd built it after raising a few million dollars from over 11,000 donors. Inside, the facility had beds and some modern equipment, yet needed much more to take care of all the patients.

Toby shared his story and some of his encounters in Africa. It started when he was a professional athlete twenty years ago and came to Kenya to train, often running on a beach in Mombasa. One day while running, a few thieves struck him on the head with a pipe, took his shoes, what little money was in his pocket, and left him for dead on the beach. After awakening, he ran over two miles to pick up his motorbike before driving into town, all with a fractured skull, finally arriving at a barren and empty medical clinic. Two days later, he received antibiotics, and it wasn't until eleven days later—plagued by complications—that he flew to London, where brain surgery saved his life.

During his traumatic experience, he'd experienced the poor state of medical facilities in Kenya and felt compelled to make things better. A year after his incident, he returned to Kenya, initially starting a foundation that gifted shoes, which led to building schools and this enormous hospital in the middle of nowhere. Now he was raising money to build a cancer center, a kitchen, a sustainable garden, and a sports area. Here was a man on an undeterred mission to give these kids a chance to live a better life.

Later that day, one of Toby's friends, Kevin, joined us. An African American, he'd attended Harvard Kennedy School before opening up a non-profit in East Africa called Cross World Africa. Their mission was to help Kenyans get into universities abroad, particularly the Ivy League, though I wasn't sure why that was a priority. I appreciated his passion for education and how he'd spun his fundraising pitch: "Don't go out drinking for one night; instead, buy books and food. Don't go out drinking for a week; we can buy cows for a family. Don't drink for a month; we can pay quarterly tuition." *That's a lot of drinking for the Ivy League,* I thought, but *it's a dose of perspective.*

Both Toby and Kevin annually ran the New York City marathon as a way to raise funds for their respective charities. I committed that I would do it with them in the next few years. But first, I had to get training. They advised me on the best way to get to Iten, Kenya's running headquarters, and left me with the departing words: "Don't try to keep up!"

Situated at an elevation of 2,400 meters (7,800 feet), Iten was a small highland town in Kenya that's been nicknamed, "The Spiritual Home of Running." Despite its dirt roads and scattering of shops and hotels, it's famed as a training center for Kenya's middle- and long-distance runners, with a magnificent backdrop of rolling hills along the eastern side of the Rift Valley.

In Iten, I found the Lornah facility, which was founded by Lornah Kiplagat, who was born and raised in Iten before moving to the Netherlands in 1999 and becoming a Dutch citizen. Lornah had competed at the Olympics and earned money through sponsorships. Then she funded the center for elite athletes—both overseas and locals. The facility was top notch with an outside swimming pool, weight rooms, and small apartments that—together with three meals a day— cost around $30 a night. While that was a lot for most Kenyans, it attracted travelers from places like Canada and Spain who were training for marathons and ultra-trail marathons.

Kenyan runners were staying outside the facility, and we'd meet up at 6 a.m. and 6 p.m. each day to run together and do hour-long ab workouts in the gym. One morning, we stopped by the small, neglected brick house—or room, I should say—of a local athlete. All he had was a small bed and two pairs of shorts, shirts, and shoes. Running was all he aspired to do; maybe it was all he could do.

Many of the local runners had sponsorship deals with athletic companies, which gifted the runners full-body sweatsuits and new running shoes. Even in the sweltering heat, they wore sweatsuits running through the valley. Why? "Train hard, win easy. When you come to the race in your singlet, you will fly." They lived by that motto. I learned a lot from the marathoners that week, even though I was seriously struggling to keep up and was always dehydrated—which was strange because I never got dehydrated. Growing up in the heat and humidity of South Carolina, I had pride in my ability to withstand the weather. I wasn't feeling myself, but I kept pushing. The Kenyans taught me much about running form, training methods, and eating habits.

How to Run

The Kenyan runners liked to talk and share their knowledge as well as train with other people, no matter what level you were. Timo Limo (who posts training pictures on Facebook) was training for the 200-meter qualifiers for the Kenyan national team and gave me some critical tips on form.

He told me to run with my hips, not my knees. Legs should arc in a large circle—think about making an arc with your knee up then extending out. The foot should strike in the middle to the ball of the foot. Don't hit the heel of the foot on the ground, or it could cause back pain. Then, the foot should spring forward, bounding like a deer. We even had a practice session that taught us how to run like a deer.

Posture was the center of the form. To run very erect—or even positioned as though you're falling back a little bit—minimized energy and effort. That was counter to my usual approach—I ran leaning over a tad, which put additional weight on the legs. Running erect meant running lighter; then, the legs could work more freely. At the same time, arms remained bent and didn't swing much;

they acted as a pacesetter, not a throttle (like sprinters use their elbow). The elbows stayed close to the body, pushing the shoulders back. This arm position helped to maintain a vertical posture. If all else fails, your running partner could smack you on the chest—which they kept doing to me to keep my back straight and to run faster.

How to Train

With the first session at 6 a.m. and the last at 6 p.m., they rotated sprint workouts, medium distance, long-distance, stationary bicycle, and abdominal exercises. There didn't seem to be any unique formula; aside from wearing their full-body sweat suits, it just depended on each runner.

Rolling hills surrounded Iten, so we're always running up and down slopes. The Kenyan runners encouraged us always to push and try to keep a constant pace while going up the hills—just as you would on the flat—without breaking stride. By doing this, lung capacity, measured by VO2 on my watch, would increase. For me, this was quite hard, mainly due to the altitude. One of my fellow runners said it would take me about four days to get acclimatized to the elevation of Iten. Indeed, the first few days were rather exhausting.

What to Eat

While there are loads of crazy energy drinks in the West, spanning many different elixirs, the Kenyan runners drank only water. Their diet consisted of light fish, vegetables, and yams, as well as rice and plantain for carbohydrates. Avoiding too much sugar was also recommended since endurance levels were more sustainable without sugar spikes.

The Kenyans had a unique, if simple way of training and running. It just required a dedicated routine: running twice a day, an elemental diet, and keen attention to running form.

During my six days at Lornah, I picked up my distance, but I felt increasingly fatigued, and my stomach felt heavy. I thought it was just the altitude and a stomach bug that I couldn't shake, so I took some antacids. That plus straining my Achilles while training on a stationary bike, I knew I wasn't going to be able to join a local half marathon the following day.

Instead, I attended a qualifying event for 400- and 800-meter runners from across East Africa. Scouts from around the world, including some American universities, attended. Many young runners competed for times, but there were also heats with older runners in their fifties and sixties. Kenyans just never stopped running. Despite my setbacks, I didn't plan to either.

I wasn't sure if it was my mental state or my body or both. I still couldn't shake the brick free, and I had a slightly protruding belly. *It must be my age, forty,* I thought. I'd been texting Innocent and planned to take the flight from Eldoret to Lodwar. I had to push on. I had to keep going. My mission wasn't complete. I wanted to experience the life of a refugee.

The villagers of Western Uganda at ReapLifeDig

Timo Limo and the runners training together at Lornah.

Brett, Jeremy, Rosa, Margo, and Jenny having dinner.

Farmers in Uganda on hay truck

Chapter 23

TO BE A REFUGEE, TO BE ANYTHING YOU WANT TO BE

"When you ask people living in desperately poor regions whether they would prefer to receive aid or work, they choose work because work gives them access to necessities and the long-term ability to procure."
—**Leila Janah** in *Give Work*

After an hour bus ride to Eldoret, I boarded the plane, receiving many curious stares. I consumed at least three coffees on that flight—more than my usual morning pick me up. But, I couldn't submit to this weakness. I wanted to discover what it was like to be a refugee with no country or identity pushed me on. I'd come to a point where I had scrapped my identity and was searching for a new one. *I have to push on,* I thought.

The city called Lodwar was one runway, a person with a cart who took the place of a baggage carousel, and a barbed-wire fence to keep people from rushing the plane to grab cargo. It was a cargo and transport center for the refugee camp. I walked around for thirty minutes, looking for a ride. The best I could find was a minibus full of boxes and supplies until someone approached me, pointing to a modern Japanese pickup truck and asking for a tip. I accepted: $20 bucks plus a

$5 tip sounded like a good deal to me. The drivers worked for the local telecom operator, appropriately named Safaricom.

It was not just hot in Turkana but "Africa hot," with the mercury consistently averaging 43-44°C/110°F. Driving through the desert along a potholed road, with the driver swerving to avoid the bumps, made me sweat profusely while my stomach churned. At one point, I had to ask them to stop so that I could dry heave—nothing came out. Back on the road, we chatted about the telecom industry and how the refugee camp was one of their most profitable areas. People were being sent money through their mobile telecom wallets (called mPesa) and used their phones to talk and text with friends and family in other countries. In Kenya, mobile payment usage was far ahead of what we had in the USA.

In the northwest of Turkana County, Kakuma is home to a UNHCR refugee camp where hundreds of thousands of people have fled from across Africa. On arrival in Kakuma, they dropped me off at a small lodge where my Congolese host, Innocent, was going to pick me up near the Kakuma airstrip—a private airstrip owned by the Catholic church and the Kenyan military where UN planes landed. When Innocent rolled in on his motorbike, he struck me as a cross between a professor and a businessman, cleanly shaven with glasses and wearing a colorful, collared shirt.

"Hallo!" He yelled, happy to meet me. "You look very good. Can you ride with me? I will take you to the hotel. Pardon my English. I'm still studying and taking my course online from a free-tuition American University."

"So, what other languages do you speak?" I asked.

"French. I'm Congolese, so we speak French as our language of instruction. Kiswahili, Lingala, and some local Turkana and Somali, just to interact with the other communities. Whatever I need. Do you speak other languages?"

"Japanese and some Chinese and Spanish…and now Kiswahili."

"Whoa." It was an exciting high tinged response. "You must be smart. The Japanese language is very hard. We have a Japanese organization here. Anyway, we can speak Kiswahili then."

"No, no, no. I can't speak that well. But we should visit the Japanese."

"We will see later, but first, the hotel."

We drove around the corner to the hotel, right next to a large dirt landing strip for the UN flight. He parked next to the fence that had jagged pricks and cut-out openings where kids ran in and out. The brick hotel wasn't much: a few rooms, a standard black water storage tank, a few people walking around cleaning the rooms. As far as I was concerned, this hotel was the Sheraton—I'd later spot one in the camp. I dropped off my bags, and then we headed in. The gate of the refugee camp marked new territory. To become an official refugee, one had to apply to the United Nations then get an ID. As for me, I wasn't supposed to have clearance, but Innocent waved to the guards, and we rode on through.

Dirt tracks lined with tin shacks, mud huts crisscrossed the camp. People walked around freely while kids roamed the streets with wild dogs by their side. Overlooking the poverty, *it seemed like a communal environment where people were relatively calm,* I thought. Arriving at a small wooden fence, we got off the bike and opened it. Behind the gate was a small brick house Innocent had built with his own hands. He had lived here in the camp for ten years and had built the house for his Congolese wife, their one-year-old son, and adopted teenager.

That evening we had an early dinner of rice and red beans prepared by Innocent's wife over a small fire. Innocent explained how he'd ended up in Kakuma. He'd been studying engineering at university and had come home one day to discover that terrorists murdered his parents and sister—decapitated. His father was a journalist who'd expressed views on the wrong side of the political spectrum. Knowing they were coming for him next, Innocent grabbed a bag of clothes and fled. Five hundred miles later, he ended up in Kakuma.

"After all of that, how do you keep such a positive outlook on life?" I asked.

"I keep myself busy. . . I keep my brain busy, and I learn everything I can." All of a sudden, the wooden gate was thrown open, and with a burst of energy came Kitsa.

"Hallo! Look at all these cameras!" This young Congolese guy, with a dapper-colored shirt and shorts and a box-cut hairstyle straight out of the '80s—was maybe eighteen years old. He grabbed my camera off the chair.

"Hey, don't grab that."

"Oh, sorry, I should have asked. Can I play with your GoPro?"

"Sure, you know how?" I was surprised.

"No, but I'll learn in a second. I live with Innocent." Within a minute, he was walking around filming and interviewing me.

"He and his older brother live here. I found them when they came to camp."

"Where is the older brother?"

"Canada. He received a Canadian scholarship for refugees."

"I will go next year! What's Canada like?" curious Kitsa.

"Wow, that's great. Like the US. You know, lots of houses, hamburgers, green forests, and very cold." That's all I could come up at the moment.

"I can't wait to eat hamburgers and see the snow! I will study game engineering and architecture there. I love video games and program my own." He pulled out his computer and started to show me.

"You better wear lots of clothes; you are African," I joked, "You program games? Show me."

"Funny man. Yes, we like to keep our minds busy here," said Innocent. I sensed that they liked to keep their minds busy as a way not to think about their circumstance.

"Let me be your video man for the trip," said Kitsa.

"Sure, be my guest."

"This is going to be so fun!" He took my GoPro, ran out the gate, and filmed down the street.

That night, I digested everything in that little hotel beside the landing strip. Innocent's story had left me devastated. How could any government allow such evil in this world? Half of me wanted to leave the refugee camp the very next day; the other half wanted to learn more about all of these souls. As depression and fatigue set in, I decided to commit to a run down the airstrip following morning—it was the only antidote I had.

Bright and early the next day, Innocent picked me up and took me to a small restaurant for breakfast of hard-boiled eggs, fried dough, and tea. I felt better, and Innocent was impressed by my exercise, saying I was the only person he had ever seen running down the airport strip. We rode motorbikes in the camp, visiting the sections from Sudan, Ethiopia, Congo, Somalia, and even Burundi. The refugee communities had become somewhat segregated, but there were also areas where they mixed and worked hard together. There was also ample support from Christian organizations that had established small schools and computer labs for people to work. Also, there were a variety of countries that had invested in helping the camp, like Japan and Switzerland. Zooming through the desert, we passed in and out of little huts and neighborhoods. Then all of a sudden, I spotted a what?! A Sheraton Hotel, Hilton Hotel, Greece Café, and an Espresso Shop.

The Somalis were the most entrepreneurial, perhaps due to greater access to funds and support from friends and family outside the camp. We met Somalis who had electronic shops, Wi-Fi businesses, and even a lady who built exquisitely designed furniture in a small, two-story warehouse. They seemed to have a knowledge of and a sense of business that others didn't. The Somali proverb, "To be without knowledge is to be without light," rang true.

The Sudanese were tall with chiseled cheekbones and had basketball courts set up in their neighborhood. Some even knew the NBA player Manute Bol, who was born in Sudan. We also met Ethiopian entrepreneurs who started hotels and espresso shops, which I frequented in the mornings.

That afternoon, we arrived at a small classroom where we would be hosting entrepreneurial training for over 100 people. During the classes and sessions, we discussed the entrepreneurial process, from brainstorming ideas to creating a business plan. The most popular ideas were firewood gathering, the importation and preservation of fresh vegetables, water filtration, and fashion. Everywhere I went in Africa, fashion trends were always a hot topic. Africans liked to dress well, regardless of their environment or limited means.

After the first day, Innocent and I convened back at his house, eating more red beans and rice.

"It's nice to see so many cultures of people working together."

"Yes, we have to. It's the only way to live."

"It's kind of like Silicon Valley, where people from all over the world work together."

"Oh yes, many different people there, Indian, Asian, white, and black." Innocent was very worldly and kept up with all the technology news.

"It's interesting because people here don't have a nationality; they don't have an identity."

"Yes, we live in Kakuma Nation; this is our home. Everyone has left behind their differences and learned to appreciate the other person no matter what tribes, nationality, or race."

"That's great, especially if you all get along. Here, you don't have to worry about some dictator like Trump."

"Hahaha. Trump will not kill you, though!" He raised his finger.

"You're right. That's one perspective. Being here is like starting over with a completely new identity."

"We can be whatever we want to be as long as we are helping out the camp and following the rules."

I nodded at his comment and felt my body become tired. "It's getting late. I better head back."

"Let's go." We hopped on the motorbike and took off.

Back at my hotel that evening, I met an older, well-built Canadian guy who asked if he could join me during my exercises. He completed the routine, and I inquired how he stayed in shape. He explained that he was a Crossfitter and how the program had changed his life by getting him in shape. Healthier mentally and physically, he could withstand the difficulties of living here, and that's what he did while raising money from churches, living with the villagers, and building wells. The Turkana people who were born in the surrounding region wanted access to the camp, as they felt the living situation was better than their own. Recently, the UNHCR permitted entry to barter, but mostly they were left on their own, so he had built an organization to help them.

That night I reflected on everything while staring at the white, cracked ceiling. Innocent had taught me much. He taught me how to live. The tragedy of his family didn't stop him from moving on. Now he had a Joelle and a child, motivating him to work even harder at every opportunity that came his way. Innocent didn't dwell on the sadness. He knew only the future, the future he created with any minuscule chance. That was a powerful realization.

For the next few days, we continued to work on formulating ideas, writing business plans, and figuring out how to fund the ideas. There were other happenings around the camp too. One was an art exhibition. There, we met

Josefina, a Chilean who worked in refugee camps teaching and exhibiting art. Art gave them a creative outlet, and it was their way to show the world how they lived. She worked on a variety of UN projects, doing her best to take her art to the world and make people happier. Art gave them a creative outlet, and it was their way to show the world how they lived. Many other artists and academics were living in the camp. It seemed that African governments in the region exiled anyone who was a thinker or a divergent voice.

On the last day of teaching, we had a competition for the best startup ideas. The winners were the water filtration business, the co-working space, and the vegetable storage concept. One student challenged me, saying: "We have the ideas, but we don't have the capital," and suggested that I didn't understand the issues they faced. I didn't ask them enough questions or listen. "I began to understand that I could have listened better, for listening is not just having the patience to wait; it is also learning how to ask the questions themselves."[23] I apologized but explained that, through this process, I could perhaps come to an understanding of their challenges. I also acknowledged that financing was a problem: "I want you to figure out how to start these businesses without capital, then work on securing it," I encouraged.

I explained that they would have to get creative and couldn't always rely on outside forces, remembering the advice from a venture capitalist while we built our company who said, "You have to be self-sufficient. Control your destiny. Let's take a look at how much your businesses need." After calculating the numbers, some came to the understanding that they could fund their businesses with no startup costs while others needed only $500 to $1,000 to get going. It was then that the entrepreneurs realized they could start their businesses on minimal investment.

We came up with ideas to raise more money. First, we'd collect funds from local government agencies. Second, the community itself could operate like a shared funding mechanism, such as a credit union in the United States, with everyone putting a little bit of money in to start. Last, I would try to secure funds from overseas. This fundraising plan led to the establishment of Kakuma Ventures, an organization that would empower them to start their own companies as they saw fit.

One of the more profound realizations that I took away from the experience was that while everyone wanted to start a business, they all wanted to pay back investors and didn't want any handouts. They wanted to build businesses with real investors that would be sustainable in the long run, enabling them to make their living and help their communities. They were real entrepreneurs. The last night before I headed out, Innocent and I mapped out a plan with excitement.

"I'll do the website and outside fundraising," I offered.

"OK, I'll work on setting up the company and a team."

"We need to get one or two businesses going so we have a proof point. How about the water?"

"That's great, but we need a filter."

"I think we can get it in Nairobi. Why don't we go there together, and you can bring it back."

"Sounds great. I can go and come no problem, but I need a day to prepare and request for a movement pass to be outside of the camp," said Innocent.

"We also need half women. Empowering women is important for the project and also for raising money."

"The women and children often get the last of the UN rations because the queue is long, and everyone wants to be served first. Men push them to the back."

"That's sad to hear. You know, refugee camps are new cities, and if corporations were smart, they'd invest here." I was dreaming out loud.

"That's our dream. We want people to stand with us so that we become self-sustainable," he agreed.

"That's the vision. If we create a platform that allows Ikea, Wal-Mart, McDonald's, Coca-Cola—and of course, the real Sheraton, Hilton, or Starbucks—to invest here, they may come."

"They need to see there are resources and opportunities here."

"Let me summarize. 200K people, mobile wallet payments, and a community of people who want to work and live together. This refugee camp is an ideal spot to do business." I convinced myself the dream could work.

"Yes. And everyone will be better off."

"Don't worry," I replied.

"And what else? What can we do tomorrow?"

"Maybe we can visit some other organizations and tell them about our plan?"

"Sounds great; I'll make a list."

I had no assurance if it would ever work or anyone would care. As Adam Braun said in *The Promise of a Pencil*, "Big dreams start with small, unreasonable acts." I had faith in Innocent and the others here. Innocent was one of the smartest people I'd ever met.

Here I was in no man's land with someone I connected better with than most Americans I'd ever met. Two people with nothing in common but the shared desire to learn about each other and do something together. Simple, right? If only the world were that easy. If only we could be global citizens tied together by mutually-interested projects, then we may all just get along. I thought, *what it must be like not to be part of a* country. *Both liberating and frightening at the same time.*

Suddenly there I was in my room—holding my head in my open palms, looking at the floor, and tears streaming down my cheeks. So many issues in my mind came to a close. Identity doesn't matter. Identity and ego are the killer of oneself and civilization, and also perpetuate racism. Women get the brunt, and that has to change if humanity will ever change. Last, I realized that no matter how dire the situation, even refugees in abject poverty wanted more than handouts. They wanted a chance, an opportunity to make their lives and the lives of those around them better. Sure, they needed the basic life necessities, but they also wanted more—that's where entrepreneurship comes in. It gave them meaning, hope, and the ability to self-sustain. This notion, I believed with my heart and soul.

The next day, Kitsa, Innocent, and I took a flight to Nairobi to find supplies for our projects. Jael let us crash at her apartment, and we frantically ran around buying supplies for our venture, including a water filtration system made by LifeStraw. We also visited iHub and two startups that were founded by American entrepreneurs. Twiga was building food storage facilities that supplied small vendors with fresh, perishable foods such as vegetables while M-Kopa was an electronics company. They'd developed a small, solar-powered home electricity system—including a light, a TV, and a cooking appliance—

which could be repaid daily with $1–$2 via mobile money. Innocent picked up one for his home.

The M-Kopa team invited us to a Maasai dinner and dance show that night to celebrate two of their young employees graduating from top US institutions. Both were aspiring entrepreneurs and had returned to Africa to work at M-Kopa with the dream of building their own companies one day. To date, M-Kopa had raised $40 million and served millions of homes across East Africa; it may well be the Apple of Africa one day. Speaking of Apple, Kitsa was running around buying electronics, including USB drives with music. Around that time, Apple discontinued some of the iPod lines, which I thought was a lost opportunity for the company's entry into Africa.

We also stopped into Sammasource in Nairobi to see how they were educating people for data science jobs. Then we checked out Kibera, the biggest slum in Nairobi, where we met with Tunapanda. Founded by two American brothers, Jay and Mick Larson, Similarly to Sammasource, Tunapanda provided tech skills to those who needed it in the slums. (Both organizations are fantastic to support). They welcomed Innocent to spend a few months with them; he later did. We walked around Kibera, which was alive with hustle and energy. Vendors hawking electrical equipment, fried fish, snacks, and drinks overran the streets.

The time I'd spent with Innocent and Kitsa had created a lasting friendship. We'd bonded over doing business and making the world a better place. They never asked for anything and were grateful for my help. What I learned working with them was that I could empower them with the right ideas, a few tools, and a little money. That was more powerful than teaching or giving them handouts, which they didn't want anyway.

We didn't expect Kakuma Ventures to be an uncomplicated venture. As someone who built schools in Somalia, Jonathan Starr said in *It Takes a School*, "I expect tremendous difficulties will arise anytime someone seeks to create something meaningful where it doesn't currently exist." Innocent has persevered, and, to this day, we still message weekly. We've received a few small grants and been accepted to the Miller Center for Social Entrepreneurship Accelerator. Rebuilding the lives of displaced people is something we want to do throughout our lives, and Kakuma Ventures would be our platform.

Innocent and I having dinner at his house.

The Sheraton Hotel (obviously fake) in Kakuma

The street of merchants

Teaching entrepreneurship at classroom in the camp

Chapter 24

HIKING KILIMANJARO: THE HOUSE OF GOD

"If you can't fly, then run
If you can't run, then walk
If you can't walk, then crawl
But whatever you do, you have to keep moving forward."
—Martin Luther King Jr.

After a few days on my own in Nairobi, my buddy, Jeremy, flew into the Kenyan capital, and we spent time exploring the city and visiting its museums. Jeremy and I met in China in 2004 and became close friends. We had a lot in common. From Michigan, he loved traveling, running triathlons, and learning languages. Having just left his job plus experiencing the passing of his father, he went on his own personal journey and visited Brett and me in Africa.

He was inspired to visit Africa as part of his journey,

Jeremy hadn't thought about visiting Africa until I made my journey. He flattered me by saying how amazing he thought it was that I explored the continent. As we spent time together, I could see how his reactions to Africa were similar to my own when I first arrived. Jeremy is compassionate and wanted to help wherever he could. At the same time, he didn't know where to start. I told him this is how I felt at the beginning as well. When we discussed what was next for me, I told him I didn't know. He encouraged me not to be scared to find my path in Africa as long as I felt it was the right thing to do.

We'd booked a tour with Kibo Slopes that not only included a trek up Mount Kilimanjaro—called the House of God by the Maasai—but also safaris in Amboseli National Park, Serengeti National Park, and the Ngorongoro Crater. They were providing transport, guides, and hotel accommodation along the way. Presto! With one reservation, we had the whole package.

Leaving the bustle of Nairobi behind, we made the two-hour drive to Amboseli National Park for our first game drive, followed by a stop in the community of Manyatta to meet the Maasai. This tribe includes more than one million people, many of whom live within the game reserves of Kenya and Tanzania. While the governments of both countries had instituted programs to encourage the Maasai to abandon their traditional, semi-nomadic lifestyles, most have opted to retain their age-old customs.

Crossing the border into Tanzania, we noticed that it was less developed than Kenya. We continued driving to Loitokitok where we met our guide, Deo smiled from ear to ear and welcomed us with open arms, literally. He showed us his blue, purple, and white tiled home both inside and out, and the three basic food and home supply stores. He used his proceeds to help build housing in the community, funded by his hiking excursions. In 2018, he started his own company called F&D Expedition.

The following day, we began our trek up Mount Kilimanjaro along with the longer and more scenic Rongai route, having opted to avoid the heavily trafficked Marangu route—also called the Coca-Cola route. It was just Jeremy and me with ten porters. At first, I thought, *we didn't need all of the porters,* but that's what came with the deal, and we were happy to have some help and company along the way—not to mention they built us a campground and gave us more than enough, freshly prepared food daily. Admittedly, *we're glamping,* I thought. *This isn't exactly roughing it.* Our guides kept encouraging us to eat more, but my stomach still wasn't right. My belly was still visibly bloated, and I wasn't digesting food properly. All I could do was drink a lot of water.

The seven-day Rongai route ascended the Mawenzi Peak before heading to Uhuru Peak, a less strenuous route than some other ways. Aside from Deo, our guides didn't say much but "pole' pole,'" translated in English as "slowly, slowly." This kind of hiking felt truly Zen: don't think, just walk, let thoughts come in and out, and continue to focus on breathing. The solitude of trekking miles upon miles every day, one could not help but go more deeply inward.

The last day of hiking was brutal, with a 1,200-meter increase in elevation. We started our hike around midnight to get to the summit in time for sunrise. The midnight moonlight was so bright that at points during the 6-hour climb, we'd shut off our headlamps and use the moon to light our path. The prehistoric rocks turned into small iced over glaciers, and as we ascended, I began experiencing altitude sickness. My head became lighter and lighter each time I stepped in the packed snow. *I must have been walking on a cloud,* I thought. At times, Jeremy had to hold out his hand, preventing me from falling down the edge of the switchbacks that would have left me hundreds of feet down a bouldering cliff. A triathlete, he was having no problems with the trek or any altitude issues and kept a steady eye on me as I pushed towards the summit.

It became so cold that my two-liter Camelback water reservoir froze, increasing the weight in my day pack. About halfway up, feeling lethargic, and the increased weight of the backpack, I sat down in dismay. *I'm not going to make it,* I thought. I could only get a few sips of water—I counted them one, two, and three, and that was it. Our other guide, who was trailing us from a distance, caught us, grabbed my pack, and lead us forward. He would stay amply ahead of us so that I wouldn't get any more water for the remaining few miles. Three sips had been enough to fuel me up the back of the House of God or Buddha, in my mind.

The final kilometer of the trail was magnificent. The sun was about to surface evenly with the horizon of clouds, blue sky, and an adjacent mountain. I looked back to see how far I'd come. That's when I had an emotional breakout of uncontrollable tears mixed with laughter. I'd never experienced anything like it before. Emotions surged through my body. Was this from the altitude or just a stream of emotions erupting from the entire journey? Townships, orphans, massacres, water wells, sharks, and slave castles. It was like flipping through scenes in a black-and-white film. It was so powerful that I couldn't control myself and had to hold my head down for a few minutes to regain composure. Soon my African journey would end.

At the summit, our guide, Deo, raised his hands and said, "Welcome to the House of God!" Jeremy chuckled at me and said, "I don't think I've ever seen a grown man cry like that!" Trust good friends always to poke fun. Once at the peak, we took photos for about fifteen minutes, then scampered down the slopes through sand and rock, going as fast as we could to reach the base.

From Kilimanjaro, we drove west to the Serengeti to a wildlife spot on the game drive. One of the top highlights for me was chasing cheetahs. Their silky fur, the way they walk, and stare at their prey—they must be the most elegant creatures on Earth! We also saw lions mating and another stalking a wildebeest—*they are the ugliest creatures and should be eaten,* I thought.

It was just about then when on one of our daily safaris, our composure unraveled. Two weeks, hanging out in a single tent, enduring miles upon miles hiking up Africa's highest peak, and suffering from the constant irritation of my stomach issues, I lost it. Jeremy was a neat freak, and I was much more go-with-the-flow and, hence, messy. Tension had been building between us, and one day while we were driving, Jeremy remarked to me to keep it tidy, and it was enough to set me off. He took it well, swallowing his words, and we parted ways a couple of days later. Jeremy headed to Zanzibar, and, upon leaving, he kindly reminded me: "Sometimes even brothers fight, buddy." It was another test of learning about myself and developing inner calmness in a heated moment. It also shined a light on a premonition that when I returned home, I'd need to remain calm, collected, and courageous when confronting a once known but now new environment since *I* had changed.

After game driving through the Ngorongoro Conservation Area—home to a wildlife-filled crater—we ended our trip in Arusha. Jeremy was off to the beach while I stuck around for the best-rated barbecue in Tanzania at Khan's Barbeque, visited a local gym, then spent a day visiting a non-profit that was introduced to me by a Japanese friend. Exclusively for girls, the Sakura Vision Women's Junior High School was helping to empower them through education, with funding coming from Japanese donors.

Back in Nairobi, I was able to catch up with Mercy. At the time, I caught a bad cold, making my stomach ache even worse. She told me to see a doctor. I insisted it was just cold and I'd be fine. She warned me that seeing an African doctor was better than going home and seeing one—they could diagnose African sicknesses. I told her I had to keep moving. I had one last adventure up my sleeve, the Horn of Africa, before leaving the continent in the hope of reaching the milestone of visiting twenty African countries.

That night she took me out to dinner at Diamond Plaza for some excellent Indian cuisine where we discussed religion. Mercy believed that faith in God was more powerful than good works. I didn't know how to answer, but I told her I just liked doing things. "Faith is just as important," she said, "everyone is on their spiritual path in life, and each individual's view should be respected." It was an important point to remember, especially after coming back from the House of God. That was a spiritual journey in and of itself. Maybe faith was what was needed to save me from my stomach ache.

Chapter 25

THE USA'S PRESENCE IN THE HORN OF AFRICA

*"We need more Americans to see the world as you, then tell them about it,
and encourage them to get out there too. Americans need a new perspective,
the kind you only get from traveling."*
—James Britt Wusterbarth

My nagging sickness and the non-stop rain in Ethiopia sadly cut the trip short. Ethiopia had so much beautiful nature, many religious sites and African tribes to visit. It was unique in that it was the only African nation never to be colonized—although there was a small period of occupation by the Italians in 1936, which thankfully left the espresso culture behind. The food typically consisted of injera—a sourdough-risen flatbread—accompanied by different kinds of spicy stews, with beef, lamb, vegetables, and legumes.

Unfortunately, my cold worsened while in Addis Ababa, and I went to see a pharmacist who gave me some medicine and told me it was just the flu going around due to the heavy rains. The medication helped clear me up a bit, but I still had to cut short my non-profit endeavors and travel throughout the country.

Roughly two-thirds Christian and one-third Muslim, Ethiopia altered my thoughts on religion in Africa, which up until this point had been quite negative.

I didn't understand why many Africans devoutly practiced Christianity when settlers had exploited them. Several times across Southern Africa, I saw pictures of a cross with a sword, representing the nefarious actions of the colonial years. It confused me.

Both Christians and Arab Muslim seafarers had settled Ethiopia. The ancient Kingdom of Aksum adopted the Orthodox church, later becoming the Ethiopian Orthodox Tewahedo Church, the largest pre-colonial Christian church in Africa. With about 36 million members, it was also the largest of all Oriental Orthodox churches[24]. Ethiopians believed that Jesus spent a significant amount of time within their borders and may have even been born there.

In my hotel, Tessa and I messaged.

"I think my trip is finally coming to an end."

"Why is that?"

"I now have a cold that I can't get rid of, and my stomach is still a problem."

"You have seen enough. You better get to a doctor or go home. You cannot keep going. I am giving you an order from your Jewish mother."

"OK, OK."

"If you aren't better in a week, then go straight back to the US or somewhere where they can treat you. This sickness has been too long."

With those thoughts and heavy rains in Addis Ababa showing no signs of letting up, I decided to make a beeline for Djibouti, a country in Africa that I'd longed to visit since hearing its name in middle school. As I landed in Djibouti, I met several US Armed Forces officers, one of whom had just flown in from Georgia to start his first deployment. The country had a lot of strategic value for the United States due to its location in the Middle East. It featured a commanding fort and a nice Sheraton hotel overlooking the Gulf of Tadjoura, where I stayed.

It was boiling in Djibouti (up to 115°F), and I was exceedingly tired, but even so, the country left a lasting impression on me. It had a completely different vibe to Ethiopia, with a Muslim-majority population that wore colorful dresses and hijabs, and the women didn't cover their faces.

At the Sheraton in Djibouti City, the capital, I met an Afghan and Iraq war veteran who was dating a local, and she told me that it was permissible to compliment women; I was concerned it might be against the law. He was from

North Carolina and now worked for a military contractor who paid him good money to be based in Djibouti and fly into war zones to fix telecom networks.

We strolled around the port city dubbed the "The Pearl of the Gulf of Tadjoura." The town had the semblance of a busy port town—some restaurants, small hotels, and shops. We stopped at a Mexican restaurant—of all the cuisines in the world—in the city square. Over a few Coronas, he told me that he was still experiencing mental scars from the war—his Humvee got blown off the road, with three of his fellow officers being killed and others losing their legs. He had signed up for the military two years before 9-11 because it was the best thing he could do after high school, and the recruiters were great salesmen. He was the only one to survive intact. He thought it was cool I was learning about Africa and encouraged me to help others learn about Africa—"to see how good we have it in the USA."

My only sightseeing trip in Djibouti was out to the salt flats, where I floated in the water. En route, there was a massive port that made anything I'd seen in Hong Kong look like Lego blocks. There were lots of Chinese mines and investment from the military and governments around the world. Although there wasn't much to see, I was glad that I went to check it out before my Africa journey came to an end.

At the airport, on the way out, I met a large, muscular, and bearded American guy who looked like he could be a Navy Seal. His name was James Britt Wusterbarth, and he was a military veteran. On this trip, he had been consulting with the Congolese Rangers in the Democratic Republic of the Congo, teaching them needed defense skills. While in Africa, he had taken time off from his current job in federal law enforcement to visit several other nearby countries. His quest to travel through fifty countries in the next few years. We spoke about the need for the USA to do more in Africa—private and public institutions. And he was so adamant that we needed more Americans to travel and get a better understanding of the world, practically. "We need more Americans to see the world like you. Then, tell others about it and encourage them to get out there, too. Americans need a new perspective, the kind you only get from traveling." I couldn't agree more.

Chapter 26

BACK IN THE USA: THE POWER OF THREE SIPS

"In judging our progress as individuals we tend to concentrate on external factors such as one's social position, influence & popularity, wealth & standard of education. . . but internal factors may be even more crucial in assessing one's development as a human being. Honesty, sincerity, simplicity, humility, pure generosity, absence of vanity, readiness to serve others—qualities which are within easy reach of every soul."
—**Nelson Mandela** in *The Prison Letters of Nelson Mandela and Conversations with Myself*

While in Djibouti, I'd managed to shake off my cold but couldn't stop the stomachache. The only thing that seemed to make it go away was alcohol, which isn't the usual remedy for stomach complaints. It wasn't until a few weeks later while at a travel technology conference in Las Vegas that I was talking to a Zimbabwean and, after telling him my symptoms, he asked if I'd gone swimming in the Nile or Lake Malawi. When I confirmed that I had, he knew immediately: "You've got snails!" He explained that alcohol makes them go to sleep, which was why I felt better after drinking. He assured me that some simple parasitical meds would knock them out. Living in Africa, he'd studied all

239

the potential life-threatening illnesses. I also texted Jenny to get her thoughts, and she said typhoid often came along with snails.

My stubbornness to refuse to see a doctor in Africa and determination just to complete my journey ended up costing me dearly and probably shaved a few years off my life, as well. The experience gave me a new appreciation of the healthcare I have access to, which isn't the case for the 250 million people exposed to these same diseases. I also realized that my health was in my hands, and one mistake could hurt my life. My dad, still watching Fox news, was equally worried about my health and insisted on sending me to his doctor, who was also an ex-Marine.

After some liver and kidney tests, his doctor confirmed that I had parasites, and I took anti-parasitical meds that cost $100 a pill. (They were just $1 each in Africa, so I had Dawn bring some back during her recent trip.) While I did feel better, my stomach remained upset with small pangs in my kidney for almost a year. But Tessa kept it in perspective.

"How are you feeling?"

"I'm doing OK. Still bloated, but I think the medication got rid of the snails, and the typhoid was easy to knock out."

"Snails and typhoid? Didn't you get your vaccine?"

"Yeah, that's what he thought it was. The typhoid vaccine was only 40 percent effective."

"If all you got was a stomachache, then it was worth it!"

"That's true. And I'm glad I don't have mosquitos buzzing in my ears when I sleep. It will take time to get back to normal, but I should be OK."

"Now you can take this time to journal about the trip. Mosquitos in your ears or was that from the malaria pills? It's a common side effect." Stunned. All along, I kept thinking mosquitos were underneath the mosquito nets flying into my ear.

"I'll just write a book about all the craziness and my stupid stories."

"Maybe. But I think you should just journal about it and then see how it goes. Writing a book is a long, arduous process."

"True. And books hardly sell anymore unless it's a bestseller. Even then."

"Right. So just take things easy for now."

My mom also worried about my health yet wasn't surprised that I'd come back sick.

"I told you not to go."

"Mom, I was fine until I swam in the lake. It was my fault. It had nothing to do with Africa."

"Well, you should have read the internet before."

"I know, I know. It's fine. I'll be OK."

"Besides, where is all your stuff?" She looked around as I emptied my bag in the laundry room.

"I dumped most of it to have just one bag."

"That's efficient. You don't need much anyway. You can only wear one pair of pants at a time."

"Yes, I realize that now."

"Took you long enough."

I glared at the washing machine. I thought about Ghana, where so many ladies tie-dyed batik shirts and hand-washed clothes. So many people in Africa don't have washing machines—how it would change their lives and health. Hans Rosling's TED Talk called *The Magic Washing Machine* because it completely changed the role of women in these societies.

"Are you going to stay here?" I think she assumed I'd take off again.

"I don't know."

"You should probably make a new home sometime. Tennessee is nice." Mom liked it here.

"Home is where your clothes are, Mom. That's an African proverb. So right now, my Home is right here, upstairs on that couch."

"You are welcome to stay as long as you'd like while you get rid of that stomachache."

"What did you do out there?" My 14-year-old niece, Izzy, chimed in.

"Here, I'll show you the pictures and videos," I said, pulling out my phone. "Here were the kids in South Africa your age, singing at a school in a Township."

"That's "Love on the Brain" from Rihanna, and their voices are so pretty. Uncle, I can't hear you. Speak up," she demanded. I spoke quietly because of some combination of not feeling well and emulating those I met in Africa who spoke softly.

"There are so many different places and people," I shouted.

"That's better; it looks interesting." She flipped through my phone.

"You don't know how good you have it."

"Yes, I do. I appreciate it. Don't tell me what I don't know." She took a bite of her Cheetos, drinking Mountain Dew.

"OK, sorry. Don't eat that crap. America just feeds us cornstarch and sugar. It's terrible for us. Let's get some lunch. I need to eat."

"You need to feed your snails." She laughed. We headed out into town and searched for food. What I wanted was a rolled-egg chapati, remember that rolex in Uganda? But she beat me to the punch. "Chick-Fil-A, please."

"I want to get a salad or veggies. Let's go somewhere else, maybe Zaxbys or TGIFs?"

"No, disgusting. I hate their chicken. TGIF is for Grandma and Grandpa. I do Chick-Fil-A only."

"It's just chicken, for goodness sake. You have so many options. Why do you have to be so picky?!"

She looked at me with a tear in her eye. "Fine. Wherever. But I'm not eating."

The conversation saddened me, and, reflecting on my time in Africa, I, too, wanted the best chicken sandwich at Nandos or even in Lesotho. I was wrong.

"Sorry. It's just been hard on me being sick and coming home. Let's get Chick-Fil-A. I agree. TIA—This is America, lots of options here, so let's take the best one."

"No problem. I hope you feel better and feed the snails." She snickered.

We sat down at a table, and just over her shoulder, I could hear the conversations of other people, what they said, and how they said it. It sounded like the screeching of nails on a chalkboard and drove me insane. Why must people talk so loudly? My niece kept asking me to speak louder as she couldn't hear me.

As we drove around, my ruminations didn't cease. So much "stuff" in this country. Brand-new cars sitting for sale in parking lots, shopping mall after shopping mall, and natural areas razed for wider highways and more buildings.

Looking out the car windows, I yearned to see a few animals walking around. And it was humid and hot in Tennessee, seemingly hotter than Africa. If it couldn't get any worse, one day while at home, I almost lost it over water running in the bathroom.

"Dad, turn off that water and turn off Fox TV," I said sternly.

"What? I have Fox TV on my headphones. You can't even hear it." He looked at me, bewildered.

"No, the water. The water is running."

"I'm rinsing off stuff in the bathroom."

"Sorry, I just can't take all that water running."

I'd learned to bucket-shower to preserve water in the desert, the large refill water bottles in South Africa, and while hiking, I'd learned the power of three sips. Three sips of water provided just enough energy to get through a workout. Now, I cherished water and the containers it came in.

"I think you've lost your mind," Dad said.

"Hey, I'm not the one listening to Fox News all the time. I'm just messing with you." I smiled and joked. Fox News didn't bother me anymore, and I'd even stop to listen to their perspective. For the most part, I'd hear a few points; then I'd tone it out and hear blabber. That's a democracy, and it is to be respected and protected. I'll just tune it out.

"I just think we can be so wasteful here. This planet is getting rundown everywhere."

"You are right. We do waste a lot. I agree with that. So many people are in need. Look at the churches, they build these massive churches in Tennessee and don't take care of the homeless. It makes no sense." Mom agreed. Dad nodded his head. My dad was the most frugal of accountants, and he wasted nothing. I was a spendthrift, and it drove him crazy. But I guess that's what happens in parent-child relationships; the children tend to become the opposite.

Her comment elucidated my thoughts on homelessness. I saw several homeless people sleeping under bridges in Tennessee and the tent towns that were popping up everywhere. While not the same volume and desperation I would see in San Francisco or skid row in downtown Los Angeles, it shocked the soul to see it spreading into the heartland. While some churches do house the homeless, it's just a short-term solution for an exploding problem. Rather than turn the other way from, I remembered to see them as souls first, and with that, empathy overwhelmed me. I spoke to those living on the street, asking them what had happened. I wanted to do something, to make a difference, recognize them as souls who deserved to be understood. Before, my natural response would have been to be fearful, even judgmental.

It was sometime after this that the grim reaper reared its ugly head. An aunt who lived with my family passed away. The burial and mourning process made me reflect on how Africans experienced death. In many parts of the continent, death reared its head around every corner, whether it be from traffic accidents or diseases. I had seen many starving to death in the slums of Lagos and the hills of Uganda. Africans see death as fatalistic, just part of life's journey. They celebrate, reflect upon, and talk about death in a way we don't in the West. I wondered if the way American's perceive death could change.

I ended my Africa introduction journey with a trip to DC, where I attended the Mandela Fellowship and met some of my new friends from Zambia (Njavwa), Malawi (Vincent), and Zimbabwe (Lily), as well as making a few more. It was great to see them and discover how the Mandela Fellowship bridged the United States with Africa by bringing fellows over for six weeks to be hosted by families and universities in different states. It was interesting to contrast the experiences of those who lived in rural places to those in big cities.

Many of the Mandela Fellows did not envision the United States as having farmland and conservative churchgoers and were surprised by how people lived in small town America. They were taken aback to discover a different America than the media portrays. This real-life experience helped them to see that, in many ways, the United States wasn't as advanced as they had previously thought, and that we, too, have our challenges as a country. Sadly, Trump cut half the funding for the Mandela Fellowship in the coming years. But this wasn't going to deter the resilient fellows. They had plans to continue working with the United States as I had plans to continue working with them in Africa.

As I came to the end of my African journey, a new one began to emerge. Did I still want to work in technology? I didn't know. I appreciated the experience in my last company and was grateful for the shares that paid my way in Africa excursions. My acrimonious attitude had vanished. With a clear mind, I realized that I had many options to start anew. The opportunities seemed endless, unlike the limited ones in Africa. I knew only one thing: I wanted to help others get those same opportunities and to address problems in the USA.

It'd be a good time to catch up on the tech scene—it'd been four years since I'd lived in Japan and traveled throughout Africa. *How do I always end up in San Francisco?* I thought. Much had changed and I wanted to see if I still wanted to play that game. At that time, I hadn't yet re-adapted and don't think I made a good impression, nor did I think I fit in anymore.

When they asked me what I wanted to do, I told them I didn't know, and I wasn't sure tech was for me. I wanted to solve the hardest and most humanitarian problems that I could. Many would tell me about technology projects working on real-world issues, and there was a new trend for that in Silicon Valley. I opened my mind to it. At the moment, I didn't want to work in a company again. I felt oddly OK with not having a plan or a defined future. I knew that I wasn't going to fall into the rat race again. Others told me to write a book. I thought a blog was enough, but they kept urging me to dig deeper, talk about how it changed my life. I headed back to Tennessee to clear my thoughts.

Back at home, I wrestled with my indecisions. Some days I would stare at the white ceiling yet thankfully with no ADHD thoughts. Other days I would sit outside and watch the trees blow. No feelings, no grand ideas. Worried, mom tried to perk me up and help me figure something out.

"You don't have to go back to Africa or even California, again. There is plenty to help out with in Tennessee. We have problems, too, like opioids, our schools are behind, and there are poor people here, too. There are lots of churches that have programs, and we have an African priest at ours, Father Pontaine." She said while cooking up my favorite chop suey dish.

Father Pontaine was from Uganda, not far from Masaka, home of the Uganda Marathon. When I met him, he was aghast that I'd been there. He mentioned that his mother had never left her village next to Masaka, where she grew up and was in awe of my travels and blog. He inspired me to take any direction that my heart and soul felt was right. Talking to him was like being back in Uganda.

"I know I can see that. I just started volunteering at the Red Cross. It's something to do. I don't know where to start."

"Anything is OK," Mom handed me a plate. She was always pretty laid-back and just wanted me to be happy.

"You won't believe what happened on my Red Cross call the other day."

"What's that?"

"I was called out to a fire and discovered that the family was from Sierra Leone—their twelve-year-old boy had set his house on fire. The child had a lot of issues adapting to school and making friends. I met his older cousin, who was studying finance at the University of Tennessee. You know what he told me?"

"What?"

"You can't just throw people like us in America. It's too hard. There is no community here, no support, no help. What can we do? You've been to Africa. You see people just walking into each other's houses, playing music, and working together. Not here. It's too tough and competitive here." This comment shocked me. But, it summed up a lot of my thoughts about the juxtaposition of the two places.

"That's sad . . . that's the difference between Africa and USA in one short scenario," she said.

Fox News was playing on the TV. Sitting at the table, I saw the screen was in plain sight while scarfing down half a plate without tasting a thing.

"Your global experience would be helpful for our country."

"Possibly, but it's not so unique anymore."

"Don't sell yourself short. You always do that. Very few, if any people, have your experience." She was right. All of our experiences are unique and should be valued.

"Thanks, Mom, I appreciate it," I said.

"You can always stick around here, we like having you around, and you need to get healthy."

"OK, but I'll probably shuttle back and forth to SF. I may start this idea to facilitate technology investment between Silicon Valley and the southeast of the USA. That would help our country."

"That's a good idea too. You liked doing that before; you don't have to change."

"Right, I can give it a shot again, and if I don't like it, I'll do something else." I thought about how Toto moved from one journey to the next.

"You know, you should share your experiences—they could help so many."

She was right again. All of our experiences should be shared because that's how to develop a mutual understanding.

"I'm making the blog, KDAlive. That's a start." I looked up from the computer, through the window, out at the trees just starting to turn a shade of orange-yellow again and took three sips of my glass of water.

"F*It, I'll write a book."

Jeremy and I coming back from two peaks at Kilimanjaro.

My tent with Kilimanjaro behind me.

The best animal picture I took the entire trip.

Mom, Dad, and Izzy greeting me at the airport.

THE EMPATHY EPILOGUE

*"We must be willing to let go of the life we
planned so as to have the life that is waiting for us."*
—**Joseph Campbell**

t's been nearly three years since I've returned from Africa and began writing this book. I finished the first draft, a methodical travel log, if you will, nearly eighteen months ago. The few people who read it said it was somewhat interesting points but was slow and sleepy. So, I attended multiple writing classes in-person and online, attended writer's conferences, and had several friends look over this version replete with carefully crafted dialogues with the actual people I met. I hope that it's a slightly more entertaining travel memoir than other's you've read.

I've taken some time to focus on my ADHD and get it under control. It also took me over a year to get my stomach back to almost normal. Sometimes there is a bright side in the darkness; in this case, the parasites knocked out my drinking habit and made me a healthier eater. I thank the snails for that.

In addition to writing this book, I've maintained my blogging. To subsidize this, I've continued consulting with tech companies. I lived in San Francisco Bay Area while spending ample time in the southeast of the USA. Transition is a challenge, and non-profit jobs are hard to come by. Still, I've been pretty happy. Not committing to a project or a job has allowed me to read, study, travel, teach junior high school, spend time with family, and do new things like singing. In many ways, not having an identity has made me happier and more adaptable to the current pandemic environment.

The one thing I've learned most during this time is that if you want to make an impact, you have to start now and can't wait to get into a position of power. That's why I continued with Kakuma Ventures. We were admitted into the Miller Center for Social Entrepreneurship program and hope to raise money after we graduate. Innocent has been relentless in finding opportunities to grow the idea.

Focused on the USA, I was determined to start with the tools I had—just like Africans do. Start small as they say in Silicon Valley. So, I began KDAlive to share my experiences with others so they can see what I've learned. If we all share our experiences—whatever they may be—we will develop a more empathetic, understanding, and supportive world. Driven by the glorification of wealth and capitalism, the USA has left too many people in the dust. While people run the daily rat race, many don't even blink an eye to help their communities or other parts of the country. It just doesn't make sense to me. If we create a more united country, the world will also benefit greatly.

Due to Covid-19, the world has changed much since I started writing this book. Undoubtedly, people will slow their lifestyles down and relook at their relationships, quality of lives, and immediate communities. Despite Trump's desire to return to massive economic growth, those days are over, and the profits over people and scale at all costs capitalistic economy will be replaced hopefully by one of humanity and well-being. People like Brett, who I met in Uganda, are leading the charge to create a better world.

As I was preparing this text, I reached out to Brett, and he surprised me yet again. He had decided to leave the WFP after fourteen years to scale the post-harvest work and go out on his own.

"The World Food Program is an amazing organization, but I felt that the post-harvest work was not getting the attention it merited, especially from a large organization that focuses mainly on disaster response. While WFP does this extremely well, the post-harvest work has the potential to end preventable hunger in Africa (and other geographies). So I made the jump away, again, from the safe, reliable UN job (and pension), and now it's time to be an entrepreneur again.

We just launched Harvest Solutions—a social enterprise focused on reducing the post-harvest loss for the 200M smallholder families. It's time to fundraise, then scale in Uganda, and continue to scale across Africa."

Before I sign out, I want to leave you with a reflection on what I learned about empathy, because more than ever, we need compassion in our culture. During my years of extended travels, I'd experienced countries as a tourist—staring out the window of a car or bus. Perhaps I would walk by and give food or money to people, but I would never take the time to understand the situation. I felt sadness or helplessness for them, but I'd do nothing more and would keep on.

In Africa, I tapped into a deeper level of empathy as I began to understand the places and cultures there. Once you can relate to people's feelings and begin to live their daily lives, you begin to understand and know what they need to make it better. Then compassion kicks into action.

What was once abnormal now becomes daily life. What was previously unfavorable now becomes desired. What you thought you needed is forgotten. Your old life is no more. Sadness turns into conviction and despair into hope. You become one with the people and are in the fight together to make things better. This understanding is a deeper layer of empathy when one can start to understand the plight of another person. I began to scratch the surface of this deep layer of empathy toward the end of my time in Africa. Always moving from place to place made it difficult for me to go as deep as an aid worker or missionary. Yet it hit me while visiting the Kakuma refugee camp and spending time with Innocent. I started to understand him, his situation, and his thoughts. I can't thank him enough for what he taught me and the experiences many others shared with me during my Africa trip.

Find that empathy and deeper level of compassion and apply it to those being affected by Covid-19, homelessness, drug abuse, and other challenges. Then and only then will we build a better community, country, and civilization.

THANK YOU

Thank you for reading about my journey through Africa. There is no telling when we will be able to travel like before COVID-19, so this may give a bit of armchair travel and hold you over until flights resume their regular schedules.

My journey meant a lot to me, so I thought I'd share it with you. If you made it this far, I hope you saw the impact that it had on me and took a few insights away that may benefit you. I've learned a lot through my travels around the world and hope that it inspires you to break out of your comfort zones and learn about different people, even if it's just down the road.

I list all of the organizations in this book on my website under the Africa category. Please visit if you'd like to learn more about them.

If you like my writing and want to hear more stories like this, perhaps about Asia or elsewhere, let me know. I've been thinking about writing a story about my four years in Japan that would also be a combination of travel and learning experiences about the culture, a fascinating one it is. If interested, please drop me a line.

One thing I've learned through my travels is how well-being differs among countries. In addition to what you just read, I also learned about what made people happy in these places, notably when they lacked the comfort of what we have in the USA. The more I learned, the more I sought out new experiences about mental health. This newly found interest lead me to spend in Myanmar at a ten-day meditation retreat and the Himalayas studying meditation and Buddhism. I explored happiness through not only the lens of Buddhist but also Judaism, Islam, Ancient Greek scholars, and many modern-day psychiatrists. From those learnings, I've developed a well-being methodology called Ultimate Well-Being. I invite you to join my program on my website at KDAlive.

Thank you again for your time and 'Be Happy' wherever you go.

ABOUT THE AUTHOR

I, Kurt Davis, am a technology entrepreneur, well-being expert, and social impact worker. The first 20-years of my career were spent between Silicon Valley and Asia, working with technology startups in finance and business development roles.

In 2017, I took off time and traveled to Africa to learn about the continent. In addition to what you just read, I learned even more about well-being in these places. It drove me to continue learning about mental health and happiness.

This newly found interest has also lead me to spend in Myanmar on a ten-day meditation retreat and the Himalayas studying meditation and Buddhism. I have explored happiness through not only this lens but also Judaism, Islam, Ancient Greek scholars, and many modern-day psychiatrists.

During the pandemic, I published a short 10,000-word e-book called *The Isolation Survival Guide*. Then I wrote this book. I'll soon publish another book about startup sales and business development entitled *Breakthrough: The Playbook for Executing a Transformational Deal*.

I am now building my platform called KDAlive which focuses on culture, well- being, and entrepreneurship. I also launched a well-being program that helps people manage their well-being through different variables. While my target audience is young professionals, I'd like to bring these ideas to high school and university students. Teaching youth about well-being as early as possible will help them live more fulfilling lives. Originally from South Carolina, I am a graduate of Davidson College and Duke Fuqua School of Business.

ENDNOTES

1   Jack Kerouac, *Dharma Bums* (New York: Penguin Press 1976).

2   Sally Frankental and Owen B, Sichone, *South Africa's Diverse People* (California: ABC-CLIO 2005), 135.

3   As of August 1st, 2020, South African History Website referenced this quote.

4   As of August 1st, 2020, the Wikipedia home page of Lesotho mentioned.

5   As of August 1st, 2020, the Wikipedia home page of Mswati III mentioned.

6   Diane Lemeiux, *Culture Smart! Nigeria* (London Bravo Ltd 2011), 43.

7   As of August 1st, 2020, the Benin homepage of the Britannica website discussed.

8   As of August 1st, 2020 the HappyDaysTravelBlog posted an article, "Walking the Slave Route in Ouidah, Benin."

9   Katherine Buchholz, "The Trans-Atlantic Slave Trade Uprooted Millions," Statista Website, June 19th, 2020.

10 As of August 1st, 2020, the IndexMundi Website of Togo vs Benin discussed political differences.

11 Bill Gates, "Why I want to stop talking about the developing world." GatesNotes Website, April 8th, 2018.

12 Brian Hicks, "Slavery in Charleston: A chronical of human bondage in the Holy City," The Post and Courier; December 8, 2016.

13 Lien De Wispelaere, "Why everyone needs to eat a rolex in Uganda," Matador Network Website, March 25, 2020.

14 Eromo Egbejule, "How to Eat a Rolex: This Popular Street Snack is Not a Watch," Ozy Website, March 2, 2020.

15 Martin Meredith, The Fortunes of Africa: A 5000-Year History of Wealth, Greed, and Endeavor (New York: Simon & Schuster UI Ltd, 2014), 382.

16 Milan Schreuer, "Belgium Apologizes for Kidnapping Children From African Colonies," New York Times; April 4th, 2019.

17 Martin Meredith, The Fortunes of Africa: A 5000-Year History of Wealth, Greed, and Endeavor (New York: Simon & Schuster UI Ltd, 2014), 680.

18 Graham Connah, African Civilizations: An Archaeological Perspective, (Cambridge, UK: Cambridge University Press, 1987) 251.

19 As of August 1st, 2020, the World Health Organization Website reported in the article, "The World Malaria Report 2019 at a Glance," December 4th, 2019.

20 International Monetary Fund, "Malawi Economic Development Report,"July, 2017.

21 D. Engels, L. Chitsulo, A. Montresor, L.Savioli, "The Global Epidemiological Situation of Shistomaisis and New Approaches to Control and Research," US National Library of Medicine and National Institutes of Health Website, October, 9, 2017.

22 Check out his Facebook Page called Harvest Solutions or email me for his contact.

23 Jacqueline Novogratz, The Blue Sweater, (New York: Rodale Inc., 2009), 86.

24 As of August 1st, 2020, the Wikipedia homepage of the Ethiopian Tewahedo Orthodox Church listed this information.

CPSIA information can be obtained
at www.ICGtesting.com
Printed in the USA
JSHW041135161220
10311JS00001B/66